The ultimate guide to

Category Management

a shopper-centric method of cooperation between retailer and supplier

Evelyn van Leur
Jan-Willem Grievink

Publisher: Category & Trade Company
Authors: Evelyn van Leur, Jan-Willem Grievink
In cooperation with Anique Grievink

Design: studioKEET graphic design, Dagmar Wynants
Final editing: D/T Tekstwerk, Ivonne de Thouars
Printing: Wilco I Printing & Binding

ISBN 978-90-822324-1-7
NUR 800
www.categorymanagement.nl

Acknowledgements

We would like to thank our relations who encouraged us to translate this guidebook in English so it can not only be used in Dutch companies within the Netherlands, but also internationally. Many thanks also to Anique Grievink, who stood at the basis of the revised Dutch version of the book and made its design and structure. Also, many thanks to all the people and organizations that helped us in the development process, in particular the companies that made their cases available, being, Arie van Doesburg of PLUS Retail, Joris Hendriks of Coca Cola Enterprises, Eric Wieberdink, Andrea Holbova of PepsiCo International, Erik Tessels of Gamma, and Christian van Someren for his input on online and omnichannel retail. For the international version we also thank Ken Hughes of Glacier Consulting, Steven van de Ridder of Picnic, Deniz Wiedhaup of Coca Cola Enterprises and Rianne van Beek of PLUS Retail.

Also many thanks to our editor and translator Ivonne de Thouars and designer Dagmar Wynants. Finally, many thanks to our families and friends who have given us the time and space and encouraged us to create this book.

Index

The first international guide to Category Management

In the early nineties, I came into contact with Category Management in the supermarket channel. In those days it was especially Brian Harris, a professor at the Southern California University, who gave a major impulse to the further professionalization of Category Management, purchasing, marketing and sales combined under the heading 'buy to sell'. Over the years, I had the privilege to lead several international conferences and courses about this subject. Now, 25 years later, Category Management, together with ECR, became a genuine profession, in which retail's three basic components - revenue, margin and cost – are ever faster and more professional driven from the consumer and shopper.

It has been over ten years since the first guide to Category Management was published in the Netherlands. This guidebook is being used in many corporations and for several educations and trainings. The field of activity now goes beyond the classical selection and management of product ranges based on consumer needs and objectives of retail formats. It is also about store presentation and informing, inspiring and activating consumers and shoppers. And in the Netherlands, this field of expertise is widely and successfully applied in the cooperation between retailers and suppliers, this will be inspiring for organizations in other countries as well.

There are many developments currently taking place in the retail industry. The emergence of online shopping alone is turning old guidelines upside down, as does the shrinking of the classical 'middle market', the mainstream segment, in favor of discount and premium retail formats. And the most important development is how the consumer conquers the power in the retail chain, mainly because of the digitization of the buying process but also because of social developments.

We are getting more and more knowledge of our shoppers and this knowledge should be applied in a manner that better pleases the customer. The challenge lies in winning the consumers' favor with a strong distinctive retail brand. And the shopper should experience this in all aspects of the store, the website and in every detail of the product range and service categories.

Category Management searches for the best solutions for our shoppers, using the retail format as starting point. The goal is adding value and thus improving the return on investment for retailers and suppliers. This is a mutual task for retailers as well as suppliers. A retailer knows everything about his format and deals with the customer's needs on daily basis. But he cannot do without the specialized knowledge of products and categories that suppliers can provide. Solid cooperation with suppliers leads to more knowledge and strength. This requires that suppliers get further insights in the way category management is being adopted by the retailer. This book aims to provide the tools necessary for excellent Category Management, based on the shopper and the retail format. It provides retailers and suppliers with a theoretical framework for projects that create added value for the shopper. By focusing on the shopper's needs, desires and concerns and providing solutions that reinforce the retail brand.

Developments in Category Management are ongoing. Therefore, this thorough revision of 'The guide to Category Management' addresses a number of developments, such as increased knowledge of the shopper and online sales. Category Management does not only find applications in food items, it is used where ever retail brands operate; in home repair, garden, electronics and nonfood items. This will be further elaborated in the specific example cases.

Finally, I hope you will enjoy reading this guidebook and that the knowledge that it conveys will contribute to a healthy future for your company and branch.

Harry Bruijniks
member of the supervisory board Euretco
member of the supervisory board Jumbo Supermarket

Harry Bruijniks gained a rich experience in food retail (Ahold en Laurus) and non-food retail.

Why this guidebook?

Until 1980 retailers purchased products which were combined to assortments. After that, retailers realized that categories were more useful and had several attractive features for both the format as the customer. Purchasing became a real profession which we called category management. After 1996, retailers started to develop all kinds of category management projects with suppliers under the direction of ECR Netherlands. The knowledge gained from these projects was converted into theories that ultimately - around the 10th anniversary of ECR Netherlands (in 2006) - resulted in the first version of 'The ultimate guide to Category Management'.

All knowledge about consumer and shopper thinking, retail positioning, category management and planograms led to considerable optimization. The result? The shopper was served better, assortments were optimized so they suited the format's positioning, and margins and costs improved. The theoretical knowledge and insights from various projects proved to be a great wealth of knowledge and experience. Category Management became the key concept in the relationship between retail and suppliers. To carry on with this knowledge and experience and make it accessible for future generations, 'The guide to Category Management' arose. A practical textbook on a subject that seems so common that we tend to forget that there are a lot of rules and commercial and scientific knowledge involved. From the very first print, this guide tried to combine the three elements: applicability for retailers and suppliers, support in business policy development and scientifically approved.

After our first edition of the guidebook, we made a radical revision. Not because the theory was found to be wrong, far from it. Retail today is more exciting than ever, the power has shifted to the shopper and the retail format as brand and the realization of that retail brand in the execution and categories is essential for success. The chapter about the shopper has been extended as well as the aspects which are important for online category management. We also added new cases.
Many of the examples used are from the Netherlands. Because in the Netherlands, Category Management is well developed, not only at the retailers but also in the cooperation between retailers and suppliers. We think the cases and examples are also recognizable to companies in other countries and a source of inspiration. In addition, we also added a number of international cases.

In our opinion, 'The guide to Category Management' remains a book that offers excellent opportunities to existing and new professionals in buying and merchandising, retail format management, category management, account management, marketing, shoppermarketing and trade marketing, to acquire knowledge and insights. And Category Management is in our opinion the art of collaboration between retail and suppliers in optimal category management which enables the retail format to grow stronger and optimally serve the shoppers' desires.

Evelyn van Leur
Jan-Willem Grievink

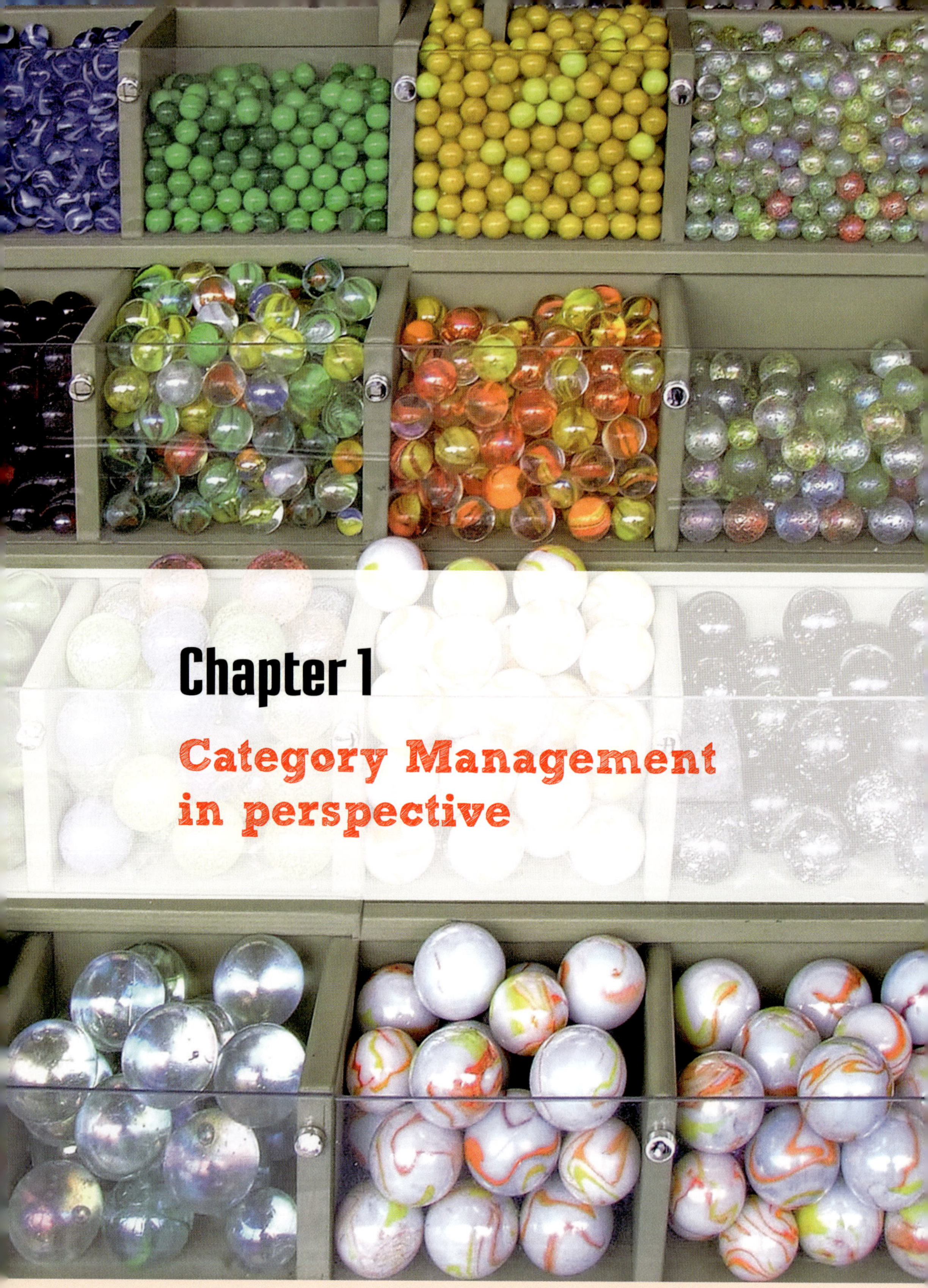

Chapter 1

Category Management in perspective

Category Management is the art of the optimal management of retail product selection and merchandising, combined with integration of data analysis and scientific processes. It is consumer and shopper driven, fact based, process oriented and based on cooperation between retailer and his suppliers. The goal is a sustainable growth and profit for the organization. It is possible to structure a Category Management model in such a way that it is applicable to nearly all retailers and vendors.

The model is the guiding principle for all of the chapters of this book. This book aims to clarify to what extent cooperation issues between trade and industry lead to choices. The particulars of the model will be explained in detail later in this book.

What is Category Management?

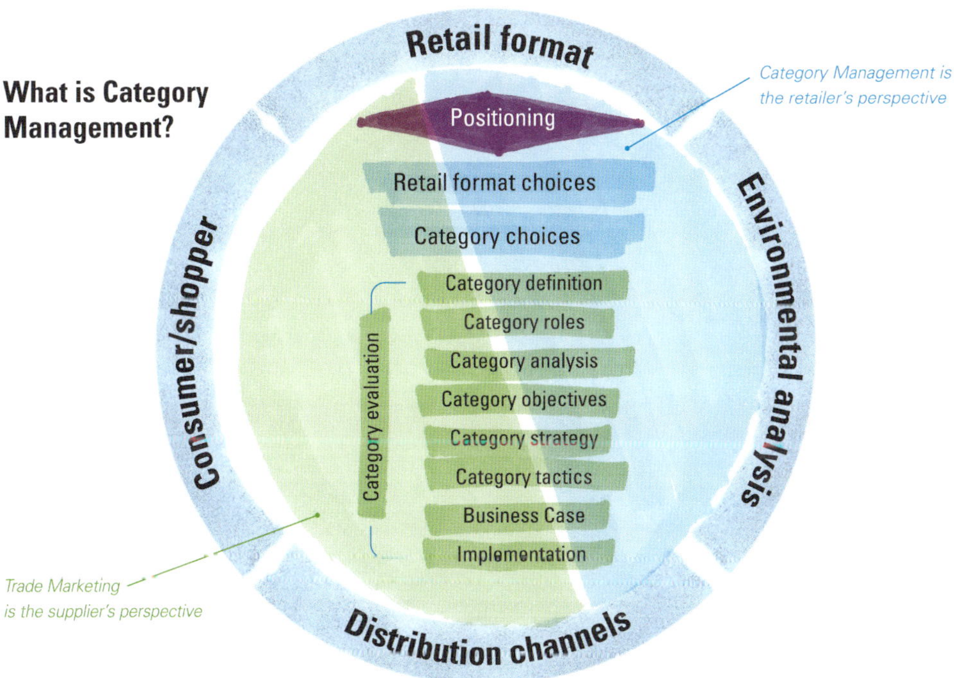

Figure 1.1

Chapter 1 is an introduction in which we provide an overview of the DNA of Category Management.
Chapter 2 details the consistency of Category Management with overall corporate policy.
Chapter 3 explains how to carry out an trend and environmental analysis.
Chapter 4 details how to carry out a shopper analysis.
Chapter 5 focuses on the retail format including characteristics and key building blocks.
Chapter 6 explains the development of a Category Management strategy and all the steps that are required.
Chapter 7 is about the differences between retailers and suppliers, and how Category Management can deal with those differences.
Chapter 8 offers a concise checklist of twenty-five questions, summarizing the everyday process of Category Management outlined in this book.

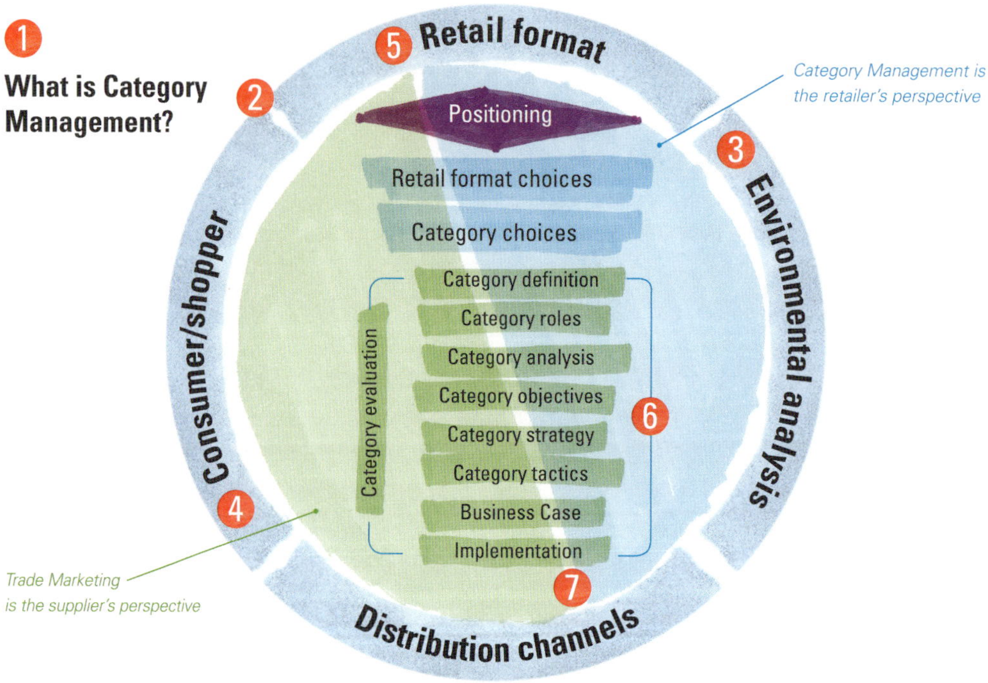

Figure 1.2
This basic diagram is derived from the famous Harris model (The Partnering Group), which is the global standard for road mapping Category Management projects. The numbers in the red dots refer to the chapters in the book. In our model, we have rearranged some components of the original Harris model as well as adding the outer circle, with trends, distribution channels and shopper insights, as wel as retail positioning, and building blocks of the retail format on top of the Harris model. This leads to the above diagram, which is used as a guide throughout the entire book. The field "Trade Marketing", in our conceptual framework is based on the same rules as Category Management, but viewed from the supplier's perspective.

Definitions

There are various definitions of Category Management, including several in the ECR literature. A simple Google search for "Category Management" yields tens of thousands hits with more than 1,000 different definitions. We have put together a definition that best corresponds to the practices of large retail formats and is the easiest to remember.

Category Management is the optimization of categories from the perspective of the shopper and retailer objective.

If you dissect this definition you arrive at the following, more detailed description. "Category Management is the art of cooperation between retailers and industry with regard to the selection and optimal management of categories in which the format and brand of the retailer is strengthened and the needs and desires of the consumer & shopper are served optimally."

The context of use and the core concepts in this book are as follows:

Trade marketing is not dealt with separately, but we consider it the territory of the supplier. It is the optimal revenue generated by the categories in the various distribution channels from the perspective of the supplier, in collaboration with the distributor (retailer).

The **consument,** in this guidebook, is seen as the person who actually consumes or uses the product.

The **shopper** is the person in the household who makes the purchase.

The **retailer** is the organization that is in direct contact with the shopper through the stores or webshop.

The **retail brand/format** is the store concept of the retailer that is labeled with a specific name.

The **supplier**, for our purposes, may be both a manufacturer (consumer products company) as well as a provider of fresh produce, or an importer or wholesaler.

Retail Perspective versus Supplier Perspective

Various terms are used for different functions in the collaboration (doing business) between retail (trade) and suppliers (industry). Depending on the organization, different definitions of these concepts and functions may be used. This may lead to confusion. The following model integrates the most commonly used terms.

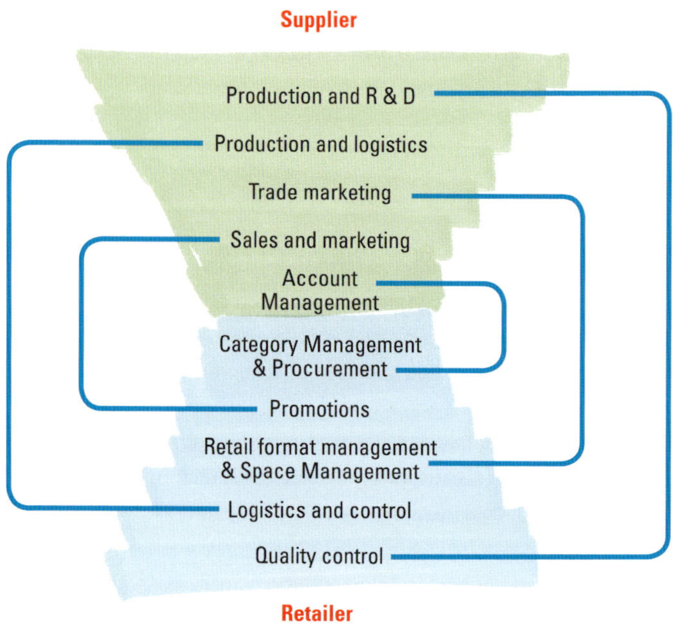

Figure 1.3
This model shows the different functions and areas of both the supplier (top) and the retailer (base). The blue lines show the core roles of the mutual consultation. The Account Manager or Sales Manager and the Category Manager are those who are the most frequently in contact with each other, sometimes supported by sales support and supply managers.

The second layer shows the supplier interacting with the Sales and Marketing Manager, and the retailer interacting with the Promotions Manager.

The actors in the third layer from the center do not have much contact with each other. The Retail Format Manager is the linchpin in the web of retail policy. If it all works out well, the counterpart of the supplier is the Trade Marketer. The fourth layer is about logistics and control: sending and receiving the goods and the associated data. The fifth layer where contact between retail and industry takes place, consists of the production department (and R&D) at the supplier and the auditors (or quality managers) at the retailers. These issues are further elaborated in Chapter 7.

Job titles can vary among retailers and suppliers

Defining job titles in a guidebook like this always incites a debate. Retailers sometimes call a 'Category Manager' a 'buyer' or vice versa, or both functions are combined in a single role. For suppliers, the same sometimes happens with different titles for trade marketing. As a result of the pragmatic operational choices of various retailers and suppliers, we can arrive at the following "ideal" description, with some (major) overlaps.

Among **retailers**, we find (in addition to the management, logistics and financial positions) commercially operational positions such as:

- Category Managers (Responsible for the categories (and products) in relation to the retail format objectives)
- Buyers (Responsible for the procurement of products, typically focusing on value in relation to retail format objectives)
- Promotion Managers (Responsible for managing optimal sales and customer loyalty)
- Space Managers (Responsible the planograms and floor planning in the store)
- Retail format Managers (Responsible for the profile and the execution of the retail format objectives)
- Unit Managers (Responsible for certain groups of categories)
- Quality Managers (Responsible for the reputation of the retail format and for maintaining the desired quality and reliability of both the suppliers and the products)

Among **suppliers** we find the following:

- Sales & Account Managers (Responsible for sales of a brand with a particular client)
- Marketing Managers (Responsible for the marketing objectives of a brand and/or the commercial objectives of a supplier)
- Trade Marketing Managers (Responsible for optimizing the revenue opportunities within retail formats and/or channels. Sometimes they are also responsible for pricing and promotions.
- Category Managers (Responsible for the development of product groups and occasionally brands, through different types of customers)
- Brand Managers (Responsible for the success of the brands in the long term)
- Channel Managers (Responsible for the revenue opportunities of the supplier within certain distribution channels)

In this guidebook, we address Category Management from the retail perspective. We do that in conjunction with the other positions with the retailer, but also in relation to Category Management's counterpart in the industry, which is most often the position of trade marketing manager.

More Profit and More Differentiation

There are four criteria for retailers that dominate any theory about collaboration between retailers and suppliers. The retailer may not always put it this way (i.e. admit it), but the topics important for him and discussed in this book are typically the result of these four criteria:

a. Does the supplier (and his product) help me to achieve higher sales?
b. What is the financial performance of the category and the supplier? Am I going to earn more as a retailer?
c. Does the supplier help me in my differentiation? Does he help to strenghten my retailbrand? Differentiation from the competition is becoming more important for the retailer and the supplier who can help with this will always have an advantage.
d. Following point a: will the availability of this product create an extra bond between the customer and the retailer? Will the relationship of the shopper with the store be strengthened? Is the product (or category) important for the shopper?

Figure 1.4
Retailers have four main criteria that they often use unconsciously to evaluate product ranges and new suppliers. Revenue and profit contribution are obvious criteria, but retailers are also increasingly considering the value that the product (or category) adds to their retail format profile as well as the potential importance of the range (or product) to the customer, asking themselves whether or not this will increase customer loyalty to the particular store. This model is, in fact, the basis for assessing suppliers and their (new) proposals. We elaborate in more detail in Chapter 7.

Category Management Model

We will use the basic model in this book frequently. What follows is an explanation of our intentions with this model. It offers a way to organize all topics related to Category Management.

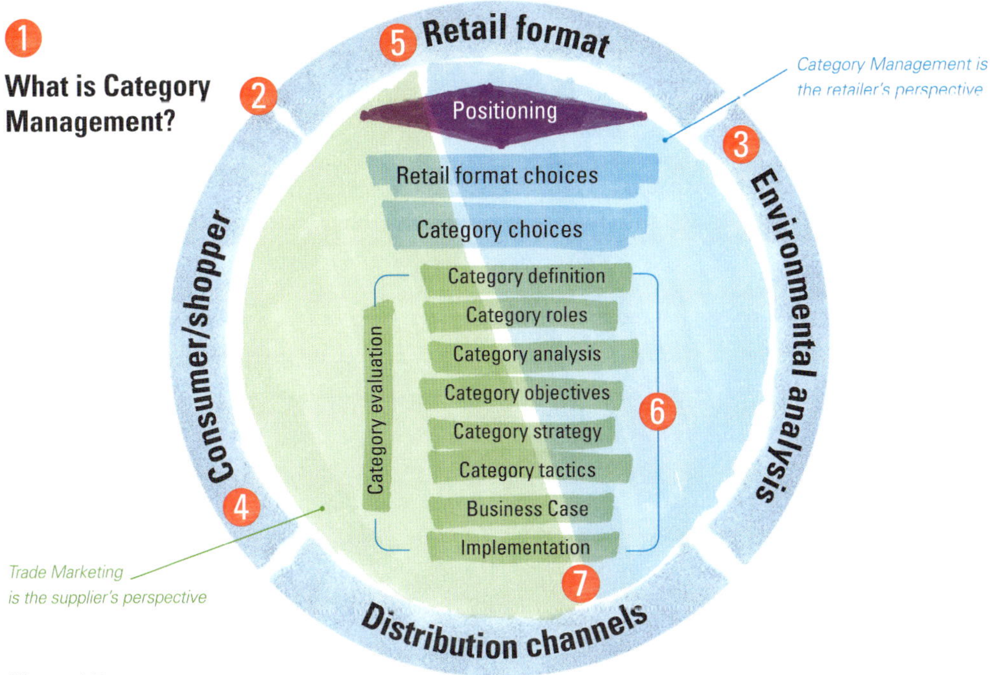

Figure 1.5

How do we read this model?

- This model is based on the behavior (needs) of the consumer as a shopper. There is, of course, a social element to this, hence the trend analysis. The shopper has several options (distribution channels or shopping places) at his disposal. Expectations and options at a gas station are different from expectations and options at a fast food restaurant or a supermarket.
- The retail format, however, affects shopper behavior and vice versa. The retail format of a full-service retailer results in different shopper behavior than that of a hard discount retailer. The retailer brand choices, the format of the store thus has an influence on the positioning to the consumer (shopper).
- In addition, retail brands use different building blocks through which they can be differentiated from other retail formats. Categories are often part of such building blocks. Retail formats require an increasingly clear profile and the quest for differentiation is increasing.
- This brings us to the center of the model where we find the category choices - the Category Management model itself. Category Management has nine steps from definition to evaluation.
- All of these steps are related to each other and are dependent on the 'forces' that may arise from the outer circle: trends, shopper insights, distribution channels and retail format.
- The way in which this model is used in an organizaterion, will have unique features for the way that the retailer organizes himself and the way in which he arranges his primary processes. This opens up opportunities for suppliers who want to do business with the retailer in question.

The Harris model is positioned at the center of the Category Management model, within ECR. Since this model is the most commonly used, we have made it the primary model in this guidebook, though slightly modified (see Chapter 6). This means that, according to this guidebook, the following is the primary objective of Category Management:

Category Management is the optimization of categories from the perspective of the shopper and retailer objective.

The needs of the consumer are central as is the collaboration with the suppliers. Of course cooperation, in principle, should lead to better results, faster processes and lower costs.

In addition to the traditional channels, there are also other channels which bring products to consumers (such as factory outlets, farm sales, market stalls and online sales). We will not repeatedly mention the existence of these channels in this book. The basic rules apply to each segment and sub-channel. We have provided models in instances where there is collaboration between retailers or outlet organizations with multiple vendors. This also applies to e-commerce, non-food retail formats, market concepts, etc.

A Category Management Plan is a Roadmap

Making a complete Category Management Plan is actually no more than a matter of progressing through the model as shown on this page and explained further on. At first addressing the shopper and social considerations, then by analyzing the channel options and the retail formats along with their positioning and choices, followed by the choices for the product range categories. Each of these components is discussed in this guidebook, with the exception of the making of the Category Management Plan itself. With the help of this model and the information in this guidebook, any Category Manager can develop his own Category Plan.

The scope of Cooperation between Trade and Industry

The way retailers and suppliers work together takes many forms. These variations largely conform to ten characteristics. You can use the checklist figure 1.6 to determine in advance the intensity of the cooperation.

Checklist

First, consider the four questions as outlines earlier on as they refer to the main question: to what extent is the product range of the supplier important for the retailer?

1. Generates more revenue?
2. Creates a larger margin?
3. Provides differentiation to the retail format?
4. Increases customer loyalty?

In addition to the ones listed above, there are six more questions.

5. Are we dealing with products in a growing market or is the market saturated?
6. Are there many similar providers from whom the retailer can choose?
7. How professional is the supplier, both on product level, as well as in the area of customer knowledge, and in terms of process efficiency?
8. Is this a strong brand that you, as a retailer, really cannot ignore?
9. How professional is the retailer and how efficient are the processes?
10. How dominant is the retail format in certain market areas?

There are, of course, more variables at play, but these can be brought back to one of the ten questions mentioned above. It can be important for the category manager to consider these questions. For example, a manufacturer is the supplier of a product in a growing market and the retailer wants to utilize the product to differentiate itself. When the retailer can fall back on three similar suppliers will give him a very different situation than the following. Suppose that the retailer with his product (even when it is a commodity) only can rely on one important supplier for his product (e.g. sugar)

It is very important for a retailer as well as a manufacturer to answer these ten questions genuinely. These answers, to a large extent, determine the position (and potency) of the co-operation.

Figure 1.6

SCORECARD FOR COOPERATION

Both retailer and supplier can use this scorecard, to rate the individual questions between 1 (worst) and 10 (best). The final score indicates whether action should be initiated or not. If the score is below 60, it is important to take action quickly! We recommend that the Category Manager also asks the opinion about the current situation from the leadership from within the own organization.

Below is a sample scorecard for the evaluation of retailer/supplier collaboration.

KEY QUESTIONS	**SCORE**
1. Revenue potential	....
2. Profit potential	....
3. Contribution to retail format/brand	....
4. Value for the shopper	....
5. Growth market	....
6. Overcapacity	....
7. Professionalism of supplier	....
8. Power of brand/supplier	....
9. Professionalism of retailer	....
10. Dominance of retail brand	....
Total score	**........**

This chart shows the ten most important characteristics influencing the relationship between retailer and supplier within a product range. Give a score of 1 (worst) to 10 (best) for each question and tally up the outcomes. If the total score is 80 or higher, you should cherish this relationship. If it is 60 or lower, it is high time for intervention and improvement.

The Future of Category Management

The rapid growth of online shopping and discounters, big data and new technologies changes the profession of Category Managers. The shopper has more choice than ever, where she shops. Also the emerging 'bluring' concepts in which retail- and foodservice are integrated, contribute to this change. Because of increasing transparency, the consumer is going to behave in a different way. There is more information about the shopper, his behavior and also about the product. All this affects every aspect of Category Management. Instead of a long period of analysis and preparation (for the inclusion of a product for example, or for a change in the planogram), the role of the Category Manager is getting more dynamic so that he can quickly respond to new insights and/or changing needs. In this guidebook we provide tools to help the Category Manager in his new role.

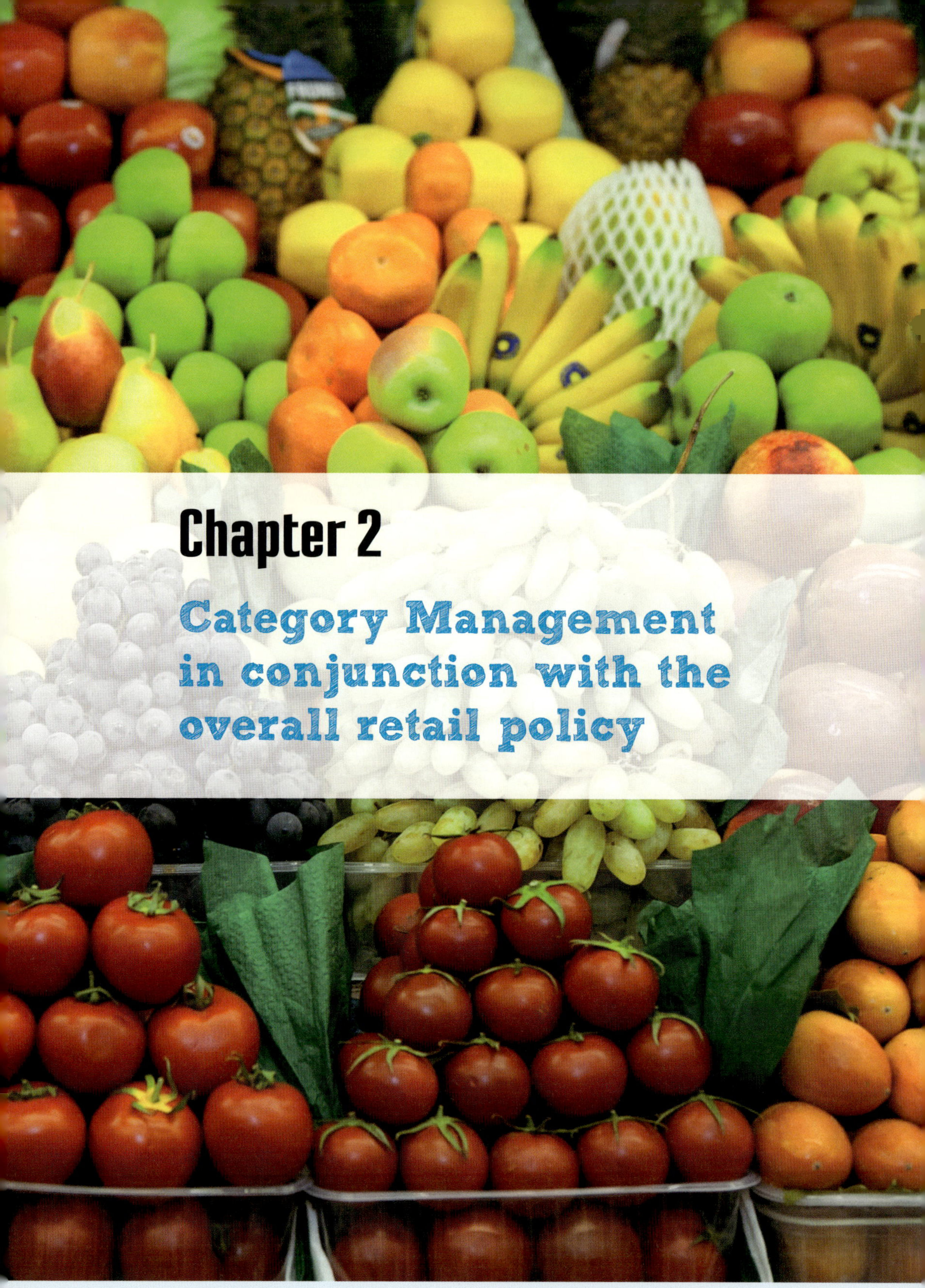

Chapter 2

Category Management in conjunction with the overall retail policy

This chapter deals with retail policies that go beyond the daily work of the Category Manager, but directly affect it. In this introduction we describe the different levels in an overall retail policy.

1

What is Category Management?

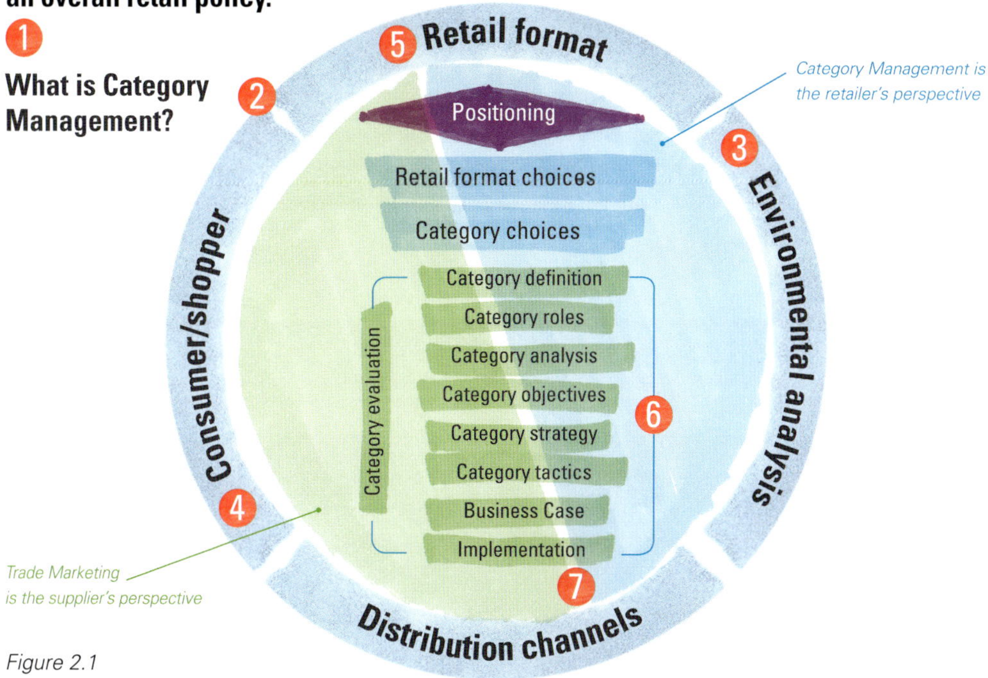

Figure 2.1

Category Management is not an isolated discipline, it is part of a retailers' overall policy. This basic model shows, as a guiding framework, the cohesion of all the aspects of the overall policy and to what extent it concerns Category Management.

- Every plan or idea of Category Management has to start with the consumer and the shopper.
- The consumer is in the centre of a changing society, where continuously changes take place with both short and long term effects.
- At the same time, shoppers have more places to shop than ever, not only within different formats of the retailer, like convenience store formats and and also in other branches like gas stations. Above all, the internet provides 24/7 shopping possibilities around the globe.
- Then there is the retail brand with its own characteristics and features.
- The retail format helps to make choices. What are the promises the retail brand makes to the shoppers and how is that proven?
- The choices of the retailer lead to a particular position in the whole competition field. We call this positioning; it distinguishes the one retail brand from the rest.
- The positioning of a retail format requires several 'building blocks'. For example assortments and services but also experience, pricing and accessibility.
- All these previous items lead to choices in terms of product ranges and products. Actually, this is where the real work of Category Management starts.
- The roadmap of a Category Manager consists of nine steps.
- All of this, of course, has an impact on the supplier. If it is correct, the supplier is much earlier involved in the process, but in the end, the overall assessment process of the retailer leads to one or more suppliers.

Consistency is critical

There is an obvious link between societal developments and the success of an product introduction. For example, the booming sales of LED bulbs had everything to do with the need for sustainability in our society. The primary aim of this chapter is to show the consistency of Category Management with consumer behaviour, trends, channel characteristics and retail positioning. The details of these chapters will be elaborated later. This summary only sketches the cohesion.

NB This chapter gives several examples from the food branch because that is the retail channel with the most detailed links. But the outlines for non-food retailers are exactly the same. Only the motivation for product use (and purchase) is different.

2.1 It all starts with the shopper

The assortment policy of a retailer starts with understanding how the consumer fulfills his needs. There a two kinds of needs, the rational, often functional needs, and the unconscious needs and wants of which the consumer is often unaware. Again, for clarity of the explanation we focus on food retailing, but other retail branches are subject to identical laws.

It appears that shoppers in the entire world buy their food in six different ways: the six 'shopping trips'. For trade and industry, it is important to have a thorough understanding of these six different shopping trips in a particular market or market area because the shopping trip and its changes determine the market's potential and assortment. In the graphics on these pages, developed by the Food Service Institute (FSIN) and EFMI Business School, you will find the six shopping trips in a coherent model. The horizontal axis shows the character of a product or service from generic low-priced products (usually referred to as commodities) to premium (indulgence) products. You can see the high or low monetary value of a consumption product's kilocalorie. The vertical axis represents the elapsed time between purchase and consumption or use of a product, divided into six different time tables. This results into the six shopping trips. We will expand the details later.

Figure 2.2 **Shopper trips determine the consumer's selection**

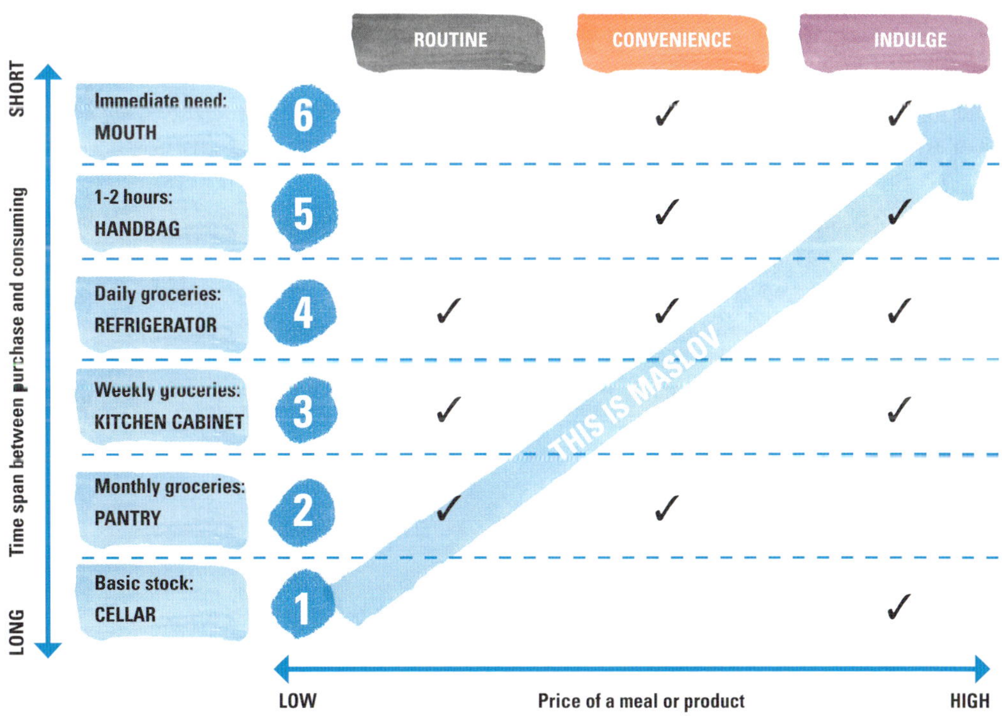

Maslov shows us that the more prosperous a society is, the less attention the consumer has for a basic stock (a well filled cellar or pantry to survive) and the more focus there is on luxurious products (for short term consumption). (FSIN analyses, based on figure FSIN and EFMI Business School Quo Vadis 2008, update 2013.)

Figure 2.2 is explained in the following pages. The diagonal line is a simplification of the well-known needs according to the Maslow's Pyramid. The left vertical axis shows the different types of shopping trips, divided by the elapsed time between purchase and consumption.
The horizontal bar at the top summarises the three ways of consumer purchasing (in food). In a routine purchase, products (commodities) are bought in a spontaneous way, without too much thinking. The second way is purchasing with mere 'convenience motives'. It means that products are bought for immediate consumption or storage. The third way of purchasing is to buy something because you want to indulge yourself or your family. Theoretically, you can use any shopping trip for each of the main reasons. However that does not occur in real life. We have indicated the most usual cases with a tick.

Shopper considerations

We dedicate a separate chapter to analyse a shopper's behaviour. For a Category Manager, it is definitively important to realize that the behaviour of a shopper goes through four different phases.

1. The pre-shopping phase: everything that happens before consumers decide to start a shopping trip. Obviously, this is the retailer's first opportunity to influence the behaviour of the potential shopper.
2. The to-shopping phase: the moment when the consumer is on his way to purchase something. He can still be affected along the way.
3. The shopping phase: the actual purchase, in the shop or online. This is when the classic Category Management manifests itself.
4. The post-shopping phase: the ultimate moment when satisfaction of the purchase is confirmed by use, additional services, etc.

Category Managers must realize that their working field not only has to do with phase 3, the actual shopping phase, but also with the processes before and after the purchase, the complete customer journey.

2.2 Environment & Trend analysis

From social trend to food trend

Social developments affect the way we do our shopping and eventually lead to the purchase of other products. The EFMI Business School developed a model (the EFMI Trend Funnel) to explain this phenomenon. Retail and industry can use this model to bring consistency in certain trends and the development of product ranges and business activities.

Example: There are more and more single households (social trend). Even within the classical multi-person household, members are living as a single person for a few days a week. Time saving and efficiency are important values for these 'loners'. Every day home cooking is not for them, but from time to time they compensate their highly efficient lives by spending a lot of time on something they enjoy (2nd layuer of funnel). Having dinner with friends or family can be one of those compensating motives. This trend leads to two types of products. On the one hand we have easy to consume, single serving meals and on the other the popular slow-food dishes.

Forecasting requires continuity

In general, many product developments are easy to predict with the use of the Trend Funnel. It is a matter of learning, to continuously see the world in an analytical way. This prediction is easier for European countries, because the Trend Funnel applies to all countries and the United States and Canada are often ahead of Europe. Although we have to make a cultural translation of these Trend Funnel conclusions, we can easily observe how social developments have resulted in new food and product trends overseas.

Figure 2.3 **EFMI Trend Funnel**

The numbers in the Trend Funnel indicate the duration of a new development. A product trend does not last as long as a food- or category trend.

The Trend Funnel is a model that allows us to translate long-term social developments and value trends, as described by scientific institutes, for food or other categories and product trends and changing consumer habits. At the top of the funnel you will find social trends like changes in the composition of households. These developments are usually long lasting and lead to changes in things that the society considers as important (the second layer of the Trend Funnel). For example, there is safety, health, quality time with family and friends, etc. These value trends are also quite long lasting, but are more 'fashion-sensitive' and lead to innovation in food trends like the things we consider important in the way we do our groceries, for instance. Do we still want to spend hours to gather this week's groceries or are we searching for more convenience? Do we want access to more healthy and honest food assortments? How much time do we want to spend in the kitchen? How important is it to cook something special for our guests at home or to tell stories about what we serve? These kinds of food trends usually last for a period of 3 to 10 years, after which they are replaced by new ones. The Trend Funnel is developed by EFMI Business School.

How to get information

Offices for national statistics like ONS or Census deliver continuous predictions that can be used for the first layer of the Trend Funnel. In Europe we also have Eurostat, the official EU statistic Association, with access to European trends. In addition, national planning associations and other planning offices provide forecasts of changes in people's value level. The first two layers of the Trend Funnel can be filled with these data and we can even recognize countries with identical patterns. The third layer is formed by food trends, which can be inferred from developments in countries that are ahead of our own country.

Sometimes it seems predicting product trends for the next 5 years is a piece of cake. The reality is however more complex. It demands skills and patience to take cultural differences in consideration. Nevertheless, the Trend Funnel is a perfect tool in the process of Category Management that periodically can be refilled with publicly known analyses. This process also requires experience and knowledge. Fast job changes often cause a brain-drain in commercial departments (both in trade and industry), which jeopardizes the quality of this process.

The challenge for Category Management is to periodically update this Trend Funnel from being general to being specific (e.g. once every two years). To some extent that is possible with publicly available information and conclusions from reports and analyses. By using these general changes, the options and consequences for assortment and promotion policy can be made concrete.

The current food trends can be summarized in seven values: Culinary, Convenience, Care & Cure, Conscious, Cute story, Cheap and Cozy. Nearly all innovations in the food industry can be related to these seven values. This leads, among other things, to an explosion of convenience products There are more and more single households (top layer of the Trend Funnel). These households are increasingly under pressure because life is so demanding (the emotion in the second layer). For a lot of households, time is a new important value, so saving time is worth money (third layer). Convenience food provides for that need. We can give the same example for health (the healthier a product, the more value for money); and products with a 'good story' (a traditional Austrian farmhouse sausage is worth more than a factory Frankfurter).

2.3 Competing channels

In both food and non-food, consumers easily switch channels to purchase something they want. They are not loyal to channels anymore. If there is have a need, any format or concept that seems to have a solution qualifies for the actual purchase. A sandwich can be purchased anywhere, whether in a supermarket, restaurant, or at the petrol station, butcher or baker. Same goes for ice cream or beverages. However, for a pair of shoes or booking a trip the online possibilities are infinite and the many traditional stores are struggling to cope with the new competitors so a category manager has to cope with new competitors with different business concepts. On top of that concept will merge that cannot be classified in one channel since they are e.g. both restaurant and supermarket.

Figure 2.4 **Example of how channels in food are divided**

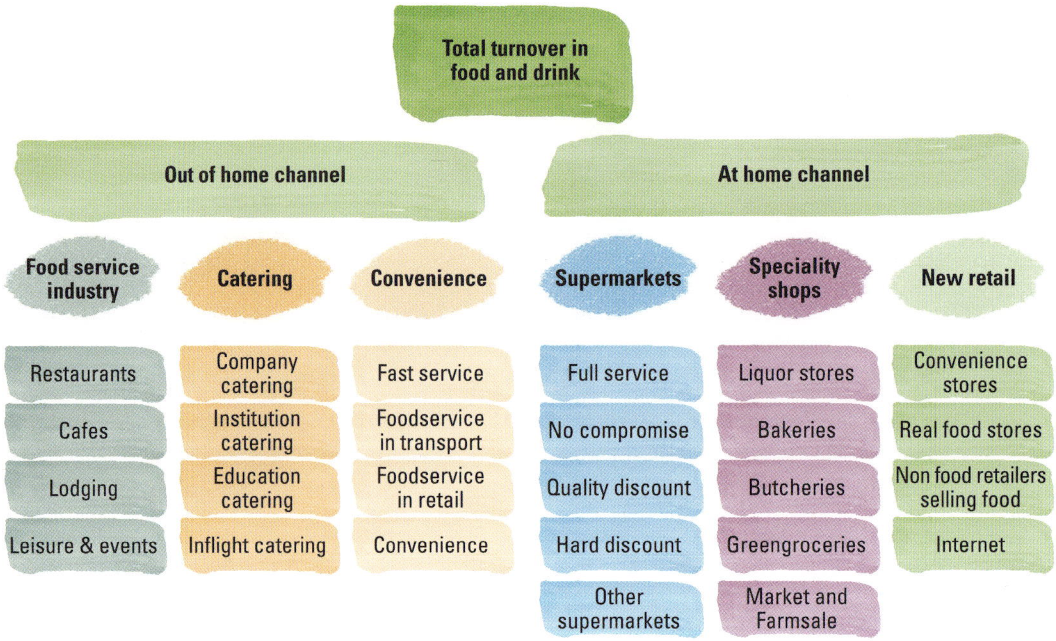

The Food Service Institute (FSIN) developed a model involving the core question: does a segment focus primarily on outdoor or home consumption? All food formats are arranged as a concept divided into the six main segments. Each of these segments has its own business concepts and profit models.

Omni channel shopping

Within the layout of the channels as made by FSIN (in the scheme you will find an example for the food branch), online shopping plays an important role in all channels. The online channel should therefore not be seen as a separate channel (which often happens) but rather as another access for the consumer to a channel. An online supermarket for example, maintains the function of the supermarket channel, but approaches the consumer online. In the out-of-home channel, internet is used for restaurant reservations or sandwiches are ordered with an app and picked up later. The ease and accessibility of omni-channel shopping, significantly encourages the consumers' switching behaviour. The choice between two online supermarkets will be based on other grounds than the choice between two supermarkets which are geographically remote. A Category Manager must adapt to changing consumers' behaviour and new unexpected competitors who disturb the status quo and change the rules. He has to learn how to switch gear with classical channel functions as the various channels have their own business concepts he must compete with. (See figure 2.4).

2.4 The retail format as a brand

A consumer wants to trust the retail brands in which he makes his purchases. For retailers, this brand perception is becoming increasingly important. Their retail format promises something to consumers and, therefore, is a brand. Previously, only products had a brand image. Nowadays the retailer is seen as preferred brand, whether that format is merely a website (e.g. Zalando or Amazon), or a retailer with many stores (e.g. Primark or IKEA).

Four success factors

All elements that can boost a retail brand can be summarized in four success factors. Category Management works with all four factors.

1. The positioning of the retail brand (the store's appeal to the shopper); a retailer uses certain building blocks, usually certain assortments (product groups) and services.
2. The way the retailer store remains up-to-date and attractive to the shopper.
3. The interpretation of the format, not only specific and differentiating product ranges (see 1), but the total package with assortment, price and service.
4. The quality of shop floor execution which is perhaps the most important precondition. Are your stores clean, are customers comfortable, do they get what they expect, etc? The latter applies mainly for a web shop; is the customer really getting what he expects (or slightly more), and is it delivered on time and without worry or stress? The retail brand appreciation will help to build trust with the customer.

Figure 2.5 **Category Management can contribute to each of these four succes factors**

In this diagram, four known Category Management techniques are plotted. Next to range, you will find replenishment, product introduction and effective promotions. The core business of a supermarket is to compose the appropriate range at the right price. But there is more. In the diagram above, we see the four most important attributes for successful retailing. Often, the shop floor execution is underestimated by Category Managers as well as by suppliers and other stakeholders. Even the most perfect plans with flawless promotions will not succeed in a cluttered shop with ineffective staff.

Category Managers must be aware of the connection between these key success factors. New or future technologies like self-scanning or interactive shopping lists can also affect the success of this speciality. Loyalty cards, i-beacons and other digital technologies have a growing influence on Category Management.

The rules of brand thinking

Many retail formats are developing into a brand, one that gets the trust of consumers. This means that retailers will place high demands on their format. All the elements of that contribute to the retail brand and format will be developed in conjunction to support the creation a leading brand.

The choice of ranges and products is obviously one of the key building blocks for retailers to transform their store into a leading brand. Therefore, Category Managers have now more to do with general policy than before. Selection failures in the assortment will damage the image and positioning of the format. We will explain the relationship between the retail positioning and its assortment policy in Chapter 5.

More than the sum of ranges

When a retail format is transformed into a brand, three things must happen consistently:

1. The instrumental elements offered, must give value for money and be appealing to your target audience. These elements are your products, shelves and displays, but also your services and guarantees. That part of your company's policy requires ongoing maintenance and upgrading. What was extraordinary yesterday, is ordinary today and may be outdated tomorrow.
2. The perception (and image) you want to create should match the previous point. Shop, sphere and surprises should strengthen the sense of satisfaction of the customer. This is about feeling, senses and psychology, a speciality most retailers have not mastered yet. Consistency, dropping a transparent and predictable story and practising the art of good story telling (let others talk about you) are techniques that can give this policy substance.
3. The shop floor execution must be in harmony with the two elements above. You can pretend to be a shop with exciting tasteful products and competitive pricing but if the consumer has a negative experience because the fruit is spoiled or the staff is chewing gum and chatting with each other or because the competitor had that new product two months earlier on shelf, something is wrong.

Figure 2.6 **What makes a retail format turn into a retail brand**

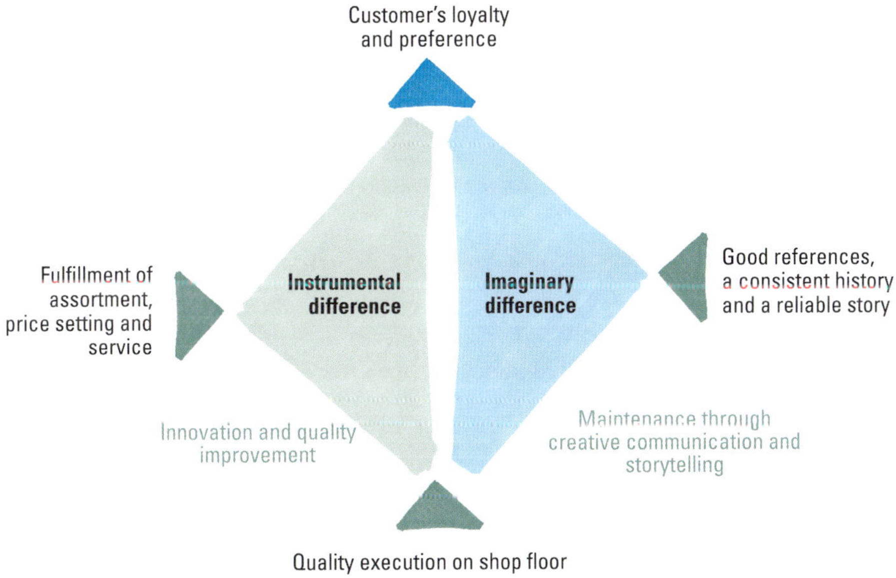

The main elements of building a retail brand are associated with each other in this scheme. The result of the three green arrows leads to consumers' loyalty and preference (the blue arrow). (FoodService Instituut (FSIN))

2.5 Choices of a strong retail brand

To stand out in the crowd, retail formats want to distinguish themselves from others. A commodity image will hardly create emotional consumers' preferences. Formats that exclusively use rational or pragmatic arguments to bind the consumer, expose themselves to risks. If consumers only come to you because you are near, it seems a safe argument but it is in fact dangerous. A strong retail brand uses four questions.

1. What kind of consumer do I want as loyal customer?
2. What attributes make sure that my customers see our shops as their preferred choice?
3. How can I ensure that shoppers are not only fans, but will even act as ambassadors towards their friends and acquaintances?
4. How do I surprize my shoppers and prevent that their buying habits in my stores become routine. In daily practice, the great mistake of retailers is not providing a clear answer to these four questions. The chapters on positioning will elaborate on the attributes retailers can use to differentiate themselves.

Summary chapter 2

- Category Management always starts with the shopper.
- Consumers are strongly influenced by developments in society which can be forecasted.
- You can often perceive in other countries how trends translate into tangible products.
- The consumer is less loyal to stores or even channels. He switches easily and clicks and bricks compete to fulfill his needs.
- Formats behave more and more like brands. Therefore, a Category Manager has to take the rules of brand building into account.
- A strong retail brand has the guts to make clear choices and Category Management must adapt to these choices.

Chapter 3

Environmental analysis

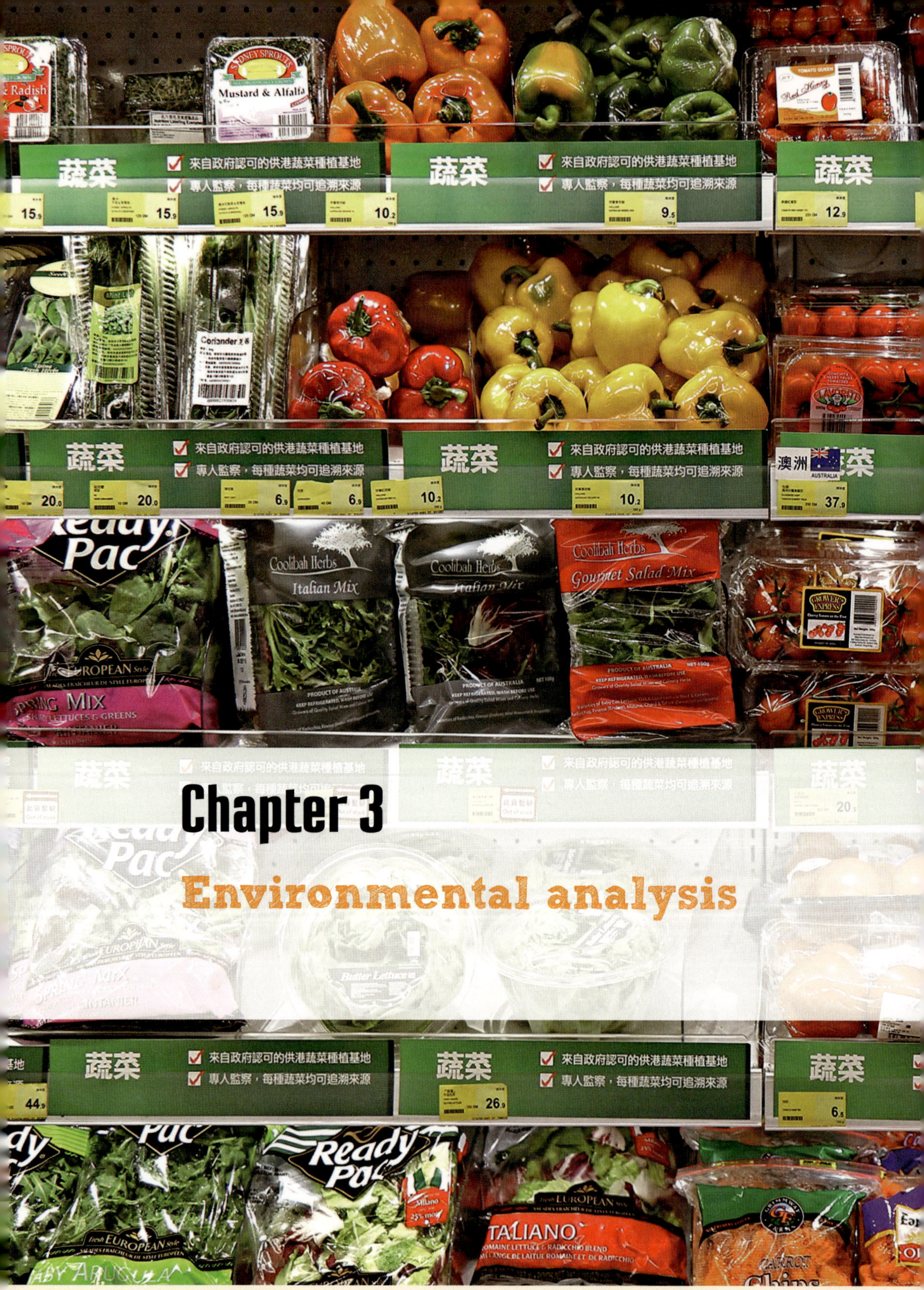

In this chapter we discuss the key elements in conducting an environmental analysis. The chapter is divided into seven parts.

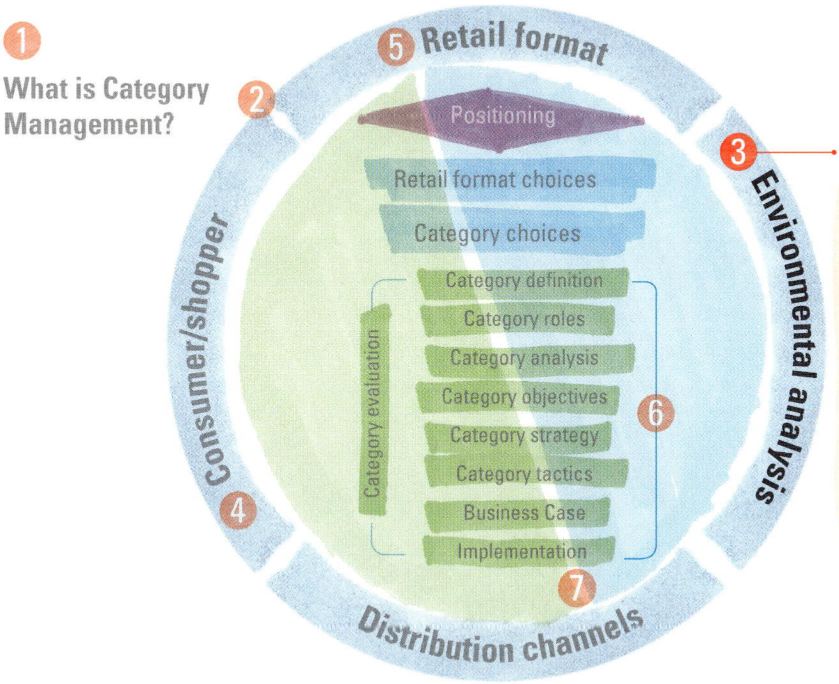

- 3.1 Why is an environmental analysis indispensable?
- 3.2 Social trends affect the product
- 3.3 Monitoring consumers' value trends
- 3.4 Developments in different channels
- 3.5 Analysing the competition
- 3.6 The retailers' vision
- 3.7 The retailers' skills and process abilities

First we explain why every Category Management Process should include environmental analysis (3.1). Subsequently, you can read why the success of categories is inseparably connected to long-term social effects (3.2).

Consumer and shopping trends should also be continuously monitored as they affect the retail format's business models (3.3). The developments in the different channels are equally important. If non-food retailers start selling drinks and sandwiches and supermarkets stunt with household items, it affects the scope of the Category Manager (3.4). Obviously, we also have to analyse the competition, as discussed in 3.5. Category Manager and suppliers should realize that the retailers' vision (the owner) can cause different rules and possibilities for a format than theory would suggest (3.6). In summary, it is necessary to make a fair assessment of the retailers' skills and process abilities as a retailer or category manager in order to make realistic plans; preferably in co-operation with multiple suppliers (3.7).

3.1 Is an environmental analysis indispensable?

Every retailer experiences the effects of social developments. For that sole reason, it is important to consider the environment. However, society not only affects retailers, but it also affects suppliers and competitors. Just being a part of society forming a random opinion, is not sufficient. For an appropriate format policy – which is in turn relevant for the retailers' category policy - a thorough analysis is required.

The foundation of external and internal analyses

A solid policy in Category Management is founded on adequate environmental analysis. The retail format management should initiate such analysis annually to get a grip on external factors like social trends, consumer trends, developments in other channels and of course the developments of directly competing formats. The Trend Funnel in chapter 2 provides some necessary clues for that process.

Translating environmental analyses and tightening the retailers' format policy, is the working area of a retail format manager. But Category Managers should get involved, because details of the analysis often provide useful information for the options in the retailers' Category Management policy. In the diagram on this page, Category Managers can note specific ideas or options during the analysis.

Figure 3.1

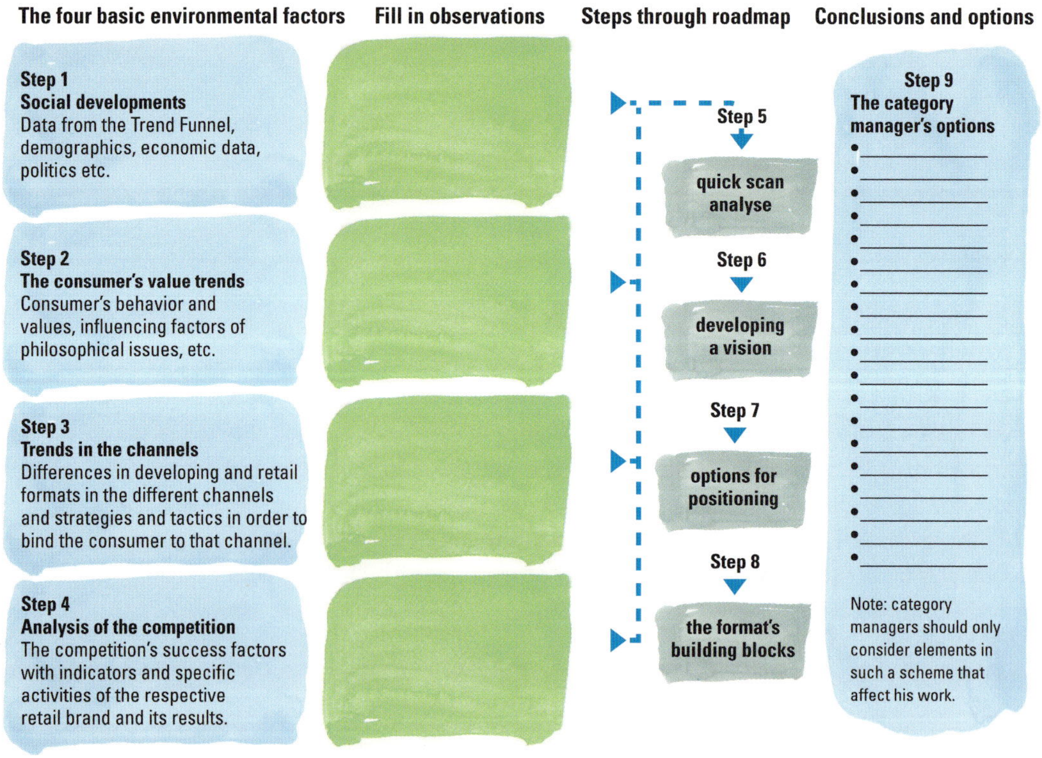

An environmental analysis consists of four levels. First, there are social changes, the resulting consequences and options (also the Trend Funnel in chapter 2). The second level concerns the consumers' value trends in your market area. The third level is about trends in the different channels in and around this market area. Which innovations attract your consumer? The last level is a conscientious analysis of direct competition in your own market area. In the diagram above you can note your conclusions (1 to 4) before you follow steps 5 to 8 and finally complete the list at point 9.

Four basic steps of environmental analysis

Step 1. Social developments
The information we obtain from the Trend Funnel is generic. Thus your own market area could show (slight) deviations. A bigger influence of the elderly, young people or families, for example, leads immediately to different food trends. Municipalities or counties often have information about local developments that are different from the national average.

Step 2. The consumers' trends value
This involves concrete changes in that what consumers consider important. A Category Manager benefits from the observation of what is (or will be) trending in his own market area.

Step 3. The channels' trends
This step refers to the differences in developments and formats in the various channels in your market area. Category Managers can also note the strategies and tactics the channels use to bind the consumer.

Step 4. Analysis of competition
In this step we give consideration to all competitors' success factors including key figures, concrete activities and their results. Especially new trendy concepts can disrupt existing markets completely.

Note that a Category Manager should only give notice to elements which will directly influence his own work.

Completing the roadmap
After analysing the four key questions, a compact roadmap shows up in steps 5 to 9.

Step 5: quick scan analysis from the Category Managers' perspective.

Step 6: what does this mean for the retail formats' policy? Should Category Managers outline the possibilities they see relating to the categories in their working field? Can the format do/mean something special in managing categories?

Step 7: which vision change has value for the formats' positioning? Is it necessary to adept the format's Unique Selling Proposition (USP) to distinguish it from the competition?

Step 8: how can the format's building blocks be changed? Are they the same as last year? Should suppliers change to 'participate' with new opportunities?

Step 9: all concrete ideas relevant to the Category Manager and the managing of his category.

3.2 Social trends affect the product

Introducing the Trend Funnel (Chapter 2), we already discussed the impact of social changes in food trends. The substantial increase in single households has implications for the way households shop, but also for the favourite time and place for groceries. And of course, this in turn affects the purchased product. The most importants social change is the growth of e-commerce. Millenials use their smartphone continiously.

Too early, too late

Most social developments will not immediately translate into retailers' actions. After all, changes evolve gradually. Responding to change is a matter of feeling and 'trial and error'. Often, it doesn't succeed. If a retailer suddenly anticipates on trends (e.g. increasing single households) with high expectations, the results are usually disappointing. Consequently the retailer reverses his policy (cleans his assortment, etc.) and will be reticent in responding to the same trend. He often discovers later that the competitor serves an increasing amount of single households and so his policy must be corrected hastily.

Tip

"Good artists copy, great artists steal". This well known quote of Pablo Picasso also applies to the translation of social trends in product innovations. Other societies have already attained a real level of social development like in the USA. In that case, it is wise to analyse how this development led to other (food) trends and products.

Analysis and testing

Figure 3.2 can help to gradually face retailers' and manufacturers' expectations of social changes. As retailers or suppliers, you can use the chart to brainstorm ideas together for fifteen minutes. What trends do you both spot in the market area and which future options are entailed? You could even test some ideas together to find out whether the trend already initiates new products or ranges.

Figure 3.2 **Roadmap to translate social trends in retail options**

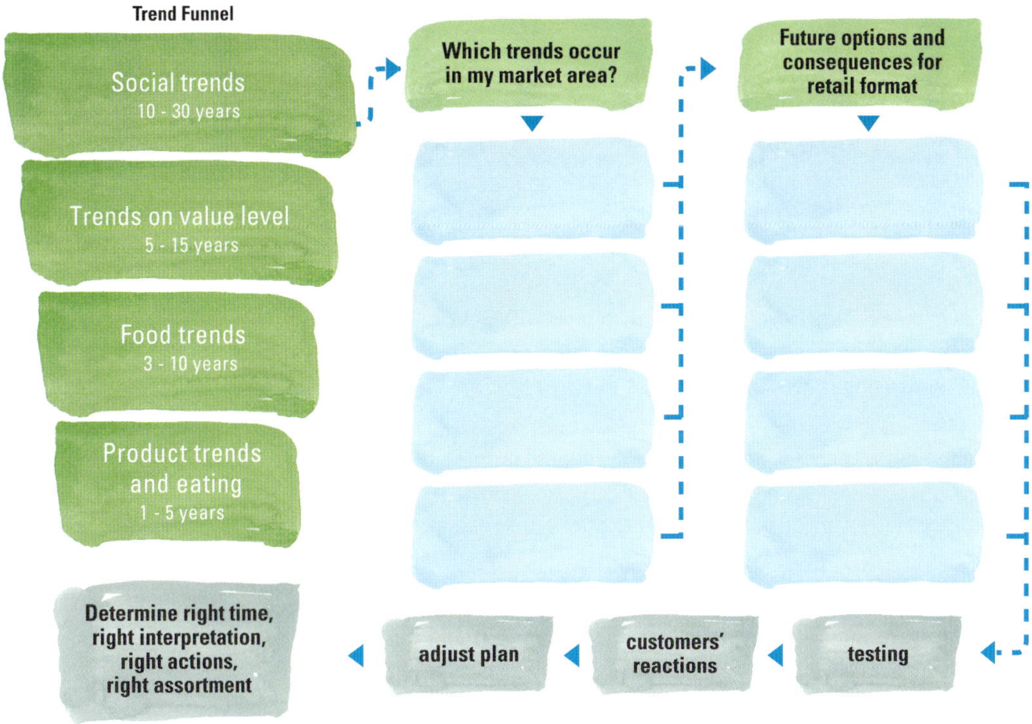

This model can function as a tool for Category Managers who wish to have short brainstorming sessions with suppliers about how both agree on the translation of the Trend Funnel into concrete options for the retailer. (EFMI Business School and FSIN)

Topics that could be placed on this trend layer include:

- Number of people per household;
- Difference between elderly (older single people) and younger people with the same household characteristics;
- Individualization;
- Ethnicity of the population (multiculturalism);
- Proportion of dual earners and emancipation;
- Ageing and leisure;
- Time management and sense of urgency of children in a household.
- Use of e-commerce and apps in purchasing process

Reports of the Eurostat often provide an excellent starting point for this analysis.

3.3 Consumers' value trends under the microscope

The second layer contains the consumers' value trends. This concerns everything consumers in a particular market area (or in the target group of retailers) consider as important or what will be important for them in the next few years. This can entail dozens of different topics like the environment, animal welfare, individualization and health. We mention a few things that could affect their shopping behaviour later on:

- Guilt about the dysfunction of the family;
- Dependence on (and use of) technology (digitization);
- Dealing with prosperity, well-being and purpose questions;
- Influences by Non-Governmental Organizations (NGO's like Greenpeace, Amnesty International, Save the Children, etc.);
- Concerns about the future;
- Safety;
- Need for transparency and honesty;
- Distrust of anything large and bureaucratically organized;
- The value of friendships and getting together with friends;
- Craving for conviviality versus individualism;
- Hobbies and leisure spending;
- Stressed feelings involved with shopping;
- Ambitions and inquisitiveness, etc.

Again, you can respond too soon to value trends. But precisely these trends have a driving force as they can move a market and accelerate developments. A second disadvantage of value trends is that translation into concrete actions can evoke feelings of disgust (or sympathy). So they are polarized. Retailers often do not make an explicit choice, but offer several options to the shopper.

Down trading lead to a new reality with hybrid consumer

The financial crisis of 2008 has globally led to trading down in shopping behaviour. The consumer saved money and liked living that way. Trading down means that the consumer holds on to a certain lifestyle which, in his opinion, is important. But he will try to fulfill that lifestyle in a smarter (cheaper) way. This has led to less spending an everyday stuffand a new reality, summed up by the term 'hybrid consumer'. This consumer is travelling with a discount airline to London to buy a Prada bag. He buys his bread at the discounter but visits the butcher for some delicious traditional ham.

The problem with this (increasing) hybrid consumer behaviour is that it does not seem logical and is not predictable. Therefore, it is hard to analyse value trends. On the other hand, it seems to be a general trend that mainstream products are less important (the mid-market) and simultaneously 'quality discounting' and 'premium product selling' are becoming more important.

Figure 3.3 **From consumers' value trends to retail options and actions**

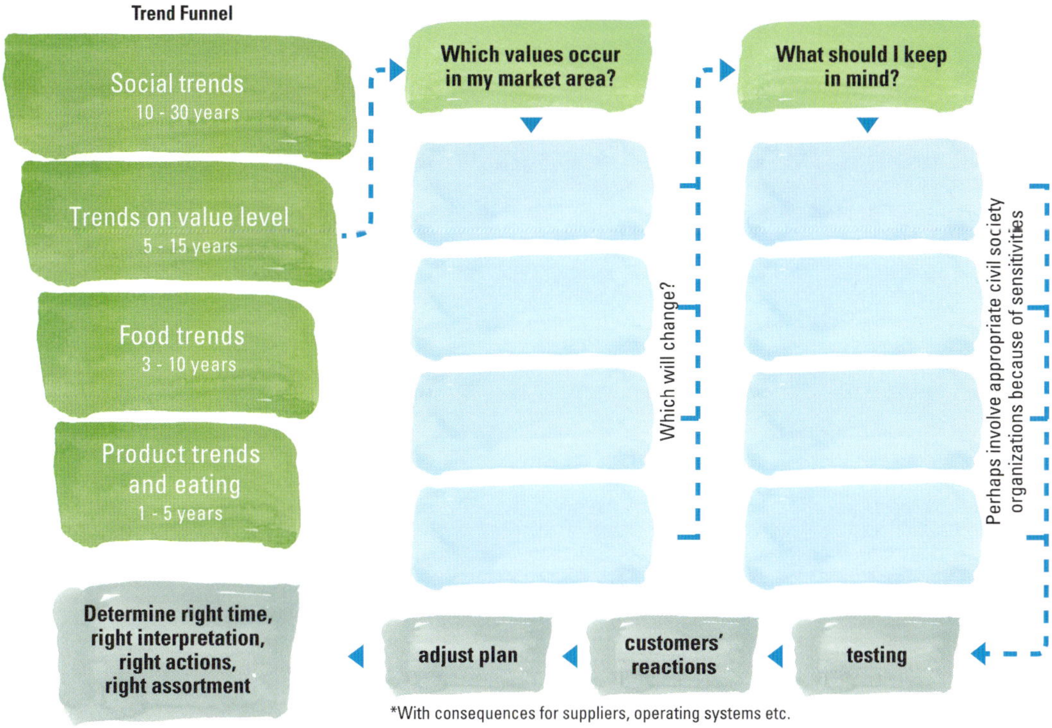

This scheme is also meant as a tool for brainstorming sessions between retailers and suppliers, now focused on an impression of consumers' values and trends. (EFMI Business School and FSIN)

Fill in trend of the branch trends e.g. food or DIY and product trends

Of course, this figure can also be used to fill in the last two layers of the Trend Funnel: the food and product trends *(for non-foods: non-food trends and non-food product trends).*

With this schedule, you can note which branch trends (eg. food or DIY) and product trends are already important in other countries and will eventually apply to your own country. It is better to watch and copy (and translate into your own culture), then to invent yourself.

An outstanding example of value trends is that average households want to spend less time in the kitchen except for when cooking is considered as an art. Then consumers exert themselves to the outmost with luxury recipes, individual ingredients, professional attributes, etc. At these moments, extra time is spent in the kitchen. But for all other meals, the time spent in the kitchen has been declining for decades, which leads to an explosion of 'convenience foods' and single dishes.

PLUS Retail lives up to fair trade

Retail Landscape Netherland

PLUS Retail is a quality supermarket in the Netherlands, with only franchisees. At a time every supermarket expands its range, exclusive supermarkets like Albert Heijn lower their prices and a discounters like Lidl rise, it is difficult to maintain your differentiation and value.

PLUS Retail defined four core values:
Quality, Attention, Local and Responsibility. Responsibility includes sustainable concepts like organic, fair trade, animal welfare and also health and food waste. But how does a category manager give a good interpretation to these concepts?

Fair trade and organic

Each category manager was instructed to consider which core value was the best fit for his category. In meat products that was responsibility: honesty, authenticity and ingredients. For fruit and vegetables the best fit was fair trade and organic.

Activities Category Management

In 2010, PLUS Retail was the first supermarket in the Netherlands that replaced all its bananas for fair trade bananas, which they sold for the same price as regular bananas. And since 2011 PLUS only sells sustainable eggs: 100% free range eggs.
In some other categories the transition went more gradually. PLUS decided to sell the Better Life chicken with the mark Better Life. However, they could not do without the so-called bloated chicken. Still the market share of the Better Life chicken increased steady, basically as fast as the supply chain could deliver them. In addition, the sustainable range expanded like an oil slick; it now includes roses, private label chocolate, tea, coffee, house wine, etc.

CASE

The transition to a fair trade supermarket is easier said than done.

What should you keep in mind if you want to do this successfully?

- First, the taste and quality of the fair trade products should be good. Your proposition may be great, but nobody wants green bananas. You must ensure that your supply is well organized and large enough throughout the year. And in periods of promotion the supply should be able to suddenly double.
- The chain should be of outstanding quality, professional and transparent. That does not always work out well. At the launch of the fair trade concept, the flavor of the pineapples PLUS Retail purchased, was not good. PLUS had to switch to another country of origin to still be able to present the necessary quality in all stores.
- The initiative should be large enough so the shopper can recognize it in the store and so it can sort effect among consumers. The third condition is that the proposition is explainable so the consumer understands its value. For example, some consumers asked why not all of PLUS Retail's fruits and vegetables were fair trade. That was easy to explain: the fair trade organization is about products and ingredients from the southern hemisphere, so especially bananas, pineapples, chocolate and coffee.
- Finally, it should be competitive and affordable. To achieve that, you must have a good understanding of your customer's needs. You must dare to pioneer and take a rocky road. And believe in your proposition and consistently propagate it.

Results

PLUS Retail achieved some valuable results: the image of their stores improved - and at a time of food scandals that is very precious. The fair trade proposition is distinctive and not easy to copy. And it has led to growth in sales. Many consumers seemed to go for sustainable bananas, eggs and chickens with the Better Live mark. The sales of the Better Life chicken grew tenfold and the market share increases monthly. That is fortunate, since the higher purchase price can only be compensated by a higher volume.

Through fair trade farmers get a better price for their products and the prosperity of these farmers and their communities increases.

Seven C's for value growth in food and non-food

Especially for food industry formats, you can summarize market growth trends into seven values, the seven C's. The completion of these values (by suppliers and retailers), will cause consumers to gradually pay more for every kilo calorie they consume, because they get something extra in return. In the non-food sector, the same trends have to be displayed in other words. Culinary can be translated by 'quality' in non-food and the value Care & Cure by 'security'. Convenience, Conscious, Cute Story and Cheap are the same in non-food areas.

Figure 3.4 **The seven C's as a currency for value growth**

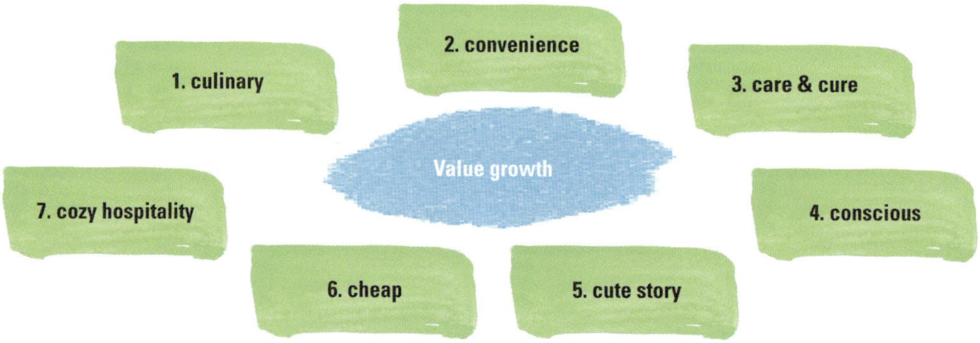

Growth in the food branch can be explained by increased productivity, controlled costs and finding new markets. Besides that, growth arizes, not because consumers buy more products but because they are willing to pay more for new products that replace their usual ones. This only occurs if the consumer obtains something extra. That can be achieved if Category Managers (and suppliers) use the seven values in the right way. If something is healthier, easier or gives more pleasure or if it is conducted in an honest way, has a good story. (FSIN and EFMI Business School)

Culinary. Consumers actually like to try different things that are supposed to be better or more tasteful. Holidays, cooking programs on TV, magazines about good food, demonstrations and new media (with recommendations from friends) cause new nice tasty products to be tested more quickly. In non-foods it is not about a good taste, but about quality. To be able to use professional tools, for example. Consumers alert each other via social media.

Convenience. Consumers constantly experience time pressure. Time is a new currency. Saving time in hard periodic tasks, is worth money. This trend has caused thousands of product changes, ranging from easy to open packaging to ready-made meals and meal or party services. In non-foods, this convenience trend is also visible.

Care&Cure. This social health value trend is encouraged by the government for various reasons such as high health care costs. Consumers also consider health increasingly important. It is a long lasting trend and its translation into concrete actions will continuously receive new impulses.
In non-foods, this trend is translated as 'safety'. A product has to be safe, without any risks.

Conscious. We could also describe this value as 'good behaviour' for it is an umbrella term for all matters related to responsible consumption and sustainability. This may vary from wanting to buy organic products to a guarantee that these cereals are not genetically modified, or the certainty that these bananas are produced without exploitation of farmers, etc. Also, animal welfare, sustainable agriculture, waste, etc., are concepts of 'good behaviour'. Communication is very important in these values. We need to show how products are produced, tell what ingredients are used, etc.

Cute story. Consumers seem to have extra appreciation for products with a traditional appearance or local origin, a good and authentic story around the product. That does not necessarily have to be organic. Mostly, the story of how something is made, where it is grown and what recipes you can make with is more important. This also explains the rise of 'real food', 'slow food' and 'local producers'.

Cheap. Less expensive luxury products that are more accessible to a larger audience by lowering the price, are an important growth drive for retail. They also cause consumers to 'leap' from commodities to luxury products. So, over time, these luxury products become commodities again.

Cozy Hospitality. If a consumer feels welcome and well respected, growth is more likely.

It is important to respond on time to the growing importance of any of these seven values in certain market areas. They have also to be translated into products, store image, promotions, etc.

3.4 Developments in markets and channels

Retailers, as well as manufacturers, are naturally inclined to take direct competitors within their own channel and region, into account. Much too often commercial activities are inspired by the competition instead of looking at the whole spectrum that can fulfill the needs of the consumers. In the examples, we limit ourselves to the food branch, but the scope is much wider. A second mistake retailers make, is focusing on the present time and paying too little attention to changes that may take place in the future.

Consumers can eat and drink anywhere. Developments in the United States and Great Britain show that consumers with high prosperity and a tendency for convenience (see sections 3.1a and 3.2), are going out for dinner more often than we imagined a decade ago. From the traditional 21 meals per week (seven days breakfast, lunch and dinner) more and more of these 'moments' are consumed outdoors in a functional way. People eat at work, on the road, together with friends, before a quick visit to the sports club, etc.

Why do we use this argument? Category Managers (and especially format managers) of supermarkets should be aware that within a decade the largest competitor might as well be a restaurant format or catering business. Moreover, trends show up earlier in out of home channels than in the supermarket. Consumers have a luxury experience (eating a special dish in a restaurant) and want to try this at home later. Later, the luxury experience will be seen as a commodity and this is the signal for supermarkets to include it in their assortment. Gradually we see that manufacturers tend to bring innovations first in the out of home channel before it enters the supermarket. Energy drinks, for example, were successfully launched out of home before they were sold in the supermarkets.

Figure 3.5

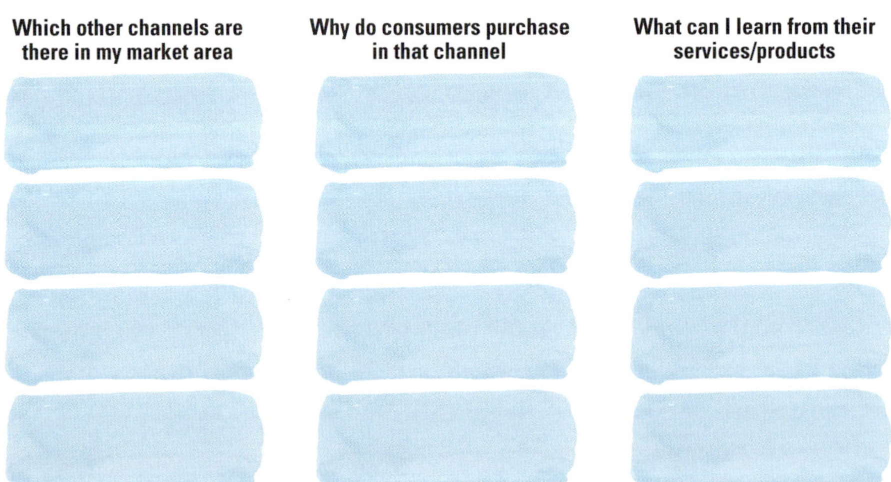

(FSIN Netherlands)

Consumers can buy their products in different channels. You can identify the channel for your own market area (first column). For the analysis, it is important to frame the spendings in different channels. And the reasons of purchase. Why do consumers purchase a certain product in this channel? Even if you can only estimate this, you can fill in the second column. And finally, it is important to see if you can learn from these channels. Because after all, many innovations come from the channels focused on tasty food (or from good cooks). Why won't you try to emulate the popularity of a baker's artisan bread in your own concept?

Category Managers in food should have a simple and quick way to examine all the other channels that sell groceries. Category Managers in other retail channels can obviously do the same for their competing channels. These three key questions should be answered by a Category Manager:

a. How is the spending in other channels at this moment?
b. Why do consumers purchase there, what is the growth potential and which growth drivers will there be in the next ten years?
c. What are typical innovations in that channel (both product and service) and what can be learned from them?

Figure 3.5 can be filled in with keywords and Category Managers can look for lessons to learn for their own format, in consultation with Format Managers.

Digitization changes traditional models

Consumers increasingly use smartphones, tablets and laptops for their purchases. Online sales are already changing the traditional retail models and will continue to do so in the next decade. In chapter 6.7 we will elaborate on that.

In which areas do these digital possibilities affect the retail process?

- Comparing products, prices and stores increases the transparency, how does this affect your strategy?
- Consumer behaviour is becoming more measurable, both online and offline. How do you get usable insights?
- More Information about the (food)chain, (food)products and ingredients. What is in it? How and where is it made? Who are the farmers or horticulturists behind the product?
- The information you can provide about your product is limitless, how should you deal with that?
- Not only are digital stores gaining in popularity, but physical stores are subject to digitization. What does this mean for the retail format?
- The places of purchase and transaction are disconnected, think about home delivery or pick-up points. What is the impact on your format and its positioning?

3.5 Competitor analyses

A proper analysis of competition is a necessary tool for every Category Manager (and Format Manager). A competitive analysis can be created in different ways. A well-known method is the simple SWOT analysis (identifying of strengths, weaknesses, opportunities and threats.

Presenting facts objectively

Another, much more detailed, method is the visualization of basic indicators of the main competing formats in your market area. When you monitor that continuously, it creates a benchmark to compare your performance with the one of your competitors.

An example of the possibilities in benchmarking, is comparing the average of competing formats in the following points:

- Space and number of cash registers;
- Parking spaces;
- Number of customers (primary and secondary);
- Absolute sales per store and sales per square metre;
- Sales growth in the last months;
- Average cash deposits;
- Turnover per hour worked;
- Number of items in assortment;
- Average number of shelf life of articles in the store;
- Percentage of out of stock items;
- Number of items in the advertising brochure;
- Turnover share of products in that brochure;
- Number of households (and people) in the market area;
- Growth forecast number of households;
- Disposable income of people in the market area;
- Drain to other markets and vice versa.
- Share of online sales.
- Use of apps.

Determining success factors

Besides the objective method of benchmarking you can also use a model that visualizes why competitors are more or less successful.

To do so, you have to search the 'driving forces' of a competitor. So you will not primarily look at the bare facts, but will try to find out why these facts apply. Figure 3.6 gives the opportunity to determine and analyse the key success factors. You can note the critical success factors for the format itself, for the building blocks of the format, for the categories that complete the core range and obviously sometimes even for a private label or an individual article.

Figure 3.6 **Four key questions behind the competitor's success**

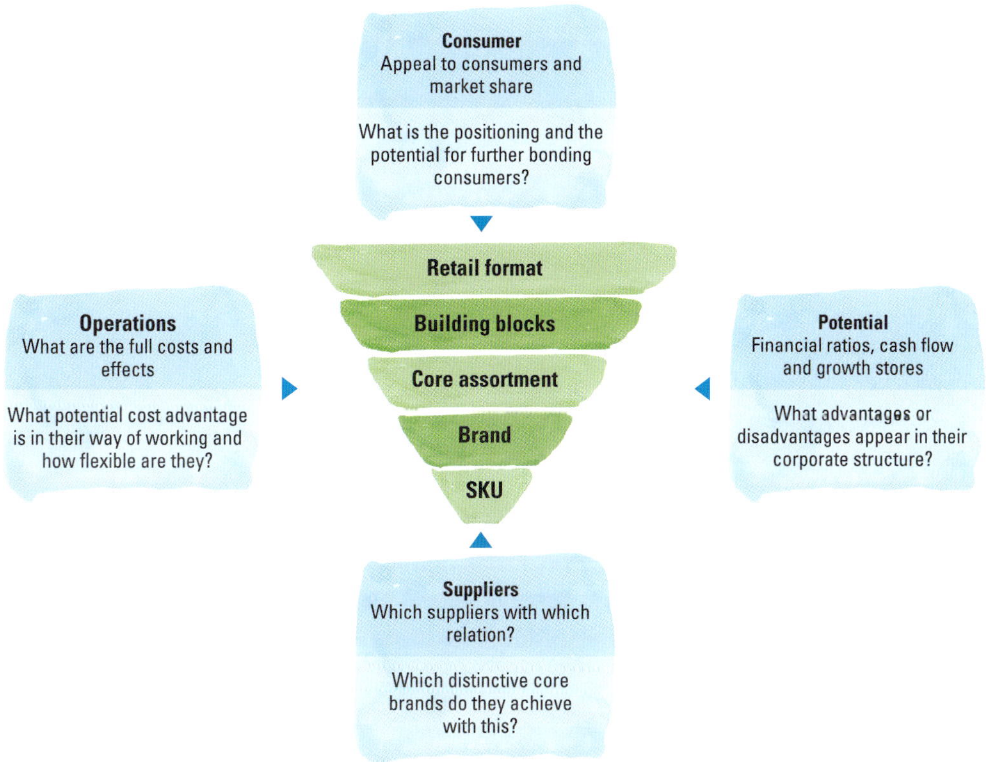

It is important that a Category Manager (but also Format Manager) answers the 'why' questions in a competitive analysis. Why is the competition different and thus more or less successful? To do that methodically (and not just based on gut feelings), the Food Service Institute developed this model. You will find the questions in the light blue boxes. You can examine the format itself, its building blocks, the core range, the brand or even actual products (the centre of the model). (FSIN 2007)

Analysing online competition

Online sales are more difficult to identify because it is harder to define all your competitors. One of the reasons for this is that the limitations of geographic borders have decreased enormously, you can buy all over the world without problems. So the number of competitors has increased enormously. There is a wide variety of actors; from small niche players to complete online department stores. To get a good image of the competition, you have to assess the category level instead of the format level. The best point to start determining your competition, is Google. After all, this is where most consumers start their online shopping trip. For Google, it is necessary to use the consumers' terminology; are they looking for sanitary napkins or feminine hygiene pads or for a light source or lamp?

Having found a potential competitor, you can note their characteristics. We have a non-exhaustive list of relevant factors included in the text box for making the online competitive analysis.

After the factors for all potential competitors have been identified, we must make choices in our own positioning. For instance, which assortment, which information do we communicate about our products, etc. You will read more about the choices in Chapter 6.

Table 3.1 **Factors to judge online competition**

Assortment ▶ Brands ▶ Width and depth ▶ Total amount of products in the store ▶ Availability/delivery period	**Price** ▶ Shipping costs ▶ Price index versus positioning ▶ Price model (dynamic, static or geographic)	**Product information** ▶ Which information is available per product? ▶ Commercial texts/USP's ▶ Describing information (attributes)	**Navigation** ▶ What structure does the navigation have? ▶ How many layers does the navigation contain? ▶ Which methods of filtering are presented? ▶ Which methods of selecting are presented?
Positioning ▶ What is the retailers' message? ▶ What is the relation between advice and purchase?	**Promotions** ▶ Does the retailer use special offers? ▶ What kind of special offers?	**Cross & upsell** ▶ Is the retailer targeting on cross selling?	**Support in sales** ▶ Does the retailer use the support of -Rankings? -Reviews?

3.6 The retailer's vision

Almost every retail organization has a certain vision, certain expectations. That vision is largely determined by the company's shareholders. If not directly the case (as in stock market listed companies), the shareholders still determine the parameters.

A vision is a company's guiding principle and sometimes the existing corporate culture is a solid framework so that the vision will not change too much.
The extent to which a vision is consistent and has a long term horizon, also determines the scope for development of Format and Category Management. The chosen business model is another variable of the organization. In practice, working with franchisees or store managers (affiliates) asks for a different way of working and other capabilities (or limitations) of the Category Manager.
Crowd funding is a new phenomenon in private investing that gradually changes the influence of banks and hedge funds. Crowd funding has a number of varieties between two extreme situations.

- There are lots of small investors with relatively little influence who want to be involved in some way.
- There are some large investors who want to get strongly involved with the company.

Table 3.2 **The way of organization affects Category Management**

Way of organization	What does this mean for Category Management and assortment policy?	Score
Listed company	Focused on maximizing profits on short and medium term. Not always room for experiments.	
Hedge fund / shareholders	Focused on maximizing profits and cash management. Similar to the previous, but more attention to the whole company's value.	
Family business	High involvement in the format's content and the interpretation of the range.	
With crowdfunding shareholders	Shareholders (sometimes employees) involved in the retail format. Chance to get these people's opinion about product innovations etc.	
Franchise model	Strict rules concerning the format's content and discipline on the central arrangements.	
Sheer entrepreneurs	Freedom in the local policy on format and range. Lots of room for experiments.	
Cooperation with entrepreneurs	Entrepreneurs often work closely together and try to 'sell' each other their successes. Stubborn entrepreneurs can be a problem for the head office's further optimization.	

The characteristics in this table can be provided with value judgements. With pluses and minuses, a Category Manager can indicate whether this offers options (+) or restrictions (-). In addition to the organizational and corporate culture, the style of leadership affects the available opportunities of individual departments to set up an independent policy.

3.7 The retailer's skills and process ability

An old law in business says that the quality of the idea itself has a limited role in the success of a good plan. Key factors for success are the forces within the company, the quality of the people responsible for implementing and whether the retailer has a well-oiled machine to process renewal. You can also think about the possibility of investing; room for extra time and attention, and so on.

An environmental analysis should therefore contain the retailers' internal factors. This goes beyond the strengths and weaknesses in the SWOT analysis. The list of internal factors can be made from the suppliers' perspective. This analysis, however, requires the ability to take a critical look at our own organization. Sometimes, for this part an external view is recommendable. Suppliers can look through a remote pair of glasses, but they must put aside the primary tendency to praise a (potential) customer.

We have listed the eligible factors for internal analysis. This schedule can serve as a guideline. Note that not all detailed questions are listed in this graphic. It provides a guide and is a first step to be honest about yourself. A second comment is that you should always make this analysis with your main competitor in mind.

People

- Do we have enough well-educated employees?
- Is there enough creativity in our teams?
- Do we spend time on external and internal analysis?
- Are we willing and able to learn from other companies?
- Do we offer enough extra training to our current employees?
- Do we dare to delegate instead of instruct?

Means

- Do we have the means (buildings, logistics, systems) to be ahead of others?
- Can we invest enough money for all necessary commercial activities?
- Can we cope with financial setbacks?
- How important is cash for our organization?
- Where does the cash come from (banks, family or other external funds)?
- Are the terms of payment adequate?
- Do we have unique access to suppliers who can provide extra advantage?
- Do we have enough skills for optimal use of social media?
- Do we have a good online infrastructure to service the customers?

Techniques

- Do we have the capacity for important changes?
- Can we outsource this capacity?
- Can we make quick and inexpensive adjustments if necessary?
- Is our ICT sufficient for the next few years?
- Do we depend on our IT or is it more effective and better to outsource or insource it?

Processes

- Are we less or more cost efficient compared to others?
- How quickly can we adjust our way of working?
- When was our last successful reorganization?
- What lessons did we learn from the changes in the last three years?
- Do we have a good view on superfluous aspects in our organization?

Structures

- To what extend is the management involved in daily operations?
- At what point does the management notice something is wrong on the shop floor?
- How many management layers does the organization contain?
- What type of span of control has the average middle management (how many people do they manage)?
- How much consultation is needed before making a decision?
- What is the impact of corporate culture on desired changes?

Figure 3.7 **Elements of the internal analysis**

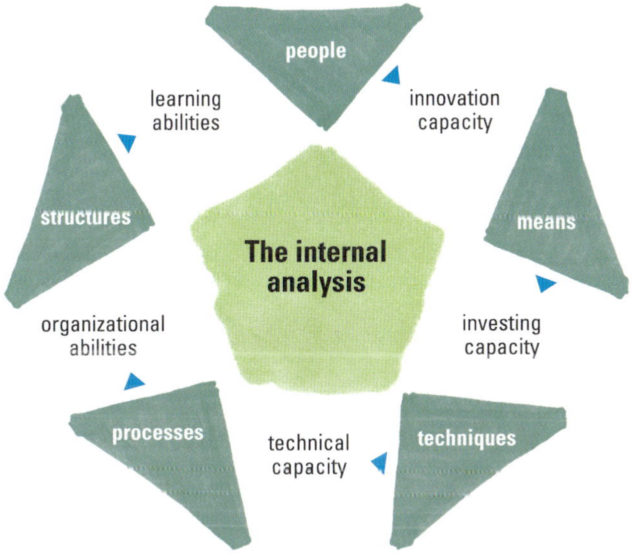

For internal analysis, it is important to ultimately frame the learning and innovation capacity of a retailer. In other words, it means his ability to adapt to changing circumstances. This has partly to do with the technical and invested capital and, ultimately, with organizational abilities. Can we organize ourselves differently if the market asks for it? Can we handle the distribution? Is our technology able to cope with that? And so on.

Summary chapter 3

- Category Management always starts with a thorough external & internal analysis
- The Trend Funnel helps categorizing relevant trends and translating social trends in consumer value trends and branch or product trends
- The 7 C's are the basis for value growth
- Monitor trends within your own channel and outside your direct market/branch or channel as they might influence your market
- Monitor & analyse the objectives of your stakeholders and the competitors within your current market and in related markets like online or food service.
- Assess the strengths and weaknesses of you own organization.

Chapter 4

The shopper

In the last years, the importance of knowledge on shopper behaviour and shopper marketing has grown significantly. Shopper marketing is about influencing the shopper's behaviour. Many marketing activities focus on the consumer or the user. Through the media, suppliers try to seduce the customer to buy their products. However, it happens frequently that a customer going to buy a specific product ends up buying something else. By focusing on the shopper and their needs, solutions to meet their expectations can be found and thus it brings category growth. This chapter shows how the purchasing process can be influenced.

Knowing the consumer's and shopper's behaviour is an important basis for the successful implementation of Category Management. If the retailer does not know his clientele, he can never enter Category Management successfully!

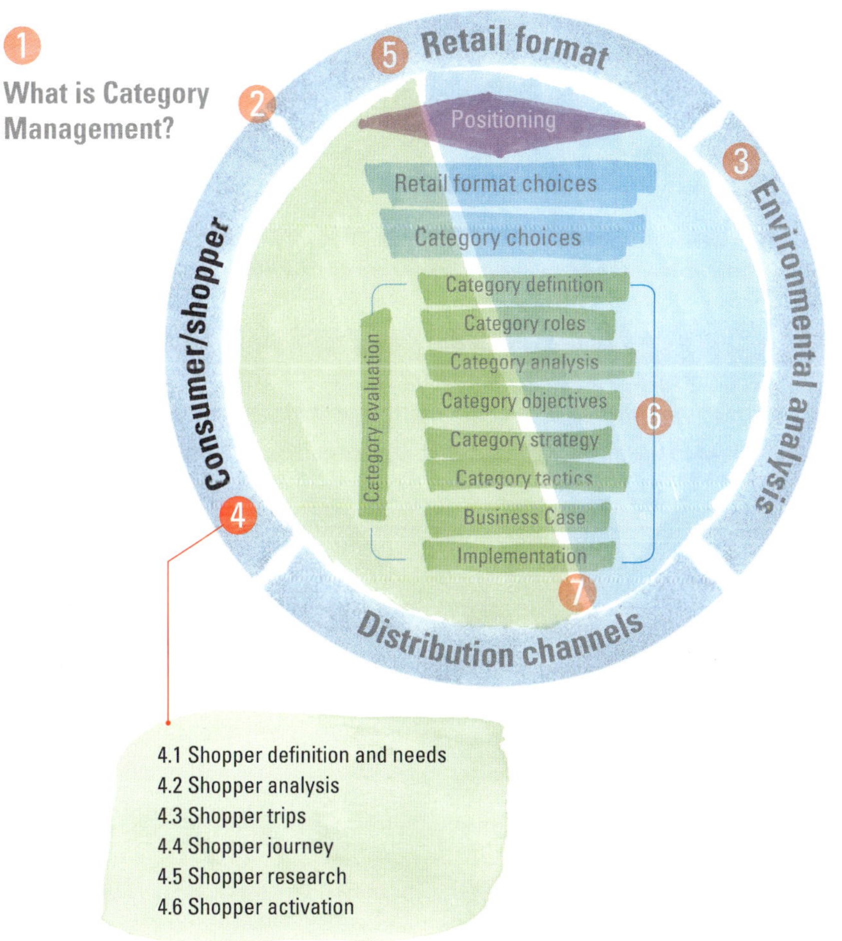

4.1 Shopper: definition and needs

The shopper is the person who makes the purchase but may not be the one who uses the product bought. A clear example of differences between consumer and shopper can be found in the case of baby food or animal feed. The baby or pet is the consumer - the shopper buys the product. The shopper decides what is bought and considers the wishes of the consumer, the one for whom the product is bought. He also compares alternatives, looks for best offers or might pick another brand if the item is out of stock. The shopper is the one who takes care of the conversion: where, when and why to convert a need into a purchase.

We often try to capture the shopper's behaviour in figures and numbers instead of understanding how the shopper executes and experiences his shopping trip. Paco Underhill is one of world's leading shopper researchers. He observes shoppers and their behaviour in the store and records all their activities. Thus he sees which route the customer takes to reach the targeted shelf, if he can find what he is searching for, if he can easily reach it and which in store communication and point of sale materials are at his disposal. Underhill also registers if a customer is bothered by other people because the product is placed in a crowded area while he wanted to shop quietly. These are some of the key factors behind success or setback. The shopper researcher draws conclusions out of these observations and gives recommendations on how the effectiveness and conversion can be increased. Two of Underhill's interesting books about shopper behaviour are *'What women want'* and *'Why we buy what we buy'*.

Shopper analysis clientele

Again and again we encounter stores that insufficiently respond to their clientele. It might seem a good idea that a hardware store near a college town is focused on cheap kitchens, while in a town with wealthy residents more emphasis is put on luxury shower cabins or doors. However, in the big cities where many immigrants live, we see limited response to their eating habits. Bags of rice and couscous of 5 kilograms would sell well here instead of the more common 500 grams. This may seem complex to implement, but software solutions make it easier to convert this knowledge of the shopper into effective stores.

4.2 Shopper analysis

In the previous section (4.1), we have made it clear how important knowledge of shopper's behaviour is if you want to define categories. Understanding the consumer's or the shopper's behaviour is essential for retailers. It is not only to gain insights of consumer behaviour, but also to understand the consumer as a person because all behaviours are personal. A better understanding of the consumer may be obtained by making a so-called 'shopper profile'. Retailers usually make shopper profiles with very pragmatic features. They describe the following obvious categories:

- Individual: who is the consumer? Is it a man or a woman? How old is he? What is his level of education? What is his occupation and what does he do in his spare time?
- Household: how many people are there in the household? What is the age group? Is it a household with or without children? What is the level of income and what are the daily activities of the persons in the household?
- Location: where does the consumer come from? How is the population density? Is it a rural or urban area? Which cultures are represented? How many people live in the area and what is their occupation?

Scheduled, these categories look like this:

Figure 4.1 **Features for a consumer and shopper analyse**

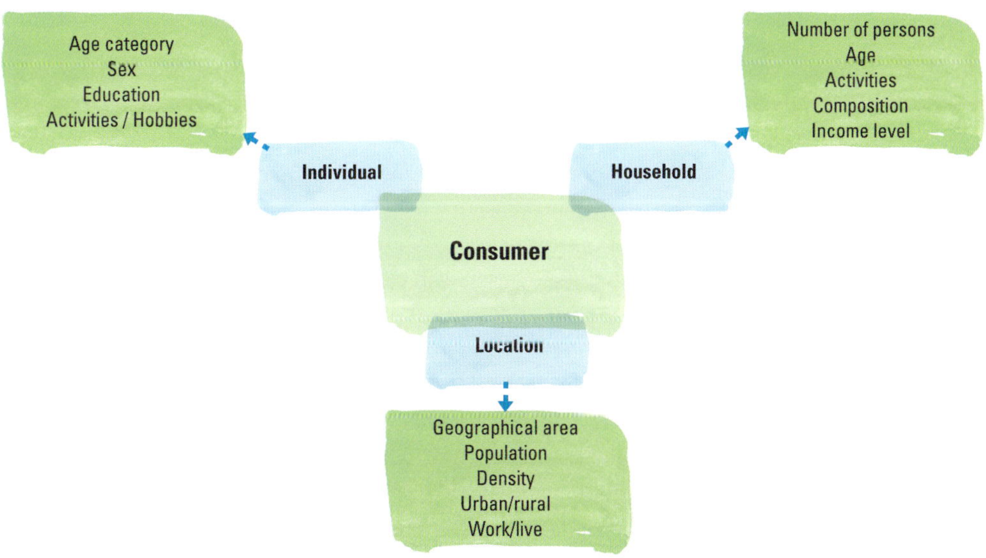

A retailer approaches his market in a pragmatic way. Three characteristics emerge from that approach: the retailer examines the local market area (bottom of the figure), the household composition in that area (right side) and the individual shoppers who visit his store (left side).

Buying behaviour analysis

In addition to the shopper profile, a number of important features should be considered while making a shopper analysis. Below you will find a list of important behavioural indicators that can be used to gain more consumer insights:

- **The Shopper Profile** can be created with variables as described in figure 4.1;
- **Shopper Penetration** is the percentage of individuals who purchase in 'my' store in relation to the total amount of individuals in the area;
- **Loyalty** is the percentage of times that a consumer purchases a product in 'my' store in relation to his total purchases;
- **Purchase Amount** is the amount spent by consumers each week in 'my' store. It is important to know what percentage this is compared to his entire budget;
- **Purchase Frequency** is the number of shopping visits a consumer makes in a given period of time;
- **Average number of Purchases** is the number of products per shop visit;
- **Win-Loss Index** is the number of products sold by a particular brand that is at the expense of another product/brand;
- **Basket Analysis** is the analysis of products that were purchased at the same time;
- **Promotional Sensitivity Index** is the increase in the number of purchased products as a result of promotional campaigns;
- **Purchase type** is to get an indication of the type of buying behaviour (planned or impulse purchase).

In the UK more (often advanced) models are used to create a shopper profile. GfK, Trendbox, Censydiam and many others develop their own analysis to capture the different consumer types.

As we described previously, it is important to understand the consumer, in addition to insights of the shopper behaviour. For a quick understanding of the consumer's reaction to promotions, product launches and range changes, it is important that retailers and suppliers exchange point-of-sale data (scanning data). A daily exchange of information at store level can bring increase in sales, reduce costs and improve relationship between the manufacturer and the retailer. The exchange of scanning data also ensures a better response to the shopper's needs. Unfortunately, not everyone is inclined to exchange these data, despite the benefits. Retailers make rational (and sometimes emotional) choices for cooperation with a supplier and ensure the openness needed for a successful and good collaboration. Therefore, suppliers and retailers should make proper arrangements in advance. The exchange of scanning data or point-of-sale data only works if both the parties have formulated a common objective.

4.3 Shopping trips

Six shopping trips in food

Consumers have several options and motives to meet their needs. We have elaborated on the food sector, but for non-food, the same process in which some trips are combined, is applied.

The shopping trips are:

1. Buying special products you deliberately want to have in stock at home. In food, we call this basement purchases. These products are bought once or twice a year.
2. Buying basic products to stock at home (cellar or pantry)
3. Buying the weekly groceries (kitchen cabinet)
4. Buying daily (fresh) items (refrigerator)
5. Buying food products you are going to consume within a few hours (the handbag).
6. Buying products you are going to consume immediately.

Every shopping trip has its own considerations, expectations and business model.

Figure 4.2 **Shopping trips define the shopper's choices**

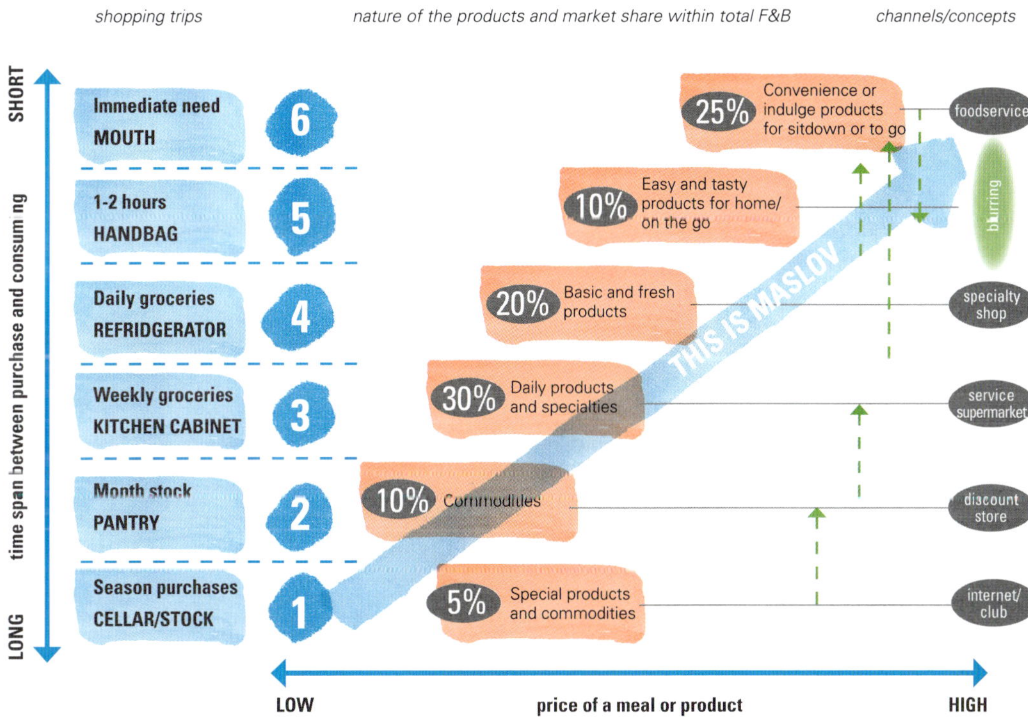

This model is explained on the following pages. The diagonal blue arrow is a simplification of the Maslow's pyramid. The orange squares represent the different types of products shoppers buy. The left vertical axis shows the different types of shopping trips, divided by the elapsed time between purchase and consumption. In the grey ovals you can see the market share of the shopper's journey within total consumer sales of food and beverage. On the right traditional marketing concepts that play an important role in each of the shopping trips are placed vertically. And the green arrows indicate in which direction a concept develops.

Almost at the top, we see three traditional channels that are suitable for the 'handbag shopping trip'. We call this
'blurring' because a (growing) group of shoppers switches easily between channels for this direction shopping trip. Note that internet shopping is not listed separately because it is integrated in each channel.
It is primarily in shopping trip 1 that internet takes the most substantial proportion. This shopping trip relates often to usually expensive items that are purchased at relatively cheap prices. Such as wine-import/club, frozen meat/fish etc.

Starting points
Figure 4.2 is based on two starting points.

a. First of all, the Maslow line (diagonal blue arrow). Maslow's theory states that as a society gets more prosperous, there is more need for premium products and individual consumption (eat what you want, where you want, at any time). The blue arrow rises to the right. In countries such as Albania and Zimbabwe, the needs at the base (bottom left) of Maslow's theory are dominant and shopping trips 1 and 2 are therefore the most important.
b. The second principle is derived from the previous one. Luxury (or premium) products will rapidly become 'normal' as a society becomes more prosperous. Luxury and convenience will be 'common' and accessible to a wider audience. For what is special today, may be normal tomorrow and outdated or generic the day after. This also means that innovations at the top are increasingly important in order to remain special.

These facts are important for assortment policy and product introductions because the life cycle of luxury products will be shorter. In case of excessive promotion, the cycle will become even shorter.
In general we can say that in the next few years shopping trip 5 and 6 (consumed almost immediately) is becoming increasingly important in prosperous countries. Out-of-home consumption (food service) is going to grow fast when the consumer's confidence is positive. In times of crisis consumers always move to a 'lower' level in Maslow's pyramid.

Offline purchasing behaviour of consumers
The customer's buying behaviour can be summarized in six different shopping trips divided over all channels. The top of the Maslow's pyramid consists of two variants: consumed directly (shopping trip 6) and take away; buy and bring something to consume within a few hours (shopping trip 5). The latter is especially trending in the Western world and is often combined with another shopping trip. Someone doing the weekly family groceries can get himself something to consume immediately (or within a few hours).

The shopping trip model
The FSIN and EFMI shopper trip model is based on six ways in which the consumer caters for his basic needs. All six have consequences for the category manager. We will explain that shortly. The shopper journey 'Internet purchases' is not highlighted separately in this model because e-shopping can be used for all shopping trips. With your Smartphone, you can buy for instance, wine for direct consumption, but also to complement your year's supply.

Shopping trip 1: *season purchases*

This is the shopping you do to maintain the desired base stock at home in an advantageous way: the basement stock. These are often luxury goods or commodities that the consumer wants to keep in stock. Most of the time, the true 'fans' of a product put this shopping trip into practice. For example: wine lovers who love their special quest for 'perks' once or twice a year. During this particular shopping trip, mutual purchases and internet play a major role. Prosperous consumers easily spend money on this trip and in total, the basement stock accounts for 5% of the total food sales. It concerns mostly expensive items purchased with a discount. Other examples are people who buy a whole cow together with others, and slaughter it (adopt-a-cow.com).

Category Manager Considerations for shopper trip 1

- Shoppers always want to have a sense of advantage during this shopping trip.
- They behave like a buyer and an expert.
- They prefer to buy directly from the source.
- Shoppers are quite willing to spend a lot of money for the purchase of these products, provided that they feel it is much cheaper to buy this way.
- Retailers can play a role in this trip if they act like a kind of real estate agent (broker) who brings the consumer in direct contact with the source.
- Retailers have to work for this shopping trip with a low profit margin and can sell large volumes to one customer.
- Retailers should be able to tell consumers the story behind these products.

Shopping trip 2: *month stock*

These are the groceries that the consumer routinely wants to have in stock at home in their pantry. Think about herbs, potatoes, sugar, beverages, toilet paper, etc. The number of items that an average household routinely stocks has grown considerably over the last 25 years. It has now reached an estimated number of 120 items per household. It is not easy to predict which articles are purchased in this shopping trip. Some households like to stock cheese and crackers while others have bags of chips and cases of beer or only coffee and toilet paper. In general, we can say that pantry items are very price sensitive (they are purchased if on sale), but that the purchase frequency is low while the purchased quantity (amount spent per purchase) is high. The total turnover of food products in this shopping trip accounts for about 10% of sales in the Western world. It is mainly the discount channel that benefits the most from this shopping trip.

Category Management considerations for shopping trip 2

Obviously, all the aspects of Category Management (see Chapter 6) play a major role. Yet we can sum up some points that need extra attention from the Category Manager:

- The alignment of the appropriate categories in this shopping trip is important. Ranges that are connected need to be logically associated with each other in the store.
- What does it mean to your existing customers if your store emphasises on this skimming shopping trip?
- What happens to the margin mix of the total store?

- How do you deal with the 'forward buying' tendency of consumers in this product group (hoarding price offers)?
- Do you want to sell large packs or a more 'normal' packaging range?
- Do cellar offers attract additional new customers in your store or reward your existing ones?
- Are your logistics sufficiently tuned? What can you do with residual stocks?

Shopping trip 3: *weekly groceries*

The kitchen cabinet shopping trip seems to have been partly described in the previous shopping strip. Yet this way of doing groceries is not about skimming. It is primarily intended for items that are needed within one week. Over the last 30 years, this shopping trip involved more and more fresh assortment, from bread (often put into the freezer at home) to meat and vegetables. For the weekly groceries the mental shopping list (whether or not on paper) is important and consumers should be tempted to purchase outside that list. For the primary customers, this trip is mainly rational. An additional bargain is fine but will not affect the choice of the store or the desired package of items. For secondary clients, these bargains are an argument to visit the store and they could purchase additional assortment. Weekly groceries are the basic scoop of a regular supermarket but supermarkets have partly taken over of the function of the specialist (daily groceries) by expanding their range of fresh products and now also fulfill partly the pantry shopping trip. Roughly, 30% of total food sales still belong to the weekly groceries but this phenomenon is under pressure.

In order to remain relevant to consumers, supermarkets have to interfere even more with other shopping trips in the future - especially with shopping trip 5 and 6 (short-term consumption). This is partly because it is the biggest growth market and also because of the success of supermarket formats which are actively engaged in short-term consumption in the United States and in Great Britain.

Category Management considerations for shopping trip 3

Category management is, as a theory, mainly built on the weekly groceries. So, it has concerns in this particular shopping trip. The assortment in the supermarket is also for 90% tuned on the weekly groceries. It means that defining the category role of this range (destination, convenience, etc.) is crucial, including the function of promotions and new product releases. See for further details, chapters 5 and 6.

Shopping trip 4: *daily groceries*

The refrigerator shopping trip was much more important 50 years ago. After all, the groceries did not last long. The mother, in a household, was still at home and had the task to take care of the meals for the family. Bakers, butchers, greengrocers and basically all the specialty stores originally derived their existence from this fact. Nowadays, the daily groceries shopping trip for daily groceries has become less important. Moreover, purchasing previously forgotten items also belongs in this shopping trip especially now that the supermarket that has taken over the traditional market for this refrigerator shopping trip from speciality stores. Very conscious customers do their daily groceries and visit the store for one or more items. However they can of course easily be tempted to purchase something extra. These extras should not be low-margin items, but rather items that contribute to the profit. The number of stores visited in this shopping trip changes. There are fewer traditional specialty stores but the stores that remain are becoming extra 'special'. They are the product champions. On the other hand, new store formats arize for this shopping journey. Neighbourhood & convenience stores and immigrant shops fill out a part of this function. Finally, the economic crisis and smaller households cause people to make smaller shopping trips. In total this refrigerator shopping trip accounts for 20% of the total food sales.

Category Management considerations for shopping trip 4

In addition to the core questions of Chapter 4, this shopping trip also has additional challenges for the Category Manager:

- How do I hold on to the clients who visit my store?
- How can I regularly surprise consumers with a high visit frequency and tempt them into additional purchases?
- Which ranges can I add (temporarily) to surprize the customer?
- How do I arrange the logistics and remaining stocks of this 'side range'?

Shopping trip 5: *short term consumption*

Purchasing something that you can consume shortly; on the road, in the office or at home. The purchased product is only in your bag briefly and disappears in your mouth a moment later. The word 'convenience' has the leading role in this shopping trip. The store should be easy to reach, with an easy selection and easy checkout, to take out and consume. This is the fastest growing shopping trip and it already accounts for about 10% of the total sales. This kind of 'meet your needs' is fuelled by the growing number of single households that often do not have the time or feel like shopping or cooking extensively. In the United States, not only conventional supermarkets have thrown themselves on this market, but also restaurants, convenience stores, caterers, take-home concepts, specialty stores and various delivery services.

Category Management considerations for shopping trip 5

This shopping trip is relatively new. Supermarkets and specialty stores have not 'grown up' with it. But Pump Shops, McDrives and small convenience stores did. Yet, supermarkets, specialty stores and new convenience stores are most likely to benefit from this growing market.

The Category Manager needs to pay extra attention to the following aspects:

- How do I use my basic assortments to add 'convenience' and 'tastefulness' in this shopping trip?
- How should I calculate the consumer price?
- How do I control the operating costs?
- How can I present a coherent range for this shopping trip for consumers who want to shop fast?
- How can I ensure that consumers evaluate positively my formula for the shopper journey as they are familiar with my store for shopping trip 3 or 4?
- How do I engineer the logistics, loss and remaining stocks of this convenience assortment?

Shopping trip 6: *direct consumption*

As a pure mouth function, this shopping trip is particularly focused on the foodservice market, the outdoor channels. It partly includes the classic hospitality function of 'going out for dinner' (for fun, so more emotionally driven), but increasingly includes also the functional outdoor breakfasts, lunches and dinners. Then, effectiveness is the number one argument and a term like 'cosy' comes later in the order of arguments. Large parts of the hospitality industry, but also catering in companies or institutions, school or sports canteens and other catering facilities in shops, stations, aircraft and hospitals, among others have to do with the functional outdoor dinner. In these channels, we see more and more standardised concepts and formats. So there is also more room for Category Management. The share of these channels within the overall food spending will grow significantly in the long term. However, in times of crisis they get the punches. About 20% of the total turnover of food and beverage (F&B) goes to shopping trip 6. In the United States shopping trip 5 and 6 represent more than 50% of total F&B sales. Because consumers have a need for functionality (ease and speed), health, variety and taste, brands have lots of opportunities. Retail formats like McDonalds and Starbucks have become such strong brands that they hardly need additional manufacturer brands. Concepts that deal with shopping trip 6 are very fragmented. The Food Service Institute maps this market annually and also provides an overview of growth trends and business concepts. Important growth factors for the direct consumption market are consumer confidence (feeling of prosperity), the growing number of single households and the increasing number of two-income households. For them, time saving (quick and easy dinner) is becoming a primary and daily assessment. This shopping trip has a strong relationship with shopping trip 5. Again, the 'night out' variant of shopper trip 6 has totally different rules. Entertainment and positive surprises are the keywords for a good night out. Food and beverages are usually just a part of the overall entertainment concept.

Category Management considerations for shopping trip 6

Category Management for shopping trip 6 has barely developed. Actually, in food services it is still in its very beginnings, but it will develop quickly, like retail developments. We thereby refer to all the steps in Chapter 6, which, simplified, can be implemented in food service. Some additional questions are necessary:

- How do I create a certain bond with my 'guests' (customers) and how do I keep in touch with them?
- How can I surprise regular guests with a functional consumer demand? How can I tempt them to a more luxurious dish and persuade them to repeat their visits?
- How often should I change my assortments?
- How do I use the brand strength of products in combination with building my own retail brand?
- How do I ensure that my main costs are variable?
- How do I create 'surprises' when I aim for the 'consumers on a night out'?

Online purchasing behaviour of consumers

The shopping trip model as introduced above, cannot be translated one on one for the online channel. This has to do with the characteristics of the online channel. The moment of reception or inclusion of the bought products is often separated from the time of purchase. The offline shopping trip model focuses on the 'purchase' and 'consumption' dimensions. The dimension 'receiving the product' should be added in online shopping trips. This decoupling causes a totally different behaviour. Shoppers buy more because the products are not directly taken but mostly delivered at home. Shopping trips 1, 2 and 3 are particularly popular in online purchases. Consumers spend an average of 6 times more with clicks than in bricks. The customer purchase frequency is between 12 and 20 times a year. The growing online business is mainly focused on creating loyal consumers and increasing their basket's size.

Each segment of a shopping trip has its own characteristics in the cooperation with industry

The business model for a retail brand that focuses on one shopping trip is very different from a retailer who focuses on another shopping trip (see figure 'the consumer's purchasing behaviour' at the beginning of this chapter). The operation costs (and therefore the necessary margin mix) increase from bottom left to top right in the model. The purchase price of assortments also rises from left below to right above. Thus it increases the price the shopper pays for an item (or meal). The exception is shopping trip 1 (replenishing the basement stock) because the average consumer will spend a lot of money during this trip. Sometimes it happens even more than for the same product in the weekly groceries.
Because all shopping trips are very different from each other, it also means that retail formats focussed on one or more shopping trips make different demands to their suppliers. This essentially implies that cooperation between industry and retailers will be different in each of these six shopping trip models. For example: the added value of the supplier will be very limited for retailers focussed on shopping trip 1, while it is highly important in shopping trip 6. The number of outlets focussed on shopping trip 6 is so large, that it is very difficult for a supplier to maintain service contacts on outlet level. This information must be included when creating a category development plan.

An overview of the differences that occur during the different shopping trips (to the extent where they have a relationship with Category Management):

- Shopper's buying motive (visit motive);
- Visit frequency of the customer;
- Amount paid by the customer;
- Store layout with assortment;
- Willingness to deviate from planned purchase;
- Openness of the organization for new products;
- Willingness (and know-how) to share and use information;
- All costs at store level;
- All logistical characteristics (package size, order frequency, delivery requirements, etc.);
- Need for renewal of the format or ranges;
- Interchange ability of suppliers and products.

This list is not complete but shows that the way Category Management is completed will totally differ. However, the guidelines in each of the channels are the same.

Shopping trips in Do-It-Yourself stores

The shopper trips in Do-It-Yourself (DIY) and garden stores vary greatly from the ones in food. First, a consumer does not visit a DIY or garden store often. Garden stores are usually subjected to a seasonal pattern in shopping trips. Actually, there are two moments: in springtime when people want to make the garden beautiful again and in the weeks round Christmas. Many garden stores therefore sell animal feed, because this attracts customers who visit the store once every 3-4 weeks and who may be tempted to buy more. Customers visit DIY stores approximately three times a year, while they do chores. While doing the work, the shopper often visits the DIY store several times a week. The aim is initially for orientation, then for information and advice and eventually to purchase the wanted product and additional items.

Figure 4.3

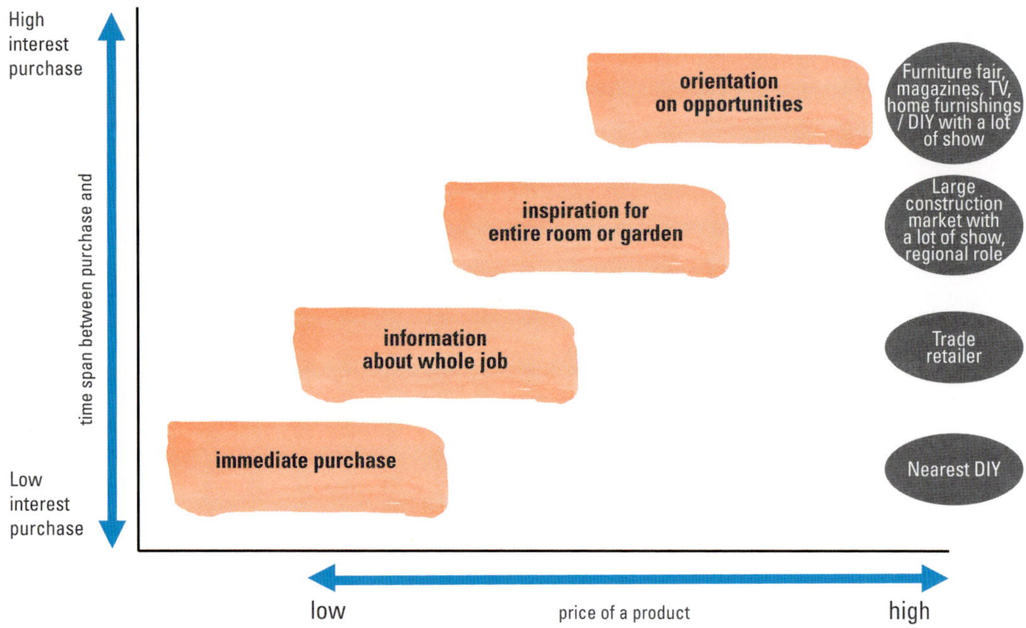

The shopping trips can often be divided into a high-interest and low-interest purchase. The price also plays a role. Many purchases in DIY stores involve a high budget. (Category & Trade Company 2014)

As a result of this, the customer visits the store less frequently, knows it less well and almost never makes an routine or repetitive purchase. You may purchase new doors for your home only once in your life or a new roller blind once in seven years. This means that navigation, inspiration, information and activation are far more important than in a supermarket.

Shopping trip 1: direct purchase

This shopping trip has to do with the motives 'direct purchase' or 'to stock at home'. This often involves products with a low value which can be purchased in any DIY store. The wanted products are often components of a job: nails, tape, glue, etc. Customers go to the nearest hardware store to purchase these items. Accessibility is an important factor as you want to find the right shelf and the right items easily.

Shopping trip 2: doing the job

This shopping trip is about construction jobs. The handyman may want information on how to get the job done and what materials and tools are needed. The shopper is out for advice or confirmation about how he will handle the job. A shopping list for a job makes sure nothing is forgotten (and that the basket is filled extra).

Shopping trip 3: inspiration for redesigning

Besides constructive advice, this shopping trip also asks for advice on decorative parts: how does the consumer want to redecorate his room or garden? How does he do the job? The partner is also often involved in the shopping process. Shoppers are willing to travel further for a store in which they expect to have a lot of inspiration. Show rooming thus plays a crucial role. The customer is inspired, but makes his purchases later in your store or elsewhere. In case of interesting special offers, a consumer can sometimes be persuaded to make the purchase now.

Shopping trip 4: guidance on opportunities

This shopper journey is often about big jobs and the handyman is just at the start of the procurement process. He wants to look for opportunities: what does it take to do this job and what are the approximated costs?

As the shopping trips in DIY and garden stores are more guided by the overall shopper journey, this directly links to the next section: Shopper Journey.

4.4 Shopper journey

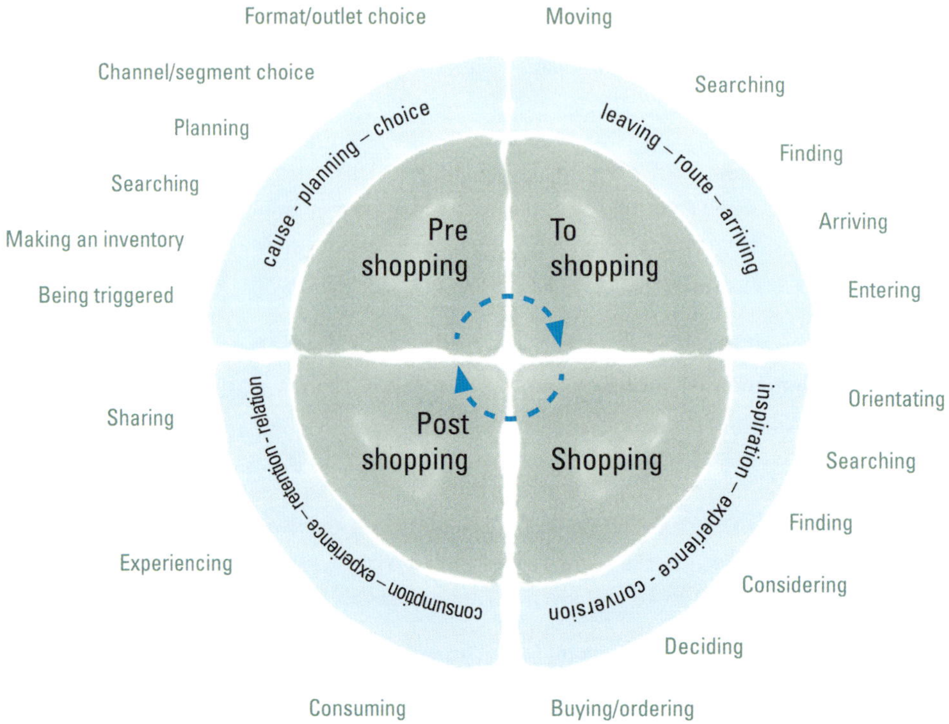

Figure 4.4
This model shows the shopper journey. It covers the complete journey, from the cause or need through the choice for a particular channel or retail brand and the actual shopping trip to the experience of using the purchased product and the satisfaction afterwards. (Marketing4Results)

Shopper journey, touch points and moments of truth

The promotional pressure and emphasis on price and promotion have increased considerably over the last few years. More and more products are sold with promotional discount. The goal of retailers and brands is to achieve category growth and gain market share and not just sales. Promotions however seldom lead to category growth. At this moment, we see many categories with increased promotion pressure, yet under pressure in terms of turnover and volume and not to mention, the profitability. Consumers become accustomed to the fact that a product can be bought during promotion campaigns and they wait for the next campaign to do their purchase. Comparing prices online already plays a major role in non-food categories.

To get out of this downward spiral, it is important to study the shopper's needs and desires thoroughly. It turns out that companies focussed primarily on the needs of the shopper and customer are about 5 times as profitable as other companies (Gulati,Ranjay:2009, *Reorganize for Resilience*, Harvard Business Press). But how do you get that focus?

The first step is, understanding the buying process from the beginning till the end and to discover the basic needs or opportunities to make improvements. We call this process the shopper journey or customer journey. It consists of four phases: the *pre-shopping, to shopping, shopping* and *post-shopping.* The time spent on the different parts of this shopper journey varies for each category.

Pre shopping

The shopper journey often begins long before someone goes to the store. It starts with a need, a desire or a problem that must be solved. Consumers will explore potential solutions, look for information and select a channel or retail brand to preview or buy a product.

For a pack of margarine the pre shopping process is obviously simpler than for a new bathroom but in both cases, there is a process that is set in motion before the purchase. Basic products will be considered according to experiences and perhaps offers but when it concerns more complex, expensive or high interest products, the orientating process will be less simple. This all happens prior to the visit to a store.

Google calls this the 'zero moment of truth'. This moment captures a chaotic process which is different for each purchase and customer. Television and magazines, but also friends, acquaintances and social media have a part in this process.

In the 'pre shopping' phase, the desire or need is converted into the journey to the store. Now the customer chooses through which channel to go: to the grocery store or to a supermarket? Is he going to a speciality store in painting to get detailed advice or to a DIY store?
The customer also decides which retail format he will visit. He can visit the nearest supermarket for a forgotten purchase but will drive a little further for weekend shopping or for a special evening.

To shopping

To shopping is the actual journey to the store. Is it easy to find, are there good parking places. Retailers can respond to this by convincing people to come to them, for example through signs along the way with 'breakfast for € 1.50'. The retail brand is important in this choice as is the image customers have of a certain category at that specific retailer.
This also goes for DIY stores. For a roll of tape any store will do but for important purchases, the customer makes a well considered choice.

Shopping

Once in the store, the customer first has to find the right shelf and the brand of his choice. At this moment, the shopper's decision tree plays an important role. A good shelf allows the customer to choose quickly and easily and find the product of his choice and can also inspire him to purchase related products. The selection always starts with the need for a meal, a drink or a lunch. Then it goes through the different segments which offer a solution and is followed by elements such as brand, size, price or packaging. In DIY stores the selection starts with a job or a desire to redecorate your home. For a job, it is helpful if everything needed is presented together or if there is at least a shopping list and advice so customers can buy everything at once. Most jobs do not need to be done often and we

From boxes & bags to meal solution: Reenergising the frozen food aisle

Background

In 2008 Ireland entered a severe economic recession which was to last several years. The impact on retail was immediate and significant, with premium and chilled/fresh foods most impacted. Therefore Green Isle Foods, Ireland's leading provider of quality Frozen Foods, expected a positive impact across their product portfolio. In times of economic downturn, shoppers generally turn back to 'basics', and the frozen aisle offers a household products that both minimize wastage (the products don't go off like fresh produce) and offer good value for money. However, that expected upswing never came. Shoppers cut back across all categories, cooking more from scratch and using Discounter stores more. The Frozen Food category in modern retail was struggling. It was within this challenging environment that Green Isle Foods working with their retail partner Tesco launched a shopper marketing initiative aimed at growth, aisle rejuvenation and shopper engagement. Tesco were similarly suffering, with the rise of Discounter shopping, and core categories such as Frozen Food needed to be protected and stabilized.

Analysis

Like any proper shopper marketing initiative, the project invested substantial time and resource in understanding current shopper behaviour, particularly in-store. Ireland's biggest multi-methodological shopper study ever commissioned on the frozen food category was designed to understand not only shopper perceptions, but to truly understand current shopper behaviour in-store. POV shopper journeys, in-aisle accompanied shops, in-store observation, qualitative in-depths and focus groups were all used to truly understand the nature of the shop and the barriers to growth. If the solution was to be successful it was imperative that an arising strategy or in-store tactic be based is solid shopper understanding and insight. Shopper was at the centre of this retailer and supplier collaborative initiative from the very beginning.

CASE

Key problem

The arising findings and barriers were as follows:

- While those shoppers who bought from the category 'sometimes/regularly' walked the aisle while shopping, the majority of shoppers at any time often bypassed the aisle completely. The majority of shopper journeys in-store did not ever make it into the Frozen Food aisle. Category non-consideration' was a major problem
- The aisle was seen as 'cold' and ' uninviting' both physically but more importantly psychologically and emotively. Shoppers used words such as boring, bland, dull, un-inviting, ever-lasting, endless and functional.
- Those who did buy only bought items they 'knew' and so the nature of the shop was SKU based rather than 'browse based' – there was little category or sub-category engagement resulting in little incremental sales.
- Shoppers often bought frozen foods 'last' on their shopper journey (due to concerns over melting) and therefore it often was either forgotten or sacrificed due to recessionary budget pressures.
- Often the aisle was simply used as a 'traffic flow' conduit for shoppers to reach the tills at the end of a shop, and so much of the actual footfall aisle traffic was navigational or 'journey based' as opposed to 'shopping based'
- While some sub-categories (like frozen fish and vegetables) were seen as of high quality, shoppers worried about the quality of many of the frozen food products.

With these challenges, it was clear that the arising action needed to be a TOTAL CATEGORY SOLUTION as opposed to just focusing on the sub-categories in which Green Isle had strong product portfolios.

Objective

The arising initiative needed to change shopper behaviour, drive more engagement for the category, increase shopper engagement and impulse incremental sales. Shoppers needed to see the aisle as a 'destination for them' as opposed to somewhere they walked through or avoided.
Shoppers needed to be disrupted from routine shopper behaviours and so it was acknowledged that any in-store execution needed to be high impact.

Approach

The final in-store execution focused on the MEAL SOLUTION, re-framing the products away from 'freezer/pantry' items and more toward a meal solution for a recession concerned family. The entire aisle was converted into a permanent 'market street' feel, with each sub-category (fish, meat, ice-cream, pizza, vegetables etc.) given its own 'shop-front' and unique look-and-feel. The 'canopies' used over each sub-category gave this illusion and resulted in presenting the category as 'many small markets' as opposed to one long endless aisle.

Materials used were vibrant and colourful, with designers using every available space to communicate in-aisle, from aisle-entrance arches to floor stickers, freezer windows to the freezer units themselves. The result was a high impact aisle that attracted significant attention from shoppers. It was transformed from an aisle that was essentially a monotonous row of white, cold, glass freezers to a vibrant street market. The visuals featured product shots (as opposed to branding) and focused shopper attention on the meals they could make as opposed to the 'products they could buy'. The sub-categories of FISH and VEGETABLES were used as the anchor categories (seen first from the middle Power Aisle) and drew those non-consideration shoppers into the space, with the design then leading them along the 'stalls' into other sub-categories.

Results and learning

On installation the transformation to the aisle was impressive and immediate. Shoppers who had only ever bought fresh vegetables were entering the frozen food aisle, lured by the visuals of the fresh produce in the vegetable 'market'. Shoppers who bought fish and burgers every week were know discovering pizza and ice-cream 'shops'. The lapsed shoppers were drawn back, the non-consideration shoppers disrupted, and those already buying browsed more, resulting in increased incremental sales.

The use of colour and the 'market feel' meant that shoppers browsed for longer. I remember one shopper saying that she felt 'warmer' in the space now – not only psychologically but physically! She wondered if perhaps the store had turned up the temperature to make her more comfortable shopping in this previously 'cold' aisle. It was an excellent example of how visuals can effect shopper mood and feelings (as of course the store temperature remained the same!).

Better sub-category segmentation also resulted in more cross-category shopping and inter-action. Until the freezers were converted to the 'market shops', sub-categories like fish, meat, potato and vegetables all bled into one space, only broken by basic in-store category signage. Afterward, it was leveraging these category cross-shops where a lot of the impulse sales were coming from – products that had always been there but shoppers were now seeing 'again'. Reminding shoppers of what the store sold was as simple as re-framing it in a new and visually appealing way. One shopper mentioned that he was delighted the store now

CASE

stocked significantly more ice-cream.
It did not. The range never changed, but the market-stall shop made it appear that the store had significant choice in each 'stall'. Shoppers always react to good in-store visuals.

Sales increased 3%, with spend per customer increasing 4% during the test/control stage. This was much lower than the positive reaction we were getting from management and shoppers on the shop floor. The reason for this low sales uplift figure was one of the key learning from the project, as it is from many category vision projects requiring significant investment: the number of stores where you run the test.

Here just one Tesco Extra store was used for the test, with a corresponding control store. However, just as the test was implemented, a new Aldi store opened across the car-park. Literally. This of course had an impact on store-traffic, but particularly in frozen food as some discounters over-trade in this area. So there were upswings in aisle traffic and impulse purchasing but of course the impact would have been far higher if such a competitor store opening had not taken place.

All good tests should be implemented in at least 5-6 stores, where aspects that lie outside the hands of the test can be factored in/out of results. Sometimes this is challenged due to budget constraints or the 'just let's get it right in one store first' attitude. Trust me – ROI is imperative for Shopper Marketing and if we want to prove what we do actually works, we will always need the numbers behind us to prove it. So invest in multi-store tests. It is always worth it to have statistically stable project results.On further roll out to the store network post-test, the POS materials were changed to have a longer life. For the initial test, standard POS materials were used, which were fine in the short-term but over the weeks and months they started to take a battering. Future roll outs used more expensive but longer-lasting POS materials to create the same effect as in the test.

Green Isle ended up investing in 'dressing' frozen sub-categories within which they didn't even have a presence (ice-cream for example) which was a good indication as to how seriously they took the 'total category solution' to this project. This was about Frozen Food, not their brand or portfolio.

This project won the Irish ECR Shopper Marketing award in 2013 and went on to be selected for the same award at the ECR Europe level, where it was acknowledged as the Runner Up. It is an excellent example of how truly understanding shopper barriers, creatively addressing them and designing high impact POS can positively change behaviours and uplift sales.

are less and less handy in jobs at home. So, orientation time is often needed in advance.
In case of decoration, inspiration is needed and we work with decorative style groups because there are many different solutions. You may want to inform the customer as soon as possible about the products that may be appealing to him. Presenting the products from the same style group together can help a consumer to choose more easily between products or styles. Now, it is important to translate this on the shelf:
A shopper journey usually begins with a number of planned sales, on a shopping list or not, but which a customer is planning to buy before he even enters the store. Once at the shelf, the consumer can be seduced to additional purchases by the presentation of additional products together.
Dog treats can be a good example. A retailer put these delicacies on the top shelf. However, by observation we see that the treats were mainly bought by children or elder people but that they had difficulty reaching them. By placing the dog treats on a lower shelf, sales increased immediately (Paco Underhill, *'Why we buy what we buy'*).

The shop visit is called the first moment of truth. It is the first moment the shopper can see, touch and evaluate the product and can decide to purchase or not.

Post shopping

Then comes the second moment of truth or post shopping: how is the use of the product? How was the transport home? Did the product arrive in good condition? How to store it? Will it fit in the refrigerator? Can it be stored in the basement? Is the product easy to use or not? And is the consumer satisfied enough to buy it again or was it a onetime purchase? And finally, can he put it in the waste bin or does he have to bring it to the bottle bank or the environmental park? In this phase, the shopper can also store the product or recommend it to others and you can see if you have created real fans.

4.5 Shopper Research

In many organizations there is a lot of knowledge about consumers. However, when the shopper is concerned, there is often much less knowledge. Shopper Research is essential, particularly to increase your conversion in the shop and to understand the barriers to purchase. There are two categories of questions to find out:

Insights behind purchase behaviour - shopper profiles: who buys the products

- Type of shopper: quick scan or just fun and orientation
- What are they excited about?
- What are the downsides or problems in installation or use?
- What are the barriers to purchase?
- What is considered and in what hierarchical order do they make these considerations?

Considerations deal about aspects like convenience, price, trendiness or sustainability. We usually call the hierarchy in these considerations, the Shopper Decision Tree. This will be discussed in Chapter 6.

The execution of the category at the retailers

- What are the experiences of the shopper at the various retailer formats with purchases within a particular category - what does the shopper think of the retailer's presentation (range, navigation, information, inspiration, price, availability, stock, service, advice on use)?
- How did the buying process work? Did the customer have to search for a long time or was it easy to find?
- Was the right information available to make the decision? Was an employee needed for explanation?
- What would be the best planogram according to the customer? What do they expect from the retail format and does the category reflect these expectations? What role do brands play in the category and what is their contribution to the retail format?

Doing shopper research can be carried out in different ways or combinations, depending on the required information. Examples include qualitative research (focus groups), quantitative research (in-store interviews or observations) or quantitative research online.

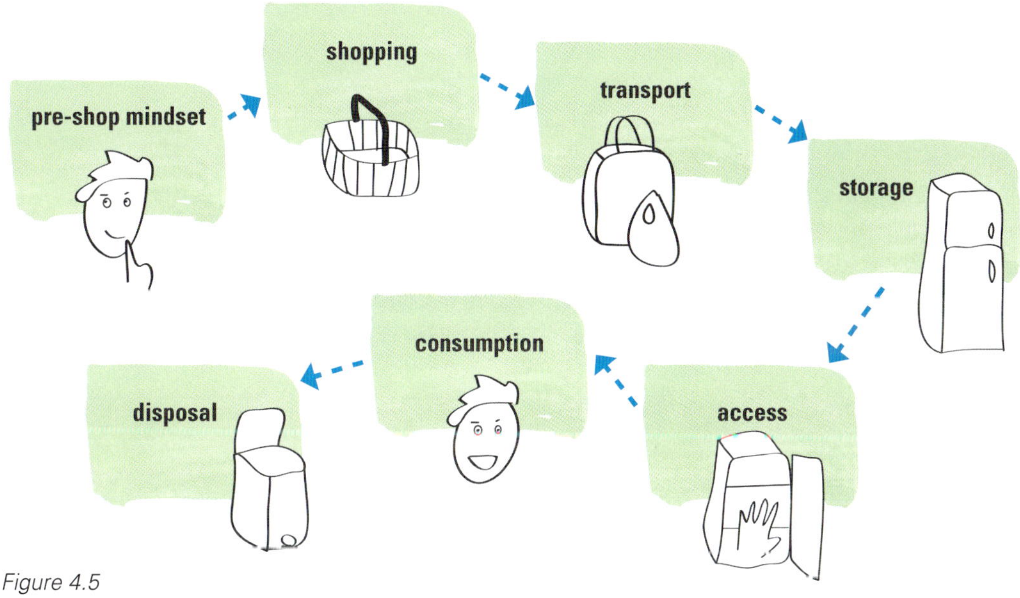

Figure 4.5

This could be the shopper journey of beer. Each phase is described, the trigger for buying beer is a party or just stock. Most steps of the shopper journey are annoying, only the consumption is pleasant. Based on this research you can think of ways to improve the shopper journey.

Neuro-marketing

Many of the shopper's decisions are unconscious or intuitive. A disadvantage of direct questions to the consumer is that he will post rationalize: he will explain his behaviour rationally afterwards. Behavioural scientists indicate and emphasise on the fact that too often, we assume that people make rational decisions. We must take greater account of psychological factors like status, security, fairness, autonomy and personal relationships. Neuroscientists have found that a MRI scan can measure the impact of images on the desire for something and what the pain is when the price to pay is considered. It starts with gaining (no gain without pain) and the balance between them: to obtain. These factors sum up together the purchase decision. This allows you to predict the success of products and to find the right experience or arguments to achieve the desired effect. Neuro-marketing is still in its experimental stage, but it will be developed further in the coming years.

4.6 Shopper activation

Shopper activation has to do with conversion. How do you transform a visitor into a shopper? It is a tactical interpretation of the final category plan.

1. Stop / navigation
2. Hold / information / inspiration
3. Close / activation

First you have to make sure your offer stands out so that the customer stops. Most of the time, he does not stop for products or POS materials. Then you have to hold his attention with the right arguments to encourage him to make a purchase. After that, a special offer might lead to the purchase. Store communication focuses mainly on the last part and skips the first two steps.
The first step is to stop the customer. So, there, you have to insert an action that gets attention. This may be a top card, a television screen or something else. The product usually does not get the needed attention because the store is already full of products. Subsequently you have to hold the attention of the customer, either by great content, an inspirational result or the right and useful information. Finally, you need a trigger to encourage the purchase. This may be an offer or a deadline.

We will elaborate on this in the tactics of the category plan (chapter 6.8).

Lay's Do Us a Flavour: The Battle Campaign Next stage co-creation & shopper marketing

Issue

The great success of the co-creation Lay's Do Us a Flavour campaign in the Netherlands in 2010 seemed almost unbeatable; the first real co-created campaign with consumers where we secured excellent collaboration with our retail partners resulted in a brand campaign that set a global standard. The campaign delivered incremental category growth: where we achieved the highest ever measured market penetration for a product launch (ie. 85% of the Dutch population participated). It became the no. 1 overall introduction, selling 6 million bags of crisps in just 10 weeks. The winner, 'Lay's Patatje Joppie' became the third most popular taste of the total Lay's range.

Solution approach

Clearly a high target, possibly unrealistic: we managed to create and deliver an even stronger campaign: Lay's Do Us a Flavour, The Battle in 2012. The biggest difference was we put down a real shopper marketing campaign for the category this time, by adding shopper (insights) into the proven combination of retail- and consumer-insights. We added a co-creation with the shopper and retailer partners, next to the original co-creation with consumers. Engaging and activating the shopper and influencing mum and her purchasing behaviour in all phases of the shopping journey, were the basic principles.

Concrete measures

1. **Based on combination of Consumer, Customer and Shopper insights**
   - The true power of the different shopper activation concepts resulted from the fact we worked with a model which uses as starting point a combination of consumer, shopper and customer insights. All shopper initiatives were checked against this insight model and the final solution was always top of mind, at the point of overlap of consumer, shopper and retailer insights and objectives. Below you will find the general category insights we used as foundation. In the co-creation with retail partners, we also

CASE

added the specific retailer, shopper and category insights.

The main Consumer insights:

- Taste is the main driver of the crisps purchase decision: 66% of the consumers/shoppers choose a particular bag of crisps for the taste.
- The Dutch have a clear opinion, they are outspoken and like to have a say in everything major. The same goes for what they eat or drink.
- The Dutch can be characterized by their passion and diligence. If they go for it, they truly go 'all the way' (e.g. Orange football supporters or King's day festivities).

The main Shopper insights

- The shopper wants to be surprized by new flavours and packaging, and is looking for temptation, especially in 'impulse' products like savoury snacks.
- The shopper is inclined to make impulsive purchases. The decision of many purchases (in crisps 40%) is made in-store.

The main Customer insights

- The retail partners are seeking distinctiveness for their own retail banner and growth & renewal in the category savoury snacks.
- The retailer is looking for added value in the category savoury snacks.
- The category role/strategy can be described as Impulse (Basket filler) and the Lay's potato crisps segment strategy as an Excitement Creator (creating excitement and stimulants).

2. Strength and execution of the shopper marketing concept & plan

▶ The shopper has had a pivotal role in the campaign, both internally and externally, in cooperation with our retail partners.

- **Internal**: shopper insights were incorporated in the campaign development as a base for all activities.
- **External**: we and our retail partners cooperated from a very early stage to develop the strongest possible shopper activation concepts that offers distinction to the retail formats and will drive shopper behaviour change.

3. Define target shoppers

▶ PepsiCo has predetermined the target shoppers for the different channels

1) Households with children: supermarkets focus
2) Young adults (18-24 yrs): Out of Home (OOH) channel and Cinemas
3) Male: OOH and Petrol Stations channel

4. **The campaign was built up in four phases (throughout 2012). A different co-creation focus was used in each phase.**

- Phase **1:** taste entries & battles: co-creation with consumers
- Phase **2:** nominations & product development: co-creation with consumers, shoppers and flavour creators
- Phase **3:** battle between the three finalists: co-creation with customers, shoppers and consumers.
- Phase **4:** introduction of the winning flavours as Lay's Limited Editions

5. The campaign was fully supported during the different phases of the **shopping trip**, PepsiCo worked on the **awareness of the campaign, the relevance for the consumer or shopper and the shopper engagement & activation.**

From consumer to shopper (pre-shop phase)

- With the campaign, PepsiCo has reached out to the consumers at home through advertising on television, online and through supermarkets' leaflets. This drove consumer's awareness and also relevance; consumers could create flavours and battle against each other (co-creation). The leaflets also generated the shopper relevance.

Before and during the purchase (pre-shop & shop phase): shopper

- This was about converting the awareness and consideration and driving the purchase decision by different shopper activations/touchpoints: bespoke shopper marketing campaigns for our retail partners (various Dutch supermarket banners and OOH partners) and relevant shopper interruption points (e.g. flyer promotions, second placement with impactful displays). PepsiCo has included the shopper to let her (mum) choose the winning flavour while shopping (co-creation shopper).

From shopper to consumer (consumption) and back to shopper (repetitive purchases) – post shop:

- With communication on all Lay's bags, consumers were again confronted with the campaign at home. They were involved and engaged in phase 1 to submit flavours and to battle, in phase 2 and 3 to vote for their favourite flavour.

CASE

Results

1. Collaboration with our retail partners

- Collaboration was the key to success for this shopper-centric campaign. We initiated cooperation in a very early stage to deliver distinctive and bespoke concepts and shopper activation (co-creation retailer) to influence the shopper behaviour. In all cases, the starting point was always the existing consumer-, shopper- and category insights and the objective of the particular partner they collaborated with. The shopper marketing concepts were developed and evaluated together. This collaboration has resulted in numerous awards and recognition from our retail partners:

1. Introduction Top 20: no. 2 introduction in the Netherlands 2012
2. Industribution Trophy: category and overall winner 2013
3. Marketing Awards: Best Trade Marketing performance, Best introduction and Fastest growing brand in the brand Top 2000
4. Golden Partner: for Sales performance, Successful introductions and Contribution at assortments' level.

And indeed we are incredibly proud of these results.

2. Experience

- Online: a total of 407,610 flavours were submitted in the Netherlands and 5,847,627 battles were played online.

Shopper activation: bespoke shopper marketing campaigns and specific shopper activations activities in all Dutch supermarkets and relevant OOH-channels.

3. Category growth

- The three finalists reached a full distribution within a couple of days and appeared quickly in the Top 5 of best rotating flavours in flat crisps during the campaign weeks.
- Extremely high sales in only two months: sold over 5 million bags of Lay's.
- Incremental category sales and increased profitability -through very limited cannibalization on the existing range/ category sales.
- The category, savoury snacks, has a particularly high penetration. Who does not eat crisps in The Netherlands? Nevertheless, PepsiCo Lay's Do Us a Flavour, The Battle 2012 added value to the category by increasing the penetration, the buying frequency, and the average weight of purchase (value). See the summary below:

	Total category	Crisps segment	Lay's
Penetration	+	++	+++
Purchase frequency	+	=*	=*
Weight of purchase (value)	+	+	++

(GfK Q3-Q4'12 compared to Q3-Q4 '11)

** In this period, the purchase frequency was stabilized because of competitors' heavy promotional pressure.*

All results were beyond the expectations.

Chapter 5

The retail brand

Retail formats are becoming increasingly important. They have grown into a brand and the strength of that brand determines to what extent the consumer trusts the retail brand and feels loyal to it. A clear identity makes not only a strong brand, but also unique features that differentiate it from other retail formats. This is called positioning.

The importance of positioning the format is an issue on the strategic level. Therefore, we focus on the techniques for positioning in this chapter (5.2). But first we will examine the format itself and demonstrate how to analyze it (5.1). This is important to determine the scope (and targets) of Category Management. Then we will look into what is needed to build up a format and what this means for the Category Manager's tasks (5.3). The choice for certain building blocks affects the choice for a supplier (5.4). And finally we will zoom in the influence of the online possibilities on the format's positioning (5.5).

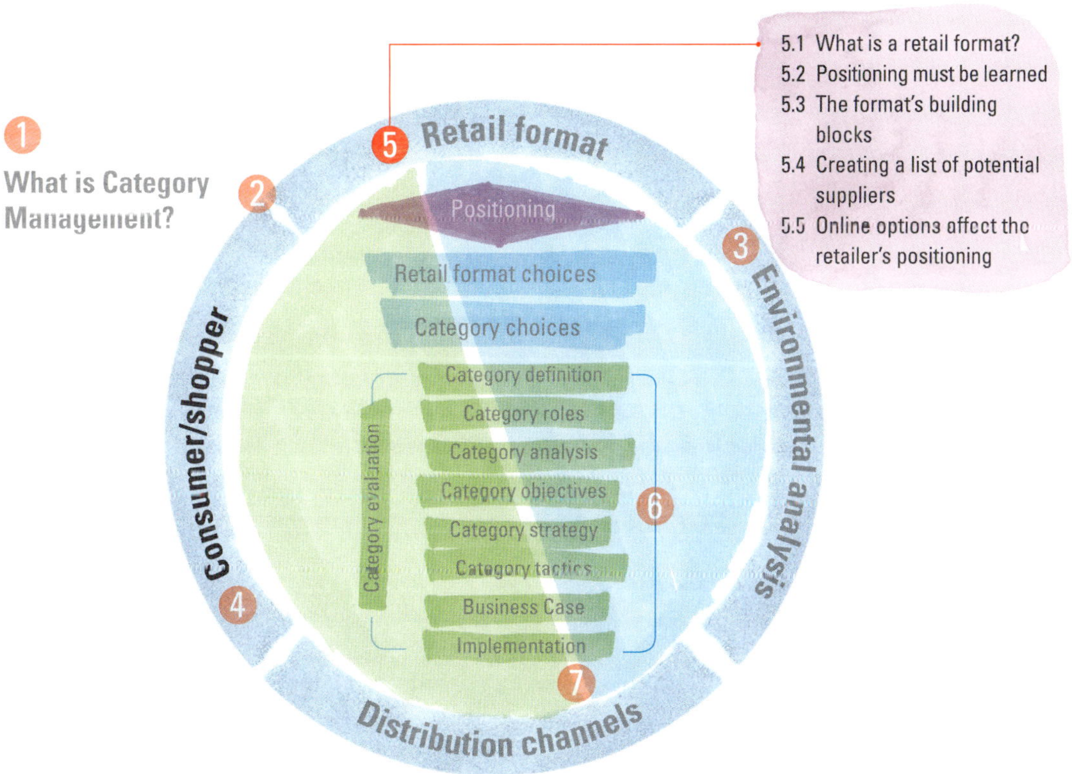

Chapter 5 is about building a retail brand and the connection with Category Management. The chapter contains 5 sections, mentioned above.

5.1 What is a retail format?

Partially, you cannot rationalize the concept of a retail format. You could describe it with terms like 'character of a store' or 'the soul of a store'. A strong retail format should appeal to the customer's sympathy. A strong brand creates a certain degree of preference or fidelity. We can analyze that and explain it logically which we will do, but there will still be inexplicable factors which cannot be caught in models or theories.

When you rationalize a retail format, it refers to the sum of products and services offered to the consumer by a store. The characteristics of a retail brand have a strong cohesion and must bear the possibility of being reproduced at different locations. Besides that, you would want the consumer who judges the characteristics of your retail format, to have the same experience you intended to create. The format is in trouble when a Retail Manager is convinced he is the cheapest whereas the consumer has a very different perception.

Figure 5.1 **What determines the retail format's identity**

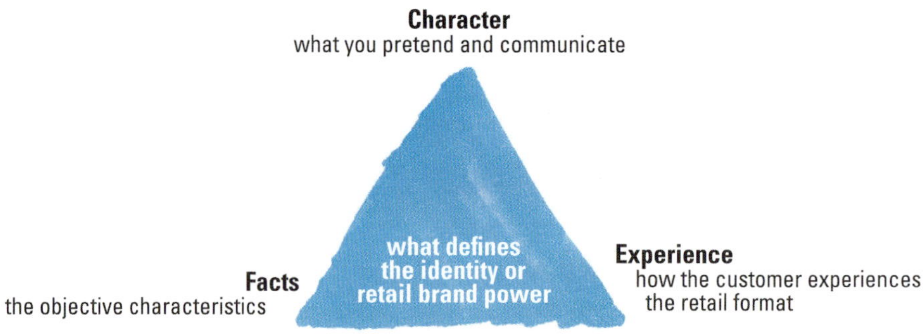

The strength of a retail brand can be described as a triangle but there must be a balance. What you intend to do and what you communicate (both at the top of the triangle), should match with how you actually act - on shop floor level (bottom left of the triangle). It should also match with the customer's perception (bottom right). If these three elements differ too much, a retail brand is weak and implausible. 'Walk your talk', 'Practice what you preach' or 'Deeds, not words' are all expressions that can be applied to this brand law.

All activities start with the brand

Because this is not a guidebook for brand builders, we will not elaborate on the brand building laws, but we want to emphasize that the strength of a retail format is determined by the balance between pretensions, reality and customer experience. The key question in all this is: does the customer find your intentions and reality relevant and enjoyable for his way of shopping?

This section about the retail brand contains the following subjects:

a. How a retail format model should be modeled
b. The outlines of a retail brand strategy
c. Four retail format targets
d. The retail brand does not stand alone but influences the whole chain
e. A retail format analysis in the form of a scorecard

5.1.1 A retail format should be modeled

Organizations want to roll out a retail format. So they should use a 'method'. For example, if an entrepreneur or manager has a jovial personality, it plays a big role in the desired level of customer service of a format, but it cannot be reproduced. However you can document desired behavioral characteristics for management and staff and 'demand' to look for people that can adopt such behavior.

In addition to the characteristics of the format as a brand (identity, see above) you can describe a format with the 6 P's of the marketing theory.

- **Product:** which assortments are offered? How are they organized into categories? Which (additional) products, which brands, which suppliers deliver the goods, and so on. The facilities and services of the retail format are also part of the product.
- **Personnel:** what are the staff's requirements? On training, behavior and skills? How do we work in the structure of the organization?
- **Place:** what are the characteristics of (and demands for) the location? Is it private property or lease and what about the living environment, the parking, additional stores, competition in the market, and influence of local administrators?
- **Price:** what is the (necessary) price? Who are your competitors? Which margin opportunities? What expectations does the local market have?
- **Presentation:** how is the decor and ambiance of the store? The presentation of the categories? The way of selling? The location and sequence of your assortment's flagships, etc.?
- **Promotion:** how do you create awareness? What is your pretension? How do you reach your target audience? How are you going to bind them?

5.1.2 The outlines of a retail format strategy

Every good policy starts with making choices. The sharper the retail format's choices, the more chances a Category Manager (and supplier) has to translate opportunities into practical assortment policy.

Monitor the correct order

Practice proves that every organization is inclined to skip steps in the process. The retailer develops a vision (dream) or a mission and immediately proceeds to concrete implementation. Especially pragmatic retailers prefer direct action. The justification of existence is assumed to be known, the financial goals are clear and well known and all activities are based upon that. However this is too short-sighted.

The scheme displays the simplified sequential steps for a successful overall strategy.

Figure 5.2 **From vision to desired effect**

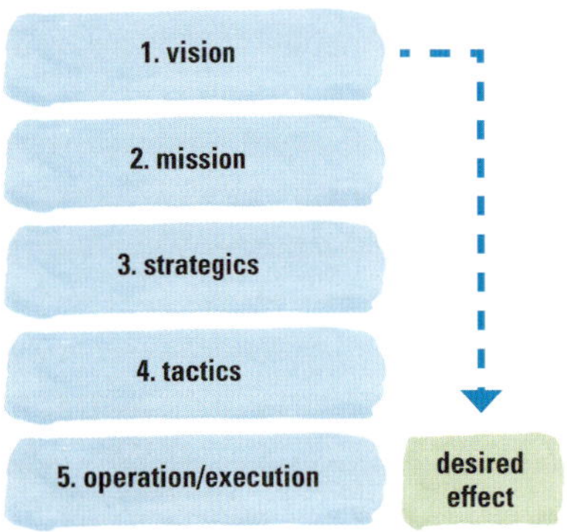

A good plan starts with a vision, describing the final picture and the desired final effect. The vision is first translated into a mission. The mission is translated into a strategic plan; which is framed with tactical preconditions (how) to carry out the strategic plan, and only then we proceed to carry out the activities (the execution).

The roadmap

1. **First the vision.** It is a description of the dream of the ultimate desired result. For example: "I want to be a store that consumers like to visit, where they can find everything, a store they are so proud of and one they want to tell everyone about. A favorite store for their shopping." And you give a character description of a store that causes the desired effect. This must match the store's identity (brand value of the format).
2. **After this comes the mission.** The mission gives in fact words to the vision but in a way that is measurable and verifiable (with all financial targets fitted in).
3. **Then, comes, the strategy.** Creating a strategy is basically dividing the mission into inter-connected components that comprize the overall plan that will lead to the mission's realization. A strategy is a roadmap that takes people, resources, objectives, priorities, etc., into account.
4. **The tactics follow the strategy.** Tactics is the way your strategy can best be achieved. Tactics are primarily aimed at supporting policies. It is filling in the boundary conditions. Tactics might mean that you want to recruit managers and staff necessarily from the area of your location.

5. **Finally, comes, the operation or the sum of all concrete actions.** Operation also includes the execution, the quality of your services or products. Building a display is an 'operational' action. Ensuring that customers can find that display and can safely take products out of it, is also part of the execution's quality.

5.1.3 Four retail targets

Within the chosen targets (mission) and with the characteristics of the retail brand in mind, you can develop a practical, shopper centered format strategy with the support of format targets. N.B. you can read about the positioning of a retail brand in the next paragraph (5.2).
A retail format strategy has actually four simple objectives. Making (more) profit is the result which is not inherent in the strategy itself. The four strategic goals for every retailer are:

Figure 5.3 **Simplified format objectives**

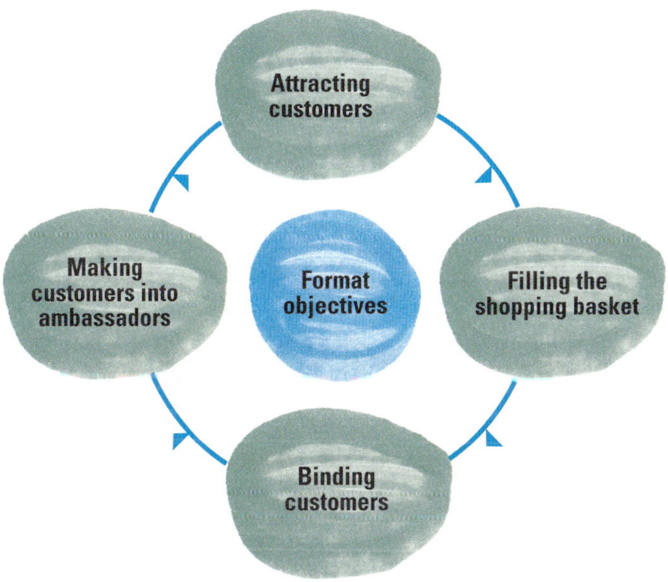

The four format objectives are easily summarized: I want to attract customers, I want hem to purchase as much as possible, I want to bind them to my store and I would like them to become ambassadors so they can enthuse others to visit my store.

The four targets of a retail format

a. **Attract customers.** The set of strategic options a retailer has (or can think of) to driving traffic to the store. Handing out shopping bags in new residential areas or allow brokers to distribute coupons to new residents, are concrete interpretations of the strategic goal to make every new resident of a market area acquainted with your store within two days.
b. **Filling the shopping basket.** The possibilities a retailer has to let customers purchase more in his store. A strategic goal may be to make 60% of your market area into primary customers. That means that they spent 80% of their expenditure on food (when it comes from supermarkets) in your store. And this could lead to the idea of quality bread (bread that always wins in blind taste tests) that obviates the local bakery.

c. **Customer loyalty.** This means that you will pursue a policy that causes customers to think three times before trying another store. Cultivate loyalty, for example by surprising your customers at each of their visit. It can be by doing slightly better than expected. Surprise and seduction are the key factors in this strategy. But saving campaigns are also tools to create a bond with your customers (even if it is temporary).
d. **Turning customers into ambassadors.** This strategy is the most difficult. You can reward customers if they attract other customers. But you can also choose to implement a policy that will naturally make them become your ambassadors. This means customers will automatically be so excited about your store that they will become 'fans'. But you can also perform a simple option like providing some nice loyal customers bags for free.

For each of these targets you can think up all kinds of interventions (tactics and actions). It is important to implement these interventions carefully (assessing what measures you can take to improve the current situation) and to learn from past activities.

The quote 'steal as an artist' is important to keep in mind. As Apple founder Steve Jobs said: "We have always been shameless about stealing great ideas." In fact, there is nothing new under the sun. Looking at other retailers, even in other countries, is much more effective than the result of a brainstorming session focused on your own ideas.

Table 5.1 **Fill in schedule for practical format targets**

	Attracting customers	Filling the shopping basket	Binding customers	Making customers into ambassadors
Concrete options				
Preconditions	It should not be easy to copy	It should not cause extra waste	It should not be temporary and not only rational	They should be able to do so freely
Ideas that worked out previously				
What we have already seen before?				
How are we going to work it out?				
What actions first?				

This fill in diagram provides an overview of the four main retail objectives in terms of customers. And with the six key questions (left) a Format Manager (but also a Category Manager) can fill in the options - possibly even with a supplier. As an example, we have completed some parameters to be shared with a supplier so he knows to what requirements his promoting proposals must comply.

5.1.4 The retail brand does not stand alone but influences the complete chain

A retail format is just one link in the complete chain an organization has to deal with. Each link will affect the format's success and the Category Manager's work. In addition, the processes within one link can be more complex and contradictory than in between the links themselves.
And if a format is very strong and dominant, its characteristics influence the rest of the chain. One of the most striking examples worldwide is the McDonalds format. The complete chain behind this format adapts to the power of McDonalds, from suppliers to packaging suppliers and recyclers.

Internal struggles

Sometimes it seems that most tensions and business conflicts occur between links in a chain. For example, it can happen between a purchasing department and the Account Manager from a manufacturer. There are often countless hidden tensions that can be causes why a well designed Category Management plan does not completely produce the desired effect. For example, at a large manufacturer there are sometimes larger differences between the sales department and the production department than between the sales department of the manufacturer and the purchasing department of the retailer. The same also applies to the retailer's purchasing department and Format Management, especially if there are franchisers on an advisory board. The diagram on the next page shows the most important processes.

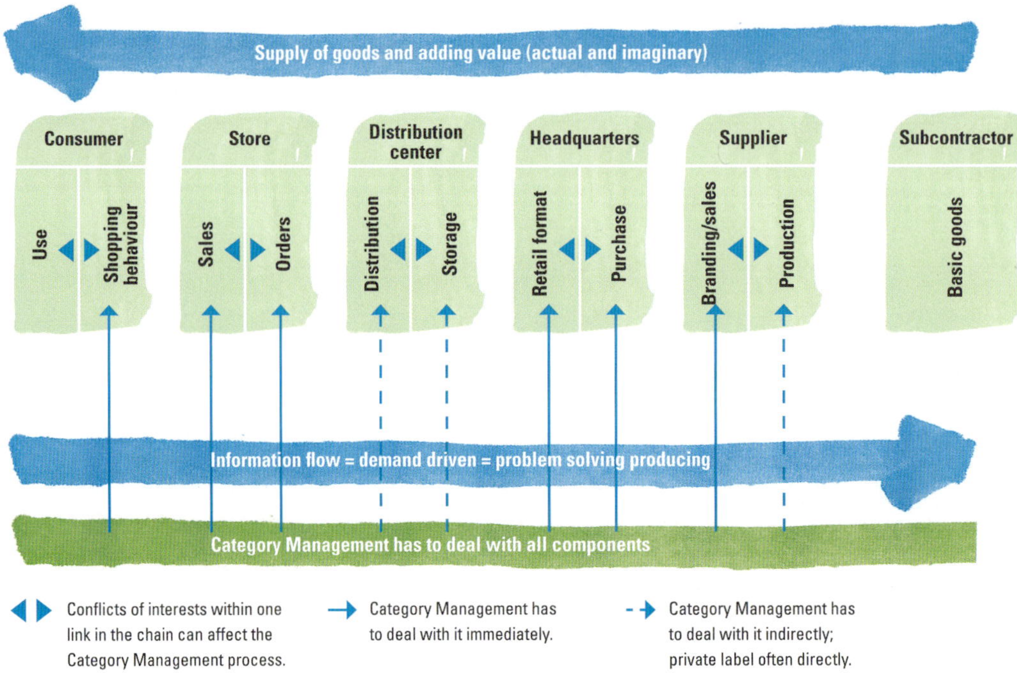

Figure 5.4

The material flows from right to left and costs will be added in the chain. A precondition is that with these costs 'value' is also added. That value is the actual value of the range, but also the perceived value (brand image). From left to right you see the flow of information that is needed to arrange the whole processes as efficiently as possible.

This scheme is not intended to explain the process but to make clear at what point analyses must be made before any interventions can be made to achieve fundamental changes in Format Management and Category Management. The internal tensions within a link can disturb a successful Category Management plan. Therefore, a Category Manager has to be honest about bureaucratic tensions within his own organization, but also needs to ask his suppliers about the possibilities and rules within their organization.
An important precondition for a supplier is that he has access to the retailer's shopper data.

5.1.5 Format analysis as a scorecard

In order to properly analyze a retail format, it is interesting to compare it with other active formats, whether or not with the same type of positioning in a given market area. A benchmark with seven different success factors is a widely used technique.

We sum up the seven key features for that kind of benchmark analysis:
1. The quality of store locations;
2. The influence of other (non-competing) stores;
3. The quality of services (including e-shopping) of the other stores;
4. The quality of business performance;
5. The quality of retaining customers;
6. The quality of operational processes;
7. The quality of assortments.

At each of these seven points a Format Manager and a Category Manager can compare the relative strength of their own retail format to others with several sub-questions. The number of sub-questions (points of attention) can be as elaborated as you want. It is important to give a grade to the current situation (rating) compared to the desired grade. The diagram on this page is an example of how that can be done.

Criterium Each question can be elaborated with different kind of subquestions.	**desired score**	**present score**	**competitor A**	**competitor B**	**competitor C**
1. The quality of the store's location					
2. The infuence of other (non competitive) stores on your store					
3. The quality of e-shopping and other services					
4. The quality of the commercial performances					
5. The quality of holding on to customers					
6. The quality of operational processes (in and before the store's location)					
7. The quality of assortments and services in the store					

Table 5.2
The seven main criteria with which we build a benchmark can be elaborated with several sub questions. A Category Manager can also ask suppliers to give grades to this list. That can provide perfect subjects for a discussion between retail format and suppliers about Category Management.

It may be clear that not all components are part of the Category Manager's direct working field. However, he must have an idea of all the factors to be able to control his own field with sufficient expertise.

5.2 Positioning must be learned

Each retail format has to position itself. It has to choose a market position that distinguishes the format from the competition. We also call it: the creation of long-term distinctive character. To do that, a retail brand can use different attributes. There are many models and theories. To keep it simple we show (widely used) positioning models in this chapter.

Which is in Chapter 5.2.1 the positioning with five attributes of the Customer Relevance Framework and 5.2.2 positioning with price and quality. We want to show this to indicate that a model has consequences on the making of a concrete translation to assortments and so on. It is because positioning itself is a part of the overall policy pyramid in which a retailer has to define his format.

Retail Policy Pyramid

In the figure on the next page we see the retail policy in the form of an inverted pyramid. We can divide the total retail policy into four parts. Prior to this, you should answer some questions: is there still a distinction in channels or has the blurring of channels already taken place? Are there also concepts (retail formats) out of the branch that threaten my position? This can also be internet shopping (we describe this separately in chapter 5.5).

A retail organization usually chooses a channel (top model) for the positioning of the format. The positioning question acts on level 1; how do you distinguish yourself from others? At level 2, you describe with which building blocks the retail brand wants to fill this positioning. Thus you prove that you are truly unlike any other format. These two policy-levels are primarily in the Format Manager's working field. Level 2, however, also concerns the Category Manager. It is because the choice of the format's building blocks (to give content to the positioning and profile) has a major impact on the primary scope of the Category Manager. At level 3 you will find the questions that lead to (related) choices for the categories and what requirements a retailer has for a category. Should the category bind or pull customers? Should it contribute more than average to the returns or not? Etc. It is only at level 4 that the content of the category assortments, products and brands will be done.

Figure 5.5 **Model of the Retail Policy Pyramid**

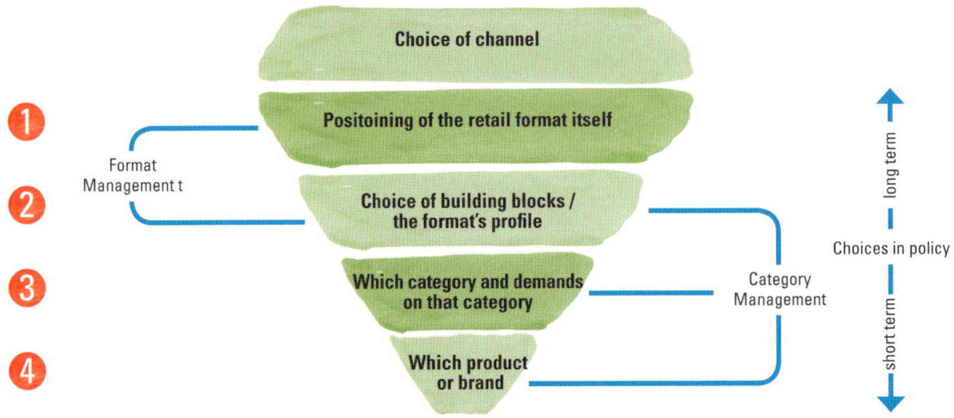

The Retail Policy Pyramid shows how a format policy is made. The top of the model involves long term choices (channel selection and positioning) and the bottom of the model is about the short term changes in category requirements and demands and whether certain products should or should not be included. The levels 1 and 2 are the property of the Format Managers, but they do define the work field of the Category Manager who is working from level 2 to level 3 and 4.

Retaining consistency

It is of great importance that each Category Manager is constantly aware of this policy pyramid. It indicates the priority order of the policy. Each decision in the upper layer changes the frameworks for the level below. Conversely, any (wrong) decision made on product or category level, will contribute to the stability of the format and its building blocks or to its invalidity.

The Category Manager's function evolves

The Category Manager's responsibility will increase in the coming years for parts that are now still covered by format responsibility. Price image, attractiveness of promotions and innovations, service of the store, perception of quality (clarity of the store, the department and store shelves and the knowledge level of the staff) will more often belong to the working area of the Category Manager.

5.2.1 Positioning with Customer Relevance Framework

In order to position, you need a solid model. Capgemini (then Ernst & Young Consulting) has developed a positioning model for ECR Europe that can also be measured by consumer research (with a score). It is called the Customer Relevance Framework (CRF). As the authors of this book have experience with this model, as a useful tool, although we realize that there are many other models possible.

The CRF model has become a basic model through which important strategic choices of big European and American retailers can be distinguished.
The model is based on American and British research and concludes that, in essence, shoppers weigh on a retail format's relevancy by five different attributes. Worldwide, these attributes are the same but they are interpreted differently in each country, based on cultural differences. In time they will be filled in differently in each country. The United States is ahead on the developments in Western Europe.

The five attributes are:

- *Access.* - The accessibility of 'doing the shopping'. This ranges from the parking lot to making the selections easily discoverable. Access is what distinguishes you if you enable the shopper to do his shopping very quickly. It concerns also the internal navigation throughout the store. The selection of the final product belongs to the core of this attribute. At a time when 'speed' is found increasingly important, 'access' is often an overlooked phenomenon.
- *Experience* - Involves questions like: Do I feel at home in the shop? Do I feel respected? Do I enjoy being in the store and do I tend to stay longer?
- *Price* - Do I feel like (or am I secured that) this shop is inexpensive and the prices are fair and consistent? Is it worth the visit? Do I feel like they have done everything to satisfy me in terms of low pricing?
- *Product* - Does the retail brand distinguish itself with its products (or range)? Do the products inspire me? Is de offering credible? Did I visit this store especially because of their range of products?
- *Service* - Am I, as a customer, treated as a valued guest in this store? Do I get answers to questions (even if I do not ask them)? Service is really about getting more than you expect, feeling satisfied by the way you have been treated and feeling welcomed in a store.

Figure 5.6 **Five unconscious shopping criteria of the Customer Relevance Framework**

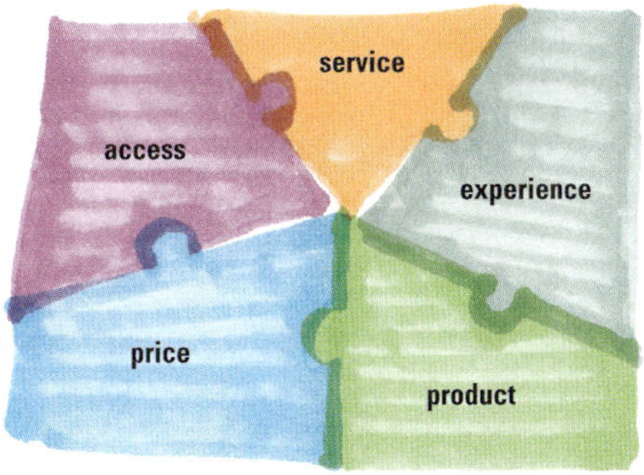

If a consumer goes shopping, he has five criteria in his subconscious mind for a store's relevancy: Price, Product, Experience, Service and Access. These are called the positioning attributes. The attributes are timeless and similar in all countries and retail formats. Only the content varies by country and time! (Capgemini)

Positioning is a matter of choices

Retailers who have the guts to choose (and do that well), are the most successful. This is one of the key lessons of the hundreds of analyzes made by Capgemini's retail experts. You have to make choices in what area you want to distinguish yourself. Champion retailers choose one of the five Consumer Relevance attributes to dominate in.

- A successful format should definitely get the highest scores on one of those five profiling attributes. In this model we work with scores between 1 (low) to 5 (high).
- Then these retail formats may still choose another attribute to differentiate themselves from others. That attribute must be scored with a 4.
- If the other attributes finally get an average of 3, the retail format has a strong profile, concludes the large-scale investigation.

The model on this page shows how five attributes could score compared to each other.

Figure 5.7 **Positioning is a matter of choices**

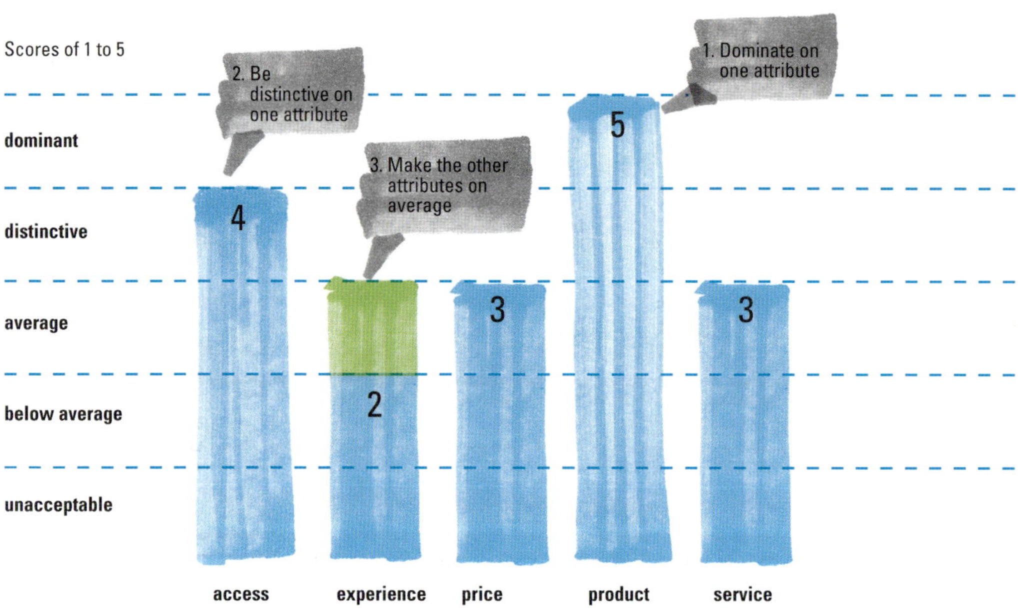

A retailer is most effective if he dominates on one attribute, is distinguishing on one other attribute and scores a 'average' performance on the other attributes. In this model on a 5-point scale, the average is a 3. Dominating is done with a 5 and differentiating with 4. All lower scores (1 or 2) must be repaired. (Capgemini Consumer Relevance Framework)

What should different kind of retail formats do?

In this chapter we are talking about supermarkets, but identical rules apply to all other retailers. It seems to be obvious that large (full) service supermarkets should dominate on 'Product'. Secondarily, they should differentiate on 'Access' or on Experience (related to market opportunities); making shopping easy or inspiring (when Experience is chosen). Access is very difficult for large stores. It is remarkable that a discount store like Aldi Süd (Germany) dominates according to the shopper on 'Access' and differentiates on 'Price'. This is logical because Germany is dominated by large-scale stores that make grocery shopping time-consuming. For supermarkets, different combinations of these attributes are possible and within the attributes different interpretations are possible. Marks and Spencer dominates with access and differentiates with product. Tesco has the trouble that its profile is not clear enough. Tesco is middle of the road (a 3-score on most attributes).

How do you fill in the positioning attributes?

In the figure we mentioned options for each possible attribute that gives meaning to the choice to dominate or differentiate. Obviously, within these characteristics choices can be made.

- For example: if 'Access' scores a 5, it means that consumers should feel that a format has made effort to find solutions for them. Aldi Süd's having a high score on 'Access' in Germany is logical. It is because Aldi has made convenient, clean stores with assortment choices that please the German customer. And this customer shops (in this format often 'skimming') according to fixed patterns and experiences that are pleasant.
- Score of 5 on the aspect of 'Price', means the format acts like a broker or agent. The format proves (guarantees) that the price asked is a perfectly fair low price for the quality offered. This is possible through price comparisons or refunds if prices are lower elsewhere, and so on.
- Score 5 on 'Experience' means the format has managed to create a very pleasant, intimate atmosphere. The store feels like an extension of the customer's own lifestyle.
- Score 5 on 'Service' means the consumer prefers this shop for the ultimate customization he experiences. He even gets things he did not ask for but finds very pleasant.
- Score 5 on 'Product' means that consumers see things that inspire them, for example, to be a better home chef. Certain (new) products enable them to improve their quality of life.

Table 5.3 **What do the scores mean to the various attributes in the Costumer Relevance model?**

Retailers aim	access	experience	price	product	service	the consumer
dominate (5)	solution	intimacy	authority	inspiration	customized	primarily visiting
differentiate (4)	convenience	care	consistency	reliable	training	prefers
average (3)	ease	respect	honestly	credible	reaction	trusts

Gaining a score of 5 on one desired attribute is not easy. A 5 score on product means for instance that the consumer will visit you primarily due to the fact that the store constantly inspires him with assortments and products. (Capgemini)

Not everything can get a high score

The big mistake Category Managers and vendors make, is that they give a high score to specific attributes and definitely on 'Product', 'Price', and 'Access'. The reality is, that a 2 or a 3 is more appropriate than a 4 or a 5. In addition, a Format Manager should dare to make choices. You can only set goal for a 5 on one attribute and go for a 4 on another. The rest needs to score a 3 at most. Conception, the company of Jan Willem Grievink has been involved in the first study in the Netherlands with this model among five supermarket formats in 2002. It was striking that not a single Dutch supermarket had a clear profile (a high score on one of the attributes). Most of them scored a 2 or 3.

Difference between pretensions and reality

Many retailers have a utopian image of the retail format's positioning force. In particular Format Managers (but also Category Managers) have the habit of overestimating themselves. There is a big difference between what a retailer wants to be (pretends to be) and the reality. In addition, the most interesting question is: how does the customer experience it? The latter can be examined.If you ask a customer what he thinks of the product or range, you cannot ask him this in one direct question. If you want to know how each of the five attributes score with your customer, you have to divide them into sub-questions to get an honest picture of how your store is experienced by the customer. In the model below the results of the market research of the supermarket formats involved in the 2002 is reported.

Table 5.4 **Differences in realities between Format Manager, export and customer experience.**

	access	experience	price	product	service
Desired reality by format	4	3	3	5	3
The current actual reality in the shops by experts	2	2	2	3	2
Rated reality by consumers	3*	2	2	3	3*

To get a fair idea about the extent to which the five attributes contribute to the positioning, it is not sufficient if only a Format Manager evaluates his own format. He should also let external professionals assess the reality of his stores (the second row). And more importantly, he should get the consumer's grades (on scale 1 to 5) on their reality. The latter cannot be achieved by requesting directly about the attributes. For that you have to hide every attribute in sub-questions the consumer understands and can judge. In the model above, the numbers (rounded) of a supermarket format in 2002 are shown. The fact that consumers give higher scores to 'Access' and 'Service' than specialists is because the consumer's reference was limited. Other grocery stores in their markets scored even worse. (Jan-Willem Grievink, ConCeption BV)

5.2.2 Positioning with price and quality

In addition to the positioning using the Consumer Relevance model, classical positioning with price and quality is also a good option to perform analysis. For example, In the Netherlands, GfK publishes such a study on supermarkets twice a year. . GfK's "Christmas report" and "Summer report" is the cause of many conversations between trade and industry and sometimes leads to sharp strategic repositioning.

If all goes well, supermarket formats should be found on a straight line, a line that demonstrates that a bigger price difference is acceptable (with, for example, a hard discounter) due to a likewise difference in quality. In the diagram we have the most inexpensive supermarket (in the perception of consumers) put in the lower left quadrant (Germany, Aldi Nord), and the most luxurious supermarket (Great Britain, Marks & Spencer) right. If all is correct, most supermarkets will be on the diagonal line. Most supermarkets' ultimate aim is to create a great quality distance relative to another supermarket, but not a big price distance. Then they reach the lower right quadrant that is extremely attractive to consumers. Factory Outlets and Duty Free shops plot themselves in that quadrant.

Figure 5.8 **Price difference vs. difference in quality**

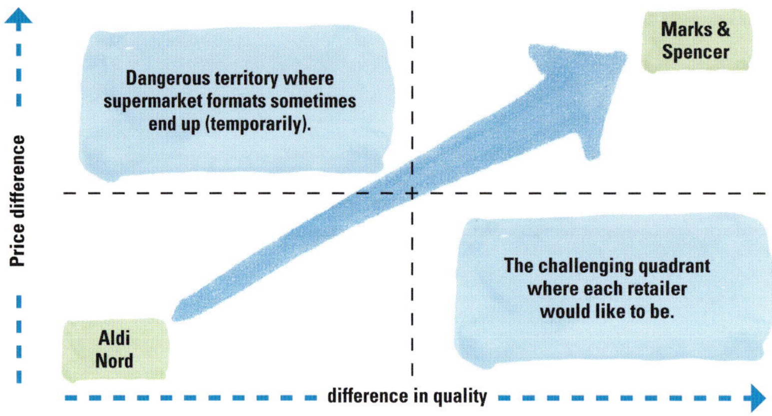

If a format delivers significantly more quality, it may also be more expensive. Marks & Spencer is experienced as 'expensive', but still appreciated for quality and convenience. Aldi is experienced as 'cheap', but consumers expect less quality here.

The most dangerous quadrant is the area where consumers experience a big price difference but little difference in quality (top left). Formats regularly end up in this quadrant and notice that customers (in mass) turn away from them. In the UK we saw that Tesco is suffering from the upcoming discounters (Aldi and Lidl) and the success of Waitrose and M&S above them.

Format profiles and the need for value creation

That the positioning of a format affects the assortments and the way it is doing business with suppliers has already been indicated. The (often used) chart on the next page is a way to segment retail formats (supermarkets). On the left horizontal axis you will find formats that primarily appear as sellers of goods and those on the right act more like a provider of solutions. On the vertical axis at the bottom you will find the formats that focus primary on cost price and at the top, the formats that focus on service.

Figure 5.9 **The format process and Category Management**

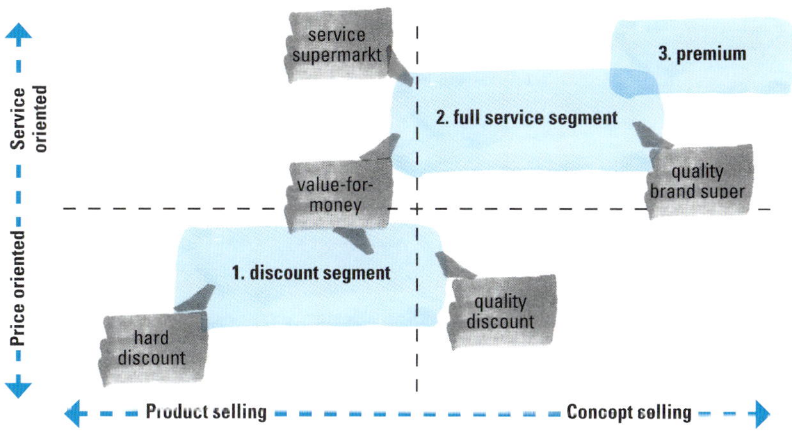

This model distinguishes on the horizontal axis the pure product and concept stores and on the vertical axis the value- or service-oriented formats. They are filled in for supermarkets, but for non-food retailers a similar arrangement applies. The model shows that the Category Manager's work for a hard discounter or a premium supermarket is totally different. (EFMI-Rabo Quo Vadis)

Positioning determines the Category Manager's scope

In the schedule we have charted five kinds of supermarket formats, which operated in Europe in 2016. The classic supermarkets, such as Coop and Sparr are in the upper left quadrant. The format that has evolved to 'brand' such as Albert Heijn, Waitrose, M&S is in the upper right quadrant. Value-for-Money formats (formerly soft discounters) as PLUS (Germany), Morrisons (UK), Casino (France) are at the heart of the model. Quality discounters Lidl, Hoogvliet (NL), Colruyt (B) are just in the right lower quadrant (but more on the half-line) and the hard discounters (Aldi, Netto and Action) act in the lower left quadrant. The model was developed by EFMI Business School and they note that gradually two large segments retail formats arize: a discount segment and a full-service segment in the middle of the market. But the middle of the market is under pressure, all over European retail segments. And the problem for market leaders is that they merely will be identified as 'middle of the market'. That is the problem for Tesco, Carrefour and Albert Heijn.

This would create space right above for a pure premium segment. Incidentally, in the background of this model other criteria play a role for a retail format. A format can have as basic premise not to be more than 10% more expensive than format X.
A picture of the food landscape, which is organized in this way, makes it clear that the work of Category Managers tend to vary. If you are a pure product seller, such as Aldi, Lidl and Action, your trade is different than when you are a concept reseller with a lot of added value in a premium segment.

Value or efficiency as a key problem

From this model are derived two main retail format's policy objectives. On the lower left side, the focus will be on increasing the efficiency and maintaining low costs. That increases the retail format's attractions; smart purchasing, achieving low operating costs and minimizing activities that disturb the efficiency. On the right top side, the focus will be on creating added value that is relevant to the consumer. These 'values' can be deduced from the Trend Funnel (see Chapter 2 and 3) and are currently the 7C's (chapter 3).

What does this mean for the Category Manager?

With a focus on efficiency

If the emphasis is on efficiency, low prices and minimal costs will be promoted into priorities. The expectations of retailers towards suppliers can also be seen in that context. This means a Category Manager should give attention to the following issues:

- More focus on increasing purchases and sales;
- Using tenders (auctions) for contracting bulk assortments;
- Emphasizing on standardization of product ranges and systems;
- Harmonizing logistics processes;
- Minimizing assortment decisions that add complexity and cost;
- Making suppliers contribute to the costs that are necessary to deviate from the conventional processes;
- Outsourcing non-standard work on store operation;
- Minimizing deviations in customer flows, operating costs, stocks and so on;
- Selecting packaging and presentation techniques which reduce store costs.

With a focus on value

Value creation in food essentially means that consumers should be seduced to buy more expensive 'kilocalories'. This only happens if the customer gets added value in exchange of the extra costs. That can be of one of the new mediums of exchange that are important to consumers (7 C's of chapter 3):

- More convenience: easier packaging or time saving dishes;
- More care & cure: more health oriented items like fresh produce, fresh meals, fresh juices, healthier versions of existing products;
- More culinary: exclusive, fine and luxurious products and constantly surprising (tempting) the consumer with unique items that make one's mouth water.
- More conscious, an appeal to 'good behavior': demonstrably sustainable products, fair trade for developing countries, biological, ecological, etc. A growing number of consumers spend money

on this value especially if it is combined with one of the other values. For example, if these products also look extremely tasty (or are extremely healthy);

- Cute story, telling a good story: products a retailer is proud of (because he has interfered with the cultivation or production) deserve to be told about. This also applies to local products, etc.

If Category Management has a focus on value it should concentrate on continuous innovation and assortment changes. Adding completely new ranges is also a part of value creation. For example, supermarkets sell more cooking-related non-food items. That is because these items have a better margin than food, while the consumer price of the article may still be lower for the shopper than at the department store, since a specialty format needs a higher margin.

Positioning is leading

The chosen positioning must always be leading in all Category Manager's further activities. However, it is interesting to compare the positioning with other (competing) formats.

The profile of a format can be improved, but a radical change of attributes is not logical. It is possible but it needs a long-term focus or requires an entirely new format. Suddenly changing an experience focus to a price focus is virtually impossible, to do it in the first place and to have the customer believe it is even more difficult. Therefore, it is always good to keep the basic principles of your format positioning in mind. Enhancing the existing attributes (features) is of course always possible.

5.3 The format's building blocks

A format does not only need a positioning (see section 5.2), but also certain characteristics to fill that position which we call format blocks. These building blocks ensure primarily that the format distinguishes itself from other formats. In supermarkets fourteen important building blocks are used for the completion of the format. Non-food formats apply derived building blocks.

In the diagram on this page a Format Manager or a Category Manager can create an overview of how the format is completed at this moment. It belongs to the format analysis to find the current building blocks and how those building blocks should be filled to realize the desired positioning with the 5 format attributes.

Figure 5.10 **The 14 most important building blocks for food retailers**

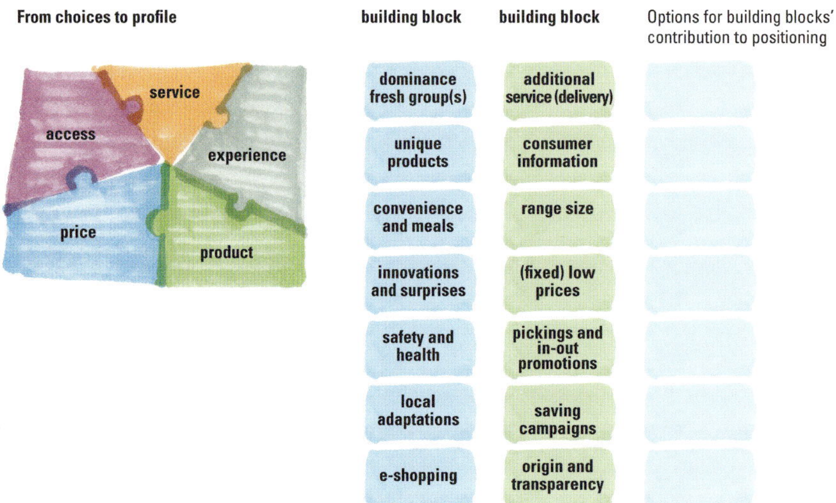

Each format profile's element leads to options and conditions for making the specific selection choices and thus for Category Management. This model provides an overview of the 14 most common types of building blocks that support a supermarket's format positioning.

The translation from format analysis to Category Management

Before we describe in detail how the Category Management theory should work in chapter 6, the diagram on this page shows the bridge between the format's building blocks and the categories' role whether they do or do not belong to them. The model is a selection method to describe (and establish) the category's role based on the function of the product groups.

Again it is important to make the difference between the desired reality, the true reality and the perceived reality by consumers. You may think you have a strong local range, but the reality is that a business owner or store manager does not present it and the consumer does not like it at all because a different format offers three times your range.

Technological changes

The emergence of new technologies changes the shopping process, but will also change the value of the building blocks. Consumers know, for example, with the help of online and mobile channels, more and more about:

- Price differences between brands and product types
- Provenance and origin of products
- Stories and reviews on products, recipes and dishes
- Reviews of others on a format, store or product
- Alternative products
- Allergens, ingredients or recipes

A Category Manager can also use this in favor of his own format. Through intensive interaction with the shopper, he can learn a lot more about behavior than before and be more responsive to customer needs. It is easy to show unique actions or products, for example. The interaction can be facilitated and bonding can be increased if you ask customers questions via social media or respond quickly to complaints, questions or needs.

5.4 Creating a list of potential suppliers

A retailer has a strong interest in suppliers that help him to differentiate from the competition. And if that supplier also ensures more profit and a customer who is loyal to the format, he has a big advantage.

Different kinds of suppliers ask for different actions
From the retailers' perspective you can classify suppliers into three categories.

a. The largest group are regular suppliers who supply most of the range: the basic suppliers. This can be a good role for a supplier, but it requires that you continuously excel in terms of cost leadership.
b. The second group consists of the key suppliers. The suppliers are important for the growth of the assortments and are the base for the format. Innovation and thinking along with the format and Category Management are preconditions.
c. The third (but most important) group is made of the priority suppliers, the strategic suppliers. This is a limited number of suppliers who greatly contribute to the differentiation of the store. Private label suppliers often belong to this group. Brand suppliers can also build a special relationship with a format when they first try their releases there, organize activities on the shop floor (tastings), develop special packaging or promotions and so on. The requirements for these suppliers are high. They must be innovative and be able to stand in the shoes of the retailer.

The supplier's significance
Tesco used a segmentation model for suppliers in relation to the (potential) significance of that supplier for the brand value of Tesco. Thereby, they came up with a division into three groups, which corresponds to the above-mentioned.

Figure 5.11 **Segmentation of suppliers in the context of their significance to the retail format**

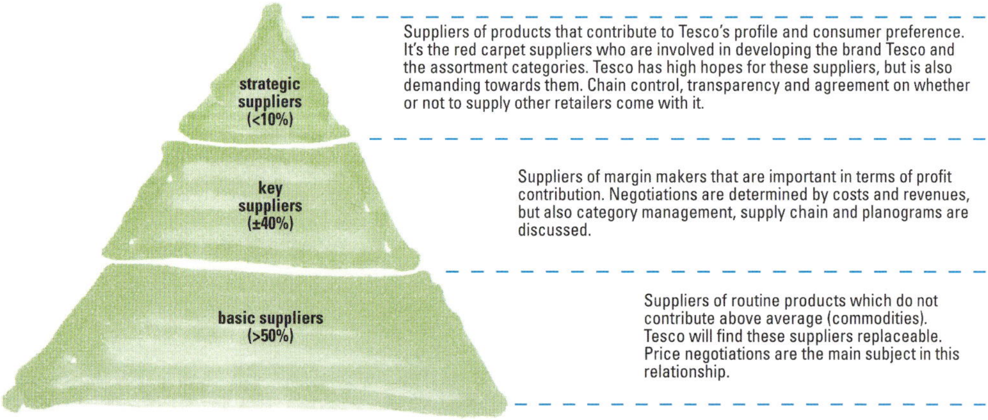

(FSIN and EFMI, Quo Vadis report 2009, model; based on Tesco)

In figure 5.11, we see that Tesco builds its distinction with a limited number of suppliers (less than 10% of the total number of suppliers). Those vendors have different requirements than the category basic suppliers who are easily interchangeable for Tesco.

The suppliers' value for the format

In order to quickly assess the potential value of a new product or supplier, many retailers use the model described in figure 5.12. This model establishes in outlines the link with the segmentation of suppliers as mentioned above. But you can also use it to estimate the value of a potential new product.

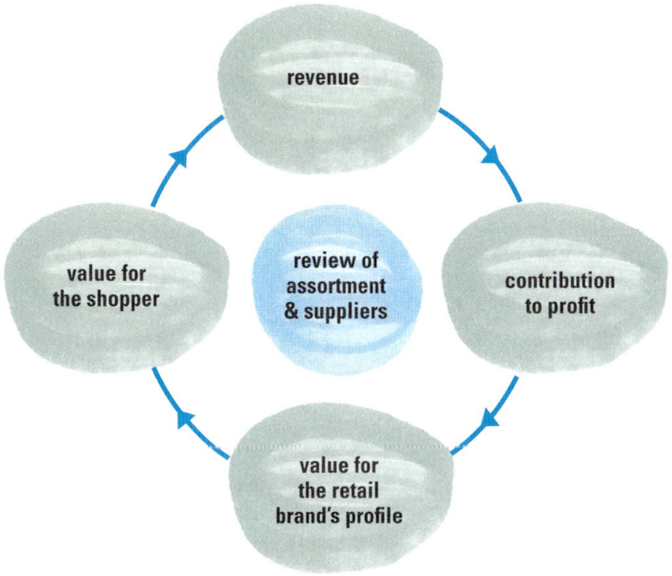

Figure 5.12

A supplier or new product (range) essentially has four possible 'values' for the growth of the format. The first is the sheer turnover value. Customers buy more. The second value is the profit contribution. Because of this product, the profit margin goes up. The third value is the creation of the format's distinction. This product (or range) helps me to distinguish myself from the competition. And the fourth value is strengthening the relationship between customer and format. If this product (or range) is of great importance for the customer, the relationship with my format will be stronger.

The retailer's contribution

A retailer has different expectations for each of the three supplier categories. He places different demands on them but simultaneously the retailer should contribute his part. We will elaborate on that in Chapters 6 and 7. Table 5.5 shows how the different suppliers are translated into differences in commercial policy. And the question is whether the retailer is able to complete his part of the information and cooperations.

Table 5.5 **What is expected from the different kind of suppliers?**

Policy scenarios to manage suppliers	strategic supplier	key supplier	basic supplier
Management involvement in the category's policy	Each level	Selected levels	Partial allowed
Frequency of meetings	Monthly	Four times or twice a year	Twice a year
Making category plans with multiple suppliers	Yes	No, unless there is a necessity	No
Giving insight to market strategy	Yes	Selected parts	Only products of supplier
Sharing necessary information	Scanning data overall category	On brand level	Limited
Annual KPI targets	Accomplished together	Negotiated and approved	Making agreements
Promotion plans	First choice in options	Negotiate for shelf space	Negotiate

In this review we see the great differences in cooperation between a 'normal' supplier (basic supplier) and a strategic supplier. A CEO or format manager will not interfere with regular suppliers, but with key suppliers. It also happens that key suppliers work with open books and while the retailer is interfering with the operations (including investments) of those suppliers. Therefore both retailers and suppliers should be well aware of the supplier's role and the consequences for the cooperation.

Overview of suppliers in relations to range segmentation

One last way to get an overview of potential suppliers is to start reasoning from the existing range structure. Retail formats build assortments with certain logic: cheap products at the bottom and premium products at the top of each range category. That can also be criteria for selecting potential suppliers.

Often a maximum of 20% of the assortment is used to create (or strengthen) a retail format. But that 20% can be found in any range and in each functional layer of the range segmentation (e.g., premium products). With a scheme Category Managers can easily create a list of potential suppliers. From that matrix he can choose suppliers with whom he can set up a specific part of the Category Management improvement process (Chapter 6).

Table 5.6 **Classification matrix for the selection of potential suppliers**

	building blocks assortment	routine assortment	fresh standard	other
Price signal products				
Private label products mainstream				
Premium products				
Generic A brands				
Premium A brands				
Premium private label				

On this model's vertical axis you will find the functional classification of ranges which involve different suppliers from price signal products (top) to premium own brands (bottom). The horizontal axis shows the most important functions of a format's product groups (a convenience store in this case). The questioning can be read as followed; if I want a supplier of premium items for a common fresh fruit group, I fill in the options in the appropriate box (third column, third or fifth purple box; depending on whether or not I want to connect my own label with it).

5.5 Online options affect the retailer's positioning

The rapid development of online possibilities has strongly changed the rules of the retail game. In the Western European countries, over 14% of the retail sales take place online. In the ongoing game of retail branding, the online channel has an even stronger influence. In all elements of the customer's journey, significant changes are taking place and we see shifts of players in it. Manufacturers sell directly to consumers through an online store, retailers create platforms to inspire consumers and media are selling products. Because of the lack of geographic contingency, the consumer can compare non- related stores online much faster than offline. For example, Amazon, one of the world's largest online retailers, has a major influence on the development of interfaces for online shopping. This also means that the area, in which a format in the online landscape is placed, is often sector-transcending. After all, consumers surf effortlessly from an electronics store to a clothing store within minutes. This should be taken into serious account when a retail format chooses an online position. Due to the high degree of transparency, online formats are compared much more on the individual product level than on format principles. This also brings along some new rules for price, product (range) and promotion. And this has an impact on the positioning in bricks, the offline positioning.

New rules and opportunities for price, product and promotion that give substance to the retail brand

Thanks to the online transparency, consumers can easily compare prices and assortments. Price comparison sites provide for that by showing all the possible offers within one environment. In many cases, the consumer's shopping trip starts no longer in your own (online) store but with Google or a price comparison site. This allows the consumer to look for an isolated product, without any influence of format principles. For example, discounters and service formats appear in one overview without the consumer even noticing it. It is therefore important to review price, product and promotion strategy in light of this transparent world. Before we dwell on that, it is good to place the online activities in a frame that is based on the greatest online challenge, namely visibility. This challenge takes place at three levels:

A. Store: the store is no longer depending on a location for success

No A1 locations or grand openings: an online store is completely invisible, until visitors are directed towards it. Generating traffic to an online store is a necessity and not comparable to visitors in the offline channel. The behavior is different, only because 40% of the people who put something in their basket actually purchase it. Even in a successful online store only 2% to 3% of the total number of visitors purchases something. So it is not only important that people find your online store, but you also have to be found by the right people. Traffic alone is not a prerequisite for success; the visitors still have to proceed to purchase.

B. Category: in physical stores much attention is paid to the store layout or the routing.

The role of the category and its position in the store is taken into consideration. Thus they can choose to place a destination category in the back of the store, so that the consumer is forced to walk through impulse or routine categories to boost up sales. In the online shopping environment the routing is totally different. If everything is optimized, the menu guides consumers directly to subcategory level and have a product overview. A good menu structure is the substitute of a routing, but does not provide the 'forced' guidance of people into the store. Here, other tools are used.

C. Product: the consumer has three tools at his disposal to find a product; search, filter and sort.

By using these three tools, the consumer is continuously changing the products on his screen. All guidelines that were founded within a physical landscape - which has major limitations on its physical boundaries - are useless online. For example, it is superfluous to make a complete planogram. This does not mean that the consumer's decision tree no longer applies online. There is still logic in the way consumers choose their products. To deploy the three tools (search, filter, sort) effectively, proper product information is required (see chapter 6.7). This ensures that there are enough angles for the customer to find his desired product. Think about product characteristics such as content and color, but the time of use may also be relevant. For example, breakfast, lunch or dinner. The information from the existing product range will have to be enriched to get the right results. The consumer navigates in a supermarket on products' shape and color. Consumers are able to find a product within minutes on a shelf with more than 500 different items. The number of products displayed online is limited to the screen size. So even though the online shelf is elastic, there are restrictions on the number of displayed products. Due to the e-commerce development that started with books which were not recognized by the cover but by the title, the interfaces were not adapted to the representation of supermarket ranges. It is only recently that the online supermarkets came to realize this.

This makes it clear why a whole industry is created around the challenge of navigation and finding products easily. Recognizing this challenge will help making decisions in price, product (range) and promotion.

A retail format that provides excellent service and therefore has always opted for a slightly higher price, will be forced to revize the pricing strategy. It is challenging to show your online visitors where the premium price is paid for, especially if you want to attract customers who are not familiar with your format's assumptions. Despite the increased transparency, it is certainly not always necessary to offer the lowest price. Formats with clear added values are able to carry on with their slightly higher price. Fast delivery, convenience, availability or the assortment's width and depth can give that added value. Furthermore, in some industries manufacturers already offer successful online propositions on the retail price. In these cases the consumer's confidence in the manufacturer is so strong that they are willing to pay the suggested list price. Examples can be found in fashion (almost every major fashion brand has its own web-shop) and electronics (e.g., major manufacturers like Samsung, Sony or Philips have their own shop).

What comes after the supermarket?

bfresh

Many supermarket organizations are experimenting with small sized stores which include ready to eat meals, food to go as well as some elementary groceries. The reason behind is that they know that the supermarket's lifecycle as we know it will end.

Background

Consumers will do less weekly shopping and buy less groceries. A food shopper will focus more on last minute decisions and fresh made products. Questions like this will activate his mind.

- When am I going to eat?
- Where will I eat?
- What will I eat?
- Where can I buy it?
- What kind of solutions are my options?

At that moment he can also activate an App to assist him in all kind of solutions for his needs. Fresh delivery will be one of the options.

One thing is for sure: a convenience solution with ultra-fresh (and healthy) foods & beverages will be one of the favorites for the ultimate demands of young adults. Especially when they work and live alone for a few days a week.

A retail sample

The Dutch based supermarket organization Ahold-Delhaize is one of the main foodretail players on the East-coast of the US. With the banners Food Lion, Stop&Shop, Giant, Martins and Peapod.

In 2015, Ahold Fresh Formats started such an experimental small store-format under the name 'bfresh'. bfresh focusses on fresh foods, smart value, awesome teammates, right in your 'hood', as they called it. It is an experimental concept to find out whether this is a scalable new concept in between a supermarket and a restaurant. It is a mix of buying and eating instore; buying online & delivery; or just come-in, grab-and-go.

Key problems

- For a convenience shopping trip, the current (large) supermarkets are a non-convenient for consumers who just want some food for now or the next few hours. They just want to grab-and-go their foods.
- There are a lot of convenience shops available, but they offer most packed (non-fresh) foods. Not very attractive for the new generations who look for fresh and healthy food solutions.

CASE

- The number of shopping trips which are just dedicated to buy something for a short term consumption, will increase very soon. The FoodService Institute NL expect this trip will double at least and reach about 12% of the total sales in Food&Beverage.
- Current supermarkets are cost- and efficiency oriented. It is hard for them to add instore fresh-food-production. It is also hard for them to add hospitality to the concept and still maintain the productivity added value they have.
- The key question is: is there an option for a supermarket format to cooperate with a format from the restaurant industry and build an integrated new concept which includes food for now and food for later as well as some of the classic supermarket products.

Objective

The main objective is to find out whether this concept will attract customers for the coming years and will achieve a top of mind position in the (already mentioned) upcoming trend for convenient meal solutions.

With this format they offer more natural and organic options than a typical supermarket, as well as vegan products, gluten-free options and specialty products. It also prepares freshly cooked seasonal meals on the premises in Little Kitchen™. While the emphasis is on fresh, healthy foods, bfresh also offers indulgence items and household, health and beauty products - a one-stop shop for urban customers",

What are the characteristics of bfresh?

- Fresh produce, meat, seafood, and full-service deli
- In-store made-from-scratch bakery
- In the in-store Little Kitchen they offer more than 30 fresh meals, made from scratch daily.
- Little Kitchen was based (in the beginning) on the knowhow and experience of La Place, the Dutch restaurant format, once established by V&D department Stores, but now owned by Ahold competitor Jumbo Supermarkets.
- Free bfresh mobile® app for ordering ahead for Little Kitchen™, savings, digital receipts and store information.
- Same-day delivery to home or work with bfresh delivery
- Electronic shelf labels to ensure price accuracy and reduce paper waste
- Small supermarket
- Store size: 10,000 square feet
- 10,000-plus items available

The idea

bfresh is created by Fresh Formats, now an Ahold-Delhaize company, established in 2014 to explore and develop new format opportunities, bfresh is a test model that the company said is a "complete withdrawal" from traditional brick-and-mortar grocery stores. A novel concept with a small-store format, bfresh is targeting neighborhood foodies who value fresh, healthy food options and affordable pricing.

"Today's grocery shoppers face several challenges including balancing food needs with tight budgets, finding convenient shopping options to fit tough schedules and feeding a strong desire to support local businesses," said Suzi Robinson, marketing manager for Fresh Formats and a developer of bfresh. "We sought to provide an easy-to-shop solution for the Allston community. bfresh is designed for anyone who loves food and wants healthy, affordable, locally sourced options in their neighborhood."

Little Kitchen with La Place experience

bfresh offers more than 30 fresh on the spot (made from scratch) seasonal meals.
The menus are daily changed, built from simple recipes. A foodretailer does not have the experience of a restaurant and cooking on-the-spot. Therefor Fresh Formats cooperated in the beginning with La Place, world-famous on these issues. One of the characteristics of La Place is that all the food preparation is done in the presence of customers. They work with simple healthy ingredients and the shoppers can see how the cooking and finishing is done. Shoppers can choose to order fresh smoothies, salads, pizza, Asian stir fry, breads, desserts, coffee and more.

CASE

Learnings: systemized gastronomy

bfresh is one of the many starting examples of blurring concepts. Blurring means that the future grocery store will change into a blend of a supermarket and a casual restaurant. It is systemized gastronomy. And that is already the main learning: you have to combine retail know-how with instore production know-how (restaurant skills).
In the beginning staff costs will be too high, weekly sales will start too low (compare to a supermarket start-up); customers need time to get involved with such a concept. For Ahold-Delhaize this is test-concept.
For the future these blurring concepts will pick a huge part of the 'stomach-share' and they take it mainly from the classic supermarket.

That means that these blurring concepts for the future have these characteristics:

- They will be able to deliver meals and foods as well as daily groceries and fresh produce.
- They can act like a caterer or a specialty (or deli-) shop.
- They use online tools to serve (and please) customers.
- A blurring format will simplify complex restaurant processes in order to harmonize with a retail business model; anyway blurring means more complexity and labor hours than a retailer.
- Blurring concepts mainly work with simple products, many of them locally sourced.
- Small suppliers get new changes to serve these formats with unique (value-add) products and services.
- In these 'blurring formats' there will be less space for national brands. More and more they work with 'home-made' products, cooked right under the eyes of the shopper.
- Sometimes the shopper wants to be treated as a guest, sometimes he wants to act like a customer and uses self-service.
- Therefor some of the formats will outsource a part of the cooking process to suppliers.

(CSP website, Ahold-Delhaize website)

Chapter 6

How to build a category plan

In the previous chapters we have emphasized on the retail format's positioning and the shopper and all preconditions that they entail. Now we get to the real Category Management part, the pure discipline of the Category Manager: Category Management: the optimization of categories from the perspective of the shopper and retailer objective. This working area is also important for the counterparts of the Category Manager in industry: the Account Managers and Trade Marketers. The better they understand the Category Manager's tasks, the better they can help to fill them and thus help the category to grow. In most cases the turnover of the suppliers will grow too, if they give a boost to the category, since they can respond better and more quickly to the Category Manager's plans.

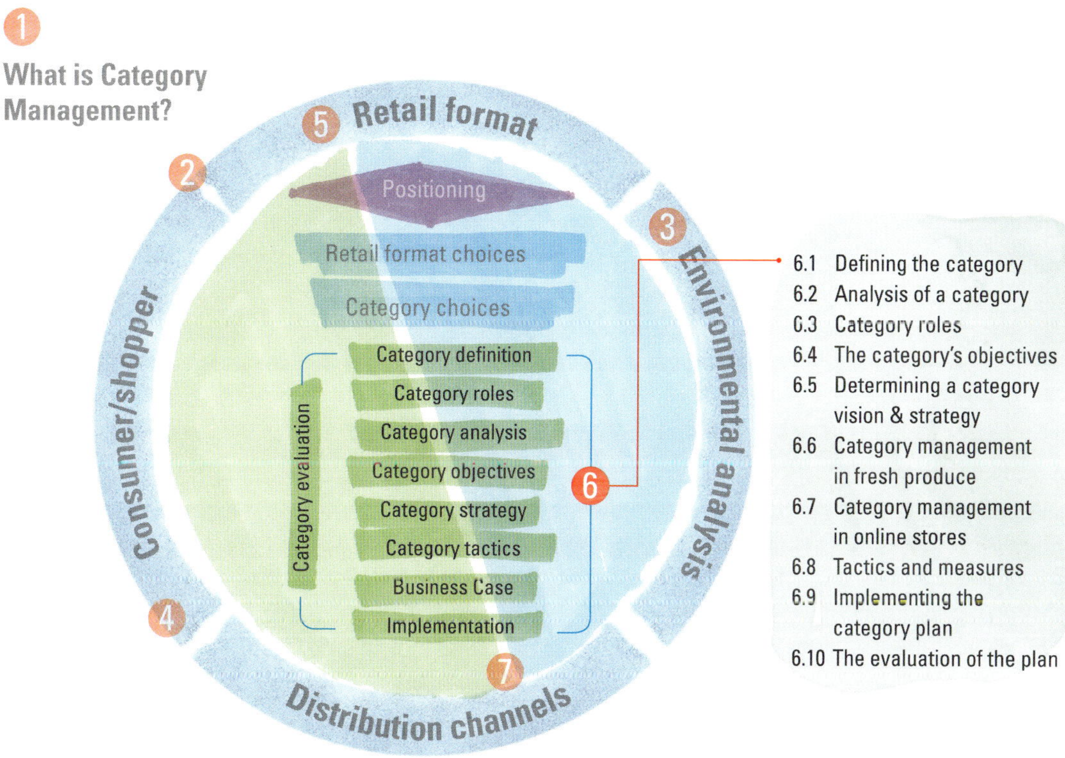

We start this chapter with the category definition. Section 6.2 explains the different category analyses: analysis of the shopper, assortment, shelf, promotion, competitive and financial analysis. Section 6.3 explains the different roles a category can have. Section 6.4 deals with the category's objectives and vision. What are the next years' drivers for growth? Section 6.5 shows how the vision and strategy are determined. Section 6.6 deals with category management for fresh produce. Chapter 6.7 focuses on online issues and approach. Section 6.8 deals with tactics of assortment, planograms and promotions. And once the management agrees on the plan and business case, we move on to the implementation.

This is discussed in Section 6.9. In order to determine whether the policy is successful and whether adjustments are necessary, the plan is evaluated periodically. The evaluation is described in Section 6.10.

N.B. the category's role, strategy and objective can sometimes lead to changing the category's definition. In fact, the flow diagram can also enhance iterative processes.

Consistency with retail format management

Category Management will always have a relationship with Retail Format Management. The Category Manager's working field is derived from the characteristics and strategic choices of the retail brand. We have discussed this in Chapters 1 and 5.

Building a category plan requires preparation. First you should determine for which category you build a plan, and then it has to be analyzed.

6.1 Defining the category

The theory of Category Management is based on shopper behavior. The shopper's current (or desired) behavior is a key factor in all models. Defining a category is an important step. If you want to be able to optimize and improve a category, you need to mark it out. However, often we see that category definitions are product oriented, instead of being based on shopper behavior. Ideally the category definition is based on consumer & shopper insights. Defining a category is not easy because it has to be measurable and logical. This is a difficult process because analyzing shopper behavior is complicated. Many supermarket products are sold differently according to their freshness, conditioning and packaging. How does the consumer interpret these characteristics? Fresh, pre-cut or deep-frozen green beans or green beans in a jar or can are all alternatives to each other. If segmentation is done with these trade-offs, it is done according to the 'shopper logic'. The ultimate category definition however, is usually not completely determined by shopper behavior, but also based on practical grounds such as raw material considerations (e.g. all types of flour together). Classifications based on technical consistency did not comply with the shopper and are therefore used less frequently. In addition, a retailer can also use other arguments to raise a range of products to a category (all frozen items together or all 'minute made' items together). This approach is called 'preferred segmentation'.

Ideal situation

Although it is complicated, it is important to determine a category definition that is based on the needs (and logic) of the target consumer group. Decisions about which products should be included in a certain category of a retailer's assortment and decisions on how those products should be priced, traded and promoted are in an ideal situation, based on two key factors:

1. A retail format strategy that clearly describes the shoppers (and consumers) who are the most important for the retailer;
2. Knowledge about the interaction between a category's different products (does one product decrease the sales of another product, or do both products together maximize sales?).

Ultimately it is about a group of homogeneous products or even supplementary to each other, for example, all products that are needed for a particular meal (breakfast, lunch, dinner or drinks) or all tools for a particular job. The shopper relates what he buys to his home. And by presenting products together, you help to trigger his memory and purchases. One way to do that is through the so called spider presentation, in which the hero of the most desired product is placed in the middle and complementary products are presented nearby.

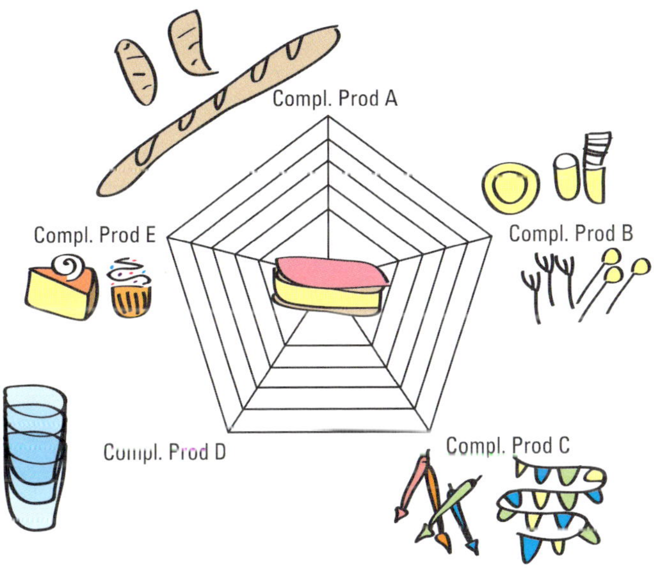

Figure 6.1
Consumers relate their purchases with their home. This may have to do with an opportunity (a party), a task (cleaning) or a space in the house (bathroom). In this chart we can see which products are associated with buying pastry. These products apply to the moment when pastry is eaten. By presenting these things together, you will make the purchases for a festive moment easier for the shopper and you will get the most out of filling the basket.

Pre-store and in store considerations

The shopper makes assessments in the store and before he goes to the store. They are summarized in the shopper decision tree which always begins with responding to a need or desire. It is based on that motive, the shopper searches for a particular solution. Certain formats or channels are visited. Once the shopper is in the store, he will look for the planned items, the products on his shopping list. He can purchase the planned item or an alternative, such as ready-to-eat, frozen, or pre-cut vegetables instead of raw. While the shopper is in the store, he also adds some items or impulse purchases. In order to fully fill the basket, it is important to explicitly place the impulse products near the corresponding planned purchases.

Figure 6.2 **Shopper Logic**

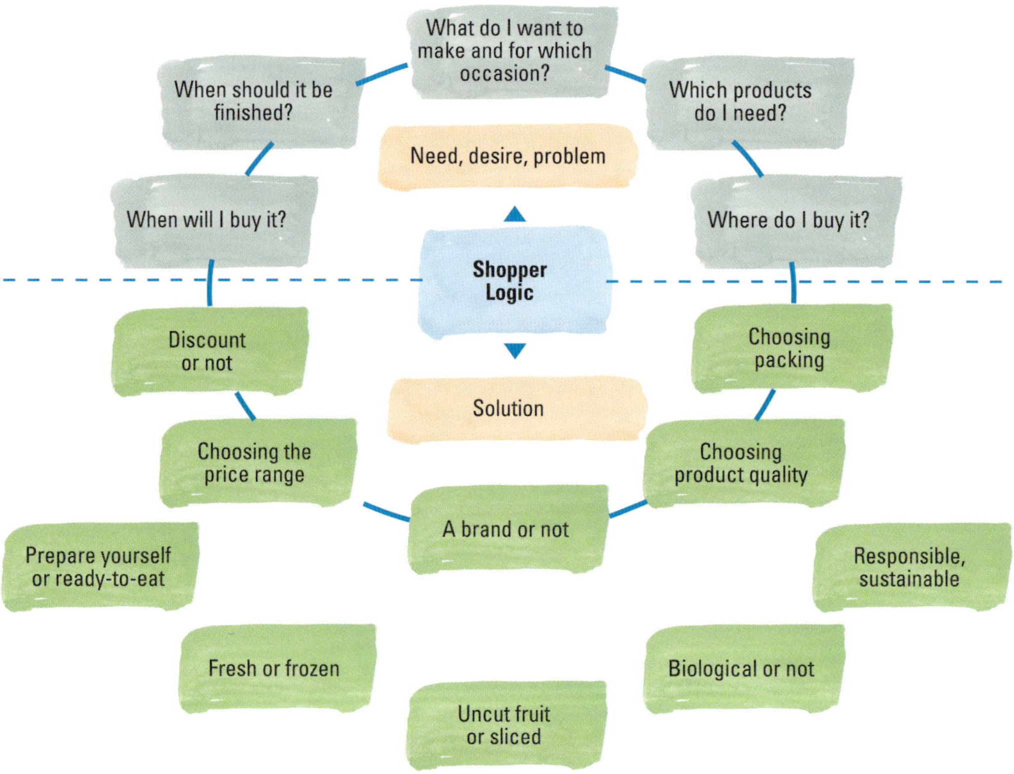

In this chart we can see the shopper's most common reasons for purchasing something. Above the dotted line you can see the personal considerations about the need, desire or problem, the place where he wants to shop and when he wants to do that. Below the dotted line you can find the considerations about the product, packaging, brand and price. This applies for all needs and channels.

The importance of logic and preferred segmentation

The shopper decision tree is of considerable importance in shopper research. Note that there is not only one shopper decision tree but several ones. There are millions of shoppers who decide to make a purchase in different ways. So there are also many different paths that consumers and shoppers follow in their choice. While taste may be the most important motive for some, for others the price is decisive. We are searching for the decision tree that applies to most customers of the retailer and best meets the retail brand.

Before we can investigate that, we should first define different hypotheses which can be tested during the research. Consumers are often accustomed to a particular segmentation and will not indicate quickly that they do not like something. But they can properly judge whether a change is nicer or better.

Examples

The importance of this analysis becomes clear when we take a cola drinking household for example. Analysis of this household's purchasing data shows that they usually buy diet coke from a certain brand, but they sometimes vary between private label and the brand. However, they often vary between different types of packaging; the first time a 2-litres bottle can be bought, then a six pack cans and next time an entire tray of cans. For this household the type of coke (light or regular) is the key product feature, followed by brand and then followed by the size or the package.

Conclusions

Categories must be defined and created around real shopper behavior facts. And finally, beware not to focus only on what people say they do, but on what they really do.

To define a category, it is important for retailers to learn to discover what is really important for the shopper. What is the motive behind his purchasing decisions and how does he navigate within a category? Is the shopper a devoted Coca Cola-drinker or does he also consider other brands? Is he most loyal to a particular brand, a particular taste or smell, a packaging, an added health value or a good price? Loyalty is measured on the percentage of purchases the shopper based on a particular product feature. A shopper decision tree can also change over the years. Small packages, for example, were traditionally designed for outdoor use, but nowadays they are used both at home and outdoors. Instead of two different categories (small and large sizes), they now form one category. This is described in the Coca Cola case on page 146.

The purpose of applying shopper logic and preference segmentation is simply to keep category definitions up-to-date with the consumer's demands. A strong category definition is an essential first step in Category Management's journey to success!

'Errors' in category definitions

A category is actually a separate manageable product group that consumers see as complementary or a substitution in meeting their demands. According to this definition, the group frozen products is not a category because it is too broad (not all products are complementary and/or substitute). The product group ice cream does meet the definition. Too often products lead the definition of a category. It is better to give consideration to the consumption moments of the shopper (e.g. 'what is for dinner tonight').

In practice the view on the relationship between categories is inadequate. Thus, because of the positioning of the retail format, it can be chosen to be set up heavily in the category bakery. Indirectly, this also means that extra attention must be paid to all bakery-related categories such as cheese and processed meat products. Another example is that a focus on ready-to-cook cannot work without paying attention to fresh fruits and vegetables. The consumer does not make the technical distinction that retailers make.

Another important phenomenon is the distinction between substitutes and complementary categories. A substitution category consists of similar products of which consumers only use one at a time (e.g. fruit). A complementary category consists of items that are commonly consumed at the same time (vegetables as part of a hot meal). For the last category more emphasis should be put on the coherence of different products.

6.2 Analysis of a category

There are 5 different analyzes:

- Shopper analysis as described in Chapter 4
- Market analysis
- Performance retailer on sales, marketing and growth, but also on retail marketing's four P's
- Competitive Analysis
- Financial Analysis

Chapter 4 describes how retailers can gain greater insight into shopper behavior. This is important if Category Management is applied in organizations. Thereafter, the analysis of the range is important; to ensure that the range is always up-to-date and meets the needs of consumers. An efficient assortment revolves around the offering of the proper products, aimed at the store's target group. That range is the basis for optimum use of store space and shelves. According to ECR, Category Management is based on four pillars: efficient assortment, -promotion, -introduction and -replenishment.

Tabel 6.1 **The four pillars of Category Management**

Efficient Assortment	Aims to offer the appropriate range, aimed at the store's target group. Forms the basis for optimum use of retail space and shelves.
Efficient Promotion	Focuses on tailoring promotions to the consumers' needs, increasing effectiveness. Operational management, including inventory for promotions, is a concern.
Efficient Introduction	Focuses on the process of developing and introducing new products that meet a yet unmet consumer need.
Efficient Replenishment	Treats the chain between consumer, retailer and manufacturer like an integrated system. Focuses on the store shelves' supply with the right products and minimum loss and exercise..

(ECR Europe; Category Management Best Practices Report)

As visible in the graphic above, manufacturers and retailers can collaborate on Category Management in the composition of assortments, shelf presentations, promotions and introductions. All these topics are related to the 'demand side' of ECR. In addition, logistical improvements in the normal flow of goods can appear on the agenda of Category Management projects. This topic covers the 'supply side' of ECR.

Benefits of efficient and effective assortments

An efficient and effective range ensures that the shopper's needs are answered better because the right products are offered at the lowest possible cost. When a range is optimized in the Category Management's process, the whole supply chain can work faster, better and be more productive. For retailers an effective assortment represents an optimum range of products and increasing profit and sales. They will collect for shoppers: making an optimal composition of offerings. For suppliers an effective assortment means that they can save costs with more profit and less out-of-stocks. The graphic below shows the benefits of an effective and efficient assortment:

Figure 6.3 **The difference between effective and efficient assortments**

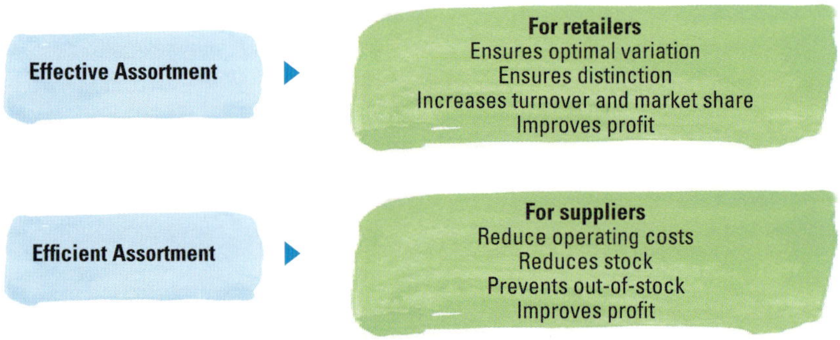

There is a difference between effective and efficient ranges. Retailers and suppliers both look differently at assortments. In this scheme the benefits of optimizing assortments for both retailers and suppliers are summarized. (The Partnering Group, Inc.)

Category analysis

Category analyses usually start with the identification of turnover, volume and contribution margins of the overall category and the segments and their development. This is done both for the overall market as the own retail format, so you can see how your format is performing compared to the market. Suppies often rely on turnover (value in euro's), while retailers are primarily looking at volume (number of units sold), because that tells something about the number of customers buying the product. And the number of purchasing customers is of great importance to a retailer. Finally, turnover has to do with shopper groups. If a store has a lot of customers with single households, the sales of single meals will be higher than in a retail format that receives less of this shopper group.
In a category analysis results are often compared with the previous year. However, it is wise to take a longer period (3-5 years) into account for a category plan to see the real trends and not only the short term effects caused by incidents like a bad summer, an introductory promotion or high promotion share.

Moreover, you can analyze the shoppers and consumers: what is the percentage of households using this product and how often or how often do they use it? What kind of households uses these products the most?

Volume = penetration x frequency x quantity

Turnover = penetration x frequency x quantity x price.

From this you can conclude where growth is possible. If the penetration already is high, you can use other means of growth than when it is low.

Offering differentiation

To what extent is the range of your retail brand distinctive compared to others? Or is there no difference for the shopper and can he find the same assortment anywhere? A retailer will prefer a distinctive range, because that gives the shopper a reason to come back to the store. Also, assortments keep changing, but the actual range is often behind on the revenue development.
A proper analysis watches the number of SKU's per price segment and sets it off against the turnover and volume in that price range. This will quickly reveal imbalances.
Finally, the execution: is the shelf easy to find and is it easy to make a choice within the shelf? Is there enough stock or do shoppers regularly miss products on Saturday afternoon? For hardware stores or garden centers: is the shelf an extension of the warehouse with plenty of products, or can you also find information and inspiration? Does it provide guidelines on how to get the job done, or inspiration for the look of the home or garden?
How are the promotions: are they only price promotions or also loyalty promotions? And what mechanism is used and with what objective?

The opportunity quadrant

Another way to provide opportunities for investigating growth of the category, is the 'opportunity quadrant'. It shows where products are placed based on an analysis of different factors, including growth of a category in the market (vertical axis) and the share of category sales by the retailer in the market (horizontal axis). The primary measures (interventions) are mentioned in the quadrants.

You can 'plot' categories and segments in the opportunity quadrant using two basic criteria:

a. The fair share of the product, segment or category. What is the share of the product in your assortment compared to the same product in other retail format's assortment? The fair share is the category's share of the retailer compared to the market share of the retailer overall. Thus you can see if the category is performing relatively better. This may be due to the type of customers that come to the retail format but also to the fact that the assortment is better connected to the format or by better execution of policy.
b. The growth of the total category compared to the overall market growth.

If a category has little growth, or even declines, it is often less attractive for retailers to pay attention to it. They like to spend their time and space on growing groups that contribute to the retail brand's differentiation. This can be a threat for a category. For suppliers, it is an important task to ensure that the category remains interesting.

Figure 6.4 **The opportunity matrix**

By creating a category matrix with on the horizontal axis the answer to the question whether there is a low or high fair share of the retailer in this category and on the vertical axis whether there is much or little growth in the category, you get an opportunity matrix. The possible measures are listed separately in the quadrants. (Nielsen)

What is the specific category strategy of competitors?

Competition analyses have been discussed in previous chapters and illustrated with models. Below, we present the basic model for competitive analysis on assortment's questions. That is a more general model. For the Category Manager's daily practice it means that he makes a competitive analysis based on assortments, brands and individual items. And he looks at price levels, the number and kind of promotions, the attractiveness of the instore presentation, the information and inspiration that is given and the omnichannel approach. Those are the lower three layers of the inverted pyramid in the middle of the model. The main questions for competitive analysis are mentioned in this model.

Figure 6.5 **Competitive assortment analysis with four angles**

The four main subjects used to compare your own range of policies with those of competitors.

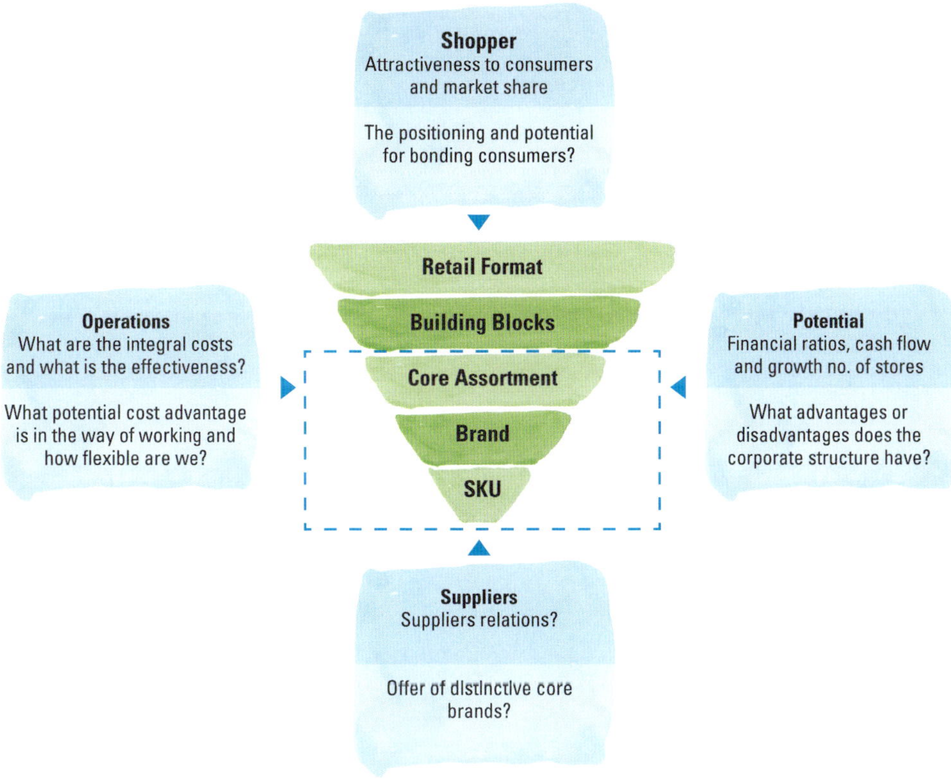

With this model you can easily visualize the 'differences' between your competitors and your own organization. The four most important factors are discussed here.

Competitive analysis around ranges

More detailed questions about a competitive analysis are shown in the chart below. A competitive analysis should not only visualize the actual differences in results but also the cause of those differences. So the operational causes, possible lower costs or a different financial position.

Table 6.2 **Competitive analysis of categories**

	shopper	supplier	operations	financial
Category results	• how many customers buy this assortment at the competitor • importance category for consumers • importance category for competitor • loyalty • purchase amount	• market share competition • market share in this category • innovation power • brands	• costs for filling shelf in % of the turnover • profit relative to stocks and cash • turnover per meter shelf • turnover rate • distribution rate	• size market • turnover • gross margin • net margin • operating cash flow
Analysis of assortment and shelf	• wide or deep assortment • number of SKU's • quality of range • type and number of brands • quality of PL • sustainability • pricing • organized, easy to shop planograms • attractiveness of the shelf • sufficient stock • information, inspiration	• share in category	• turnover per m^2 • turnover rate • staffing costs • profit on investments • days on shelf before expiry date • rotation, stock, waste	• turnover category • profit contribution category • cash contribution category • return on inventory investment
Analysis of pricing and promotions	• pricing compared to competition • number and type of promotions • effect of promotions	• price differences compared to competition • share in category	• % accurate predictions • costs of discounts, price adjustments and promotions • out of stock	• volume promotion in % turnover • incremental volume promotions • true profit contribution of category

This table can be used to research to what extend 'the competition' has a different assortment. It takes the shopper behaviour, suppliers, the way the store handles the assortment and the assortment policy's financial effects in account.

Less is more

In the last years, there has been a tremendous growth in number of SKU's in stores. Over the last 10 years the assortments of supermarkets have almost doubled. However, a larger choice is not always more pleasant for the customer: it means he has to make more effort to find a product and the choice between different products is harder. Thus, there is a balance between the desired choice and the number of products offered. This varies from product to product. Consumers are willing to delve into a product of high interest and to make some effort to find their favorite decorative style. But purchasing routine products such as drywall or margarine should be easy and quick. A large choice is an impediment to buy these products. Easy to shop and a wide selection are two important aspects that can also be contradictory. Many examples prove that an assortment reduction has led to growth in the category's volume and turnover. The consumer experiences a range reduction (with a new planogram) often like a wider choice because the category is easier to shop and the choice between the segments and brands is easier. Even though there really is something to choose, there is less duplication within the range. More choices lead to consumers being uncertain about the correctness of their choice. They have a higher feeling of satisfaction with their choice within a narrow range than within a wide one. Studies show that a smaller range can uplift the conversion tremendously. The choice is easier and the stress of choosing decreases. By putting some items on multiple facings, you will make the choice much easier while the stopping power remains.

Ranges are constantly changing. Therefore it is important to investigate regularly if a range still matches the turnover. The rise of a new segment may decrease the sales of another segment. It is wise to delist items in time to create space for the growing segments.

Financial analysis

As part of the analyses, a good financial analysis should not be forgotten. What does a certain range really add? How much does the shelf space cost? What is the percentage of waste? What is the turnover rate and the cost of capital of the inventory? Do you have to deal with leftovers? The category's financial performance is essential for a Category Manager (his position is based on it). This is sometimes underestimated by suppliers. A Category Manager will determine the space in the store and attention in the routing by the category's financial potential. This will also affect the relationship between the supplier and the Category Manager.

In the format's process as well as in Category Management's organization, KPI's are needed to measure and manage the category's performance. These KPI's are usually presented in a dashboard or scorecard. A proper financial analysis should contain all sorts of costs, also related to the category role. Experience shows that many Category Management practitioners have forgotten this versatility, not just junior Category Managers. It is difficult to calculate the actual results of category management projects for the organization's profitability, but it is very important to value this as well. An estimate of the revenue potential and all costs often makes a good business case, based on which the category plan can be approved by the Board and deployment can be started.

6.3 Category roles

A retail format has several objectives: attracting and filling customers, bounding customers and making fans. This is achieved with different categories that fulfill different roles. The category's role determines the retail format's function for the shopper: is it a traffic builder, impulse category, determinative or routine?

Before you can describe a category's objective, you must recognize its category role within the retail format. This determines the goals you can achieve and the strategy you can choose.

The category role and its options

Category role

The category role is primarily determined by the retail format. This goes mainly for categories that are strategically important to the retail format and determine the store's character. As the use of (marketing)instruments is based on the category role, agreement on that role is very important. We have already discussed this in detail in chapters 1 and 3.

The format positioning is the starting point of an assortment policy, so retailers reflect early on the category role and strategy. This will take place before the cooperation between retailer and manufacturer starts. It provides guidance in determining priorities and helping giving direction to joint projects of retailers and suppliers.

We want to emphasize again that in determining the category role, it is not only important to reflect on the category's meaning for the format, but also on the significance for the shopper. It is the acknowledgment of the consumer's buying motifs and moments that provides the fundament to optimize a category in terms of shelf performance, effective promotions and the development of new products.

Determining the category role

The choice of a category role is probably the most fundamental step in the Category Management process. We focus on four points that are important to determine the category's strategy (and later on, the tactics). They are listed in the diagram below.

Figure 6.6 **Before we choose a category rol**

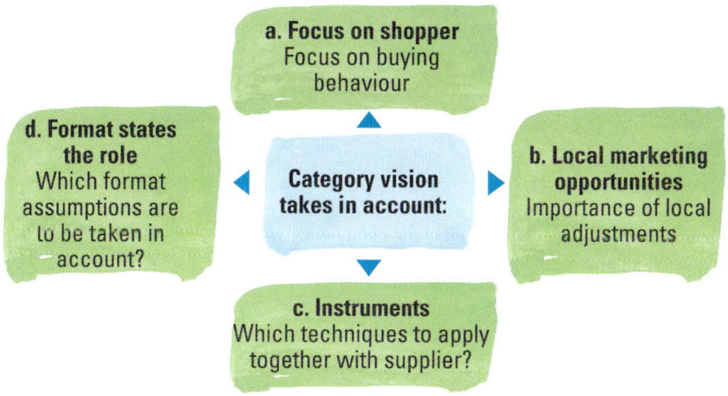

Before we begin to actualize a category vision, it is important to limit the possibilities. Of course we start with the shopper, but we will also examine the local marketing opportunities, techniques that enable suppliers to provide and the discipline of the retail format itself.

a. The shopper should always be leading in the use of marketing tools

If you want to deploy marketing tools, it is very important to take account of the retail format's shopper insights and shopper profile. Understanding those insights is often mentioned as one of the 'wins' of performing a Category Management project. Suppliers are inclined to reason (too) much from their brand's or product's viewpoint, regardless of the retail brand. The retailer knows his format, but sometimes it is difficult to translate this into clear needs for assortment and promotions. Because the format's positioning and shopper profile should guide the use of marketing tools, the retailer can try to describe these needs in an early stage instead of during the project. Statements on this subject are not necessarily bound to a particular category.

b. Local marketing and knowledge are often necessary, but difficult to fill in centrally

Evaluation of several pilot projects has shown that improvement proposals are developed top down, based on the average consumer and that it is assumed that this can be easily implemented at store level. However, the reality is far from this. There are several examples that point out that knowledge of the local market and the local retail environment are strong determining factors that should be taken into account seriously. This is at least true in case products have a strong regional distribution such as buttermilk or beer. Suppliers often develop new local segmentation tools to make this manageable. Software developments are becoming more and more sophisticated so it takes less time and effort to respond to local conditions.

c. Local freedom versus format discipline

Local freedom at store level often is described by head offices and marketeers as an obstacle. Local deviation demands a lot of effort to optimize the use of marketing instruments per store. However, in some categories the local implementation on the shop floor is crucial. A Category Manager that combines centralized control with perfect local interpretation is the winner. Retailers sometimes do not allow this or do not (yet) have the resources. In this case, effective and efficient use of Category Management requires a balance between centralized management, local freedom and discipline at store level. It is a matter of higher cost versus high quality revenues that are difficult to express in direct numbers.

d. Determining the tools: do it together

In analyzing the category we already mentioned that cooperation between manufacturer and retailer offers added value. The same goes for the choices in the retail marketing mix according to the results of analyzes. Determining the assortment, instore presentation, planograms and promotions together delivers better results than each party could individually achieve.

The category role has to support the format positioning

After all considerations, partly based on the qualitative and quantitative analysis, we can now determine the category role. In the analysis we have considered the consumer as a shopper, the retail format and its local adjustments, the capabilities of the supplier, the general market opportunities and the analysis of the numbers. Measurement techniques that can be used in this phase are, for example, a shopping basket analysis, point of sale data, consumer data, panel data, an analysis of impulse purchases and a financial analysis.

Determining the category role can be arguable

The category role is leading for the category strategy. Determining a category role is less simple than may seem. A Category Manager can have a different perspective on that role than a Format Manager or a supplier. It is therefore important that all stakeholders make clear how they see the role. Above that, the potential of a category should also be considered with a longer term horizon. The question how the category can develop in the following three years, is of great importance. Every decision made in the process of determining a category role, should be supported by analysis. While many retailers develop general category roles, which are tailored to their individual strategies and targets, we will treat five examples that illustrate typical category roles. ECR defined five roles we point out in the box below. In addition, individual retail formats sometimes define other roles, but you can usually trace them back to the five we explain below.

The five main category roles

Destination

These assortments determine the retail brand's identity. They help to profile the format as a preferred store. The ranges consistently prove the format's added value. For these categories the retail format is famous. This can only be a limited number of categories, about 4 to 7. The retail format will excel in these categories and give them extra attention in the store and in their communication. To achieve this you should invest: in assortment development, signage, information and training the staff. If a format chooses bread & bakery as a destination category, then availability until closing hour is important. The fact that the waste may be greater, is included in the KPI's. Stores that have virtually no waste, probably do not have bread left at closing time. Profitability is not the main KPI for a destination category, that should be shopper appreciation. A retail brand chooses a destination group to represent its format.

Routine

Shoppers will in general purchase these products because they belong to the routine package of a household. Routine categories support the format in getting a preferred position because you can purchase your usual products too. In that case, it often involves consistent, competitive consumer value. This goes for approximately 50% of the categories. Managing routine categories may sound less appealing than managing destination categories, but the game can be so much more complex. Routine categories should bring profits to the retailer. These assortments are not very distinctive for a supermarket. But it is important that consumers who visit your store, also buy these categories. The assortment may be compact but competitive. Switching consumers to other shops must be prevented. An easy-to-shop shelf and the prevention of out-of-stocks is very important.

Traffic builder

These are categories that attract customers to the store to because they have for example a special offer. Promotions of high-priced items with substantial savings. Traffic builders have a high consumer value, like meat, detergent and beer, and an attractive benefit. A retailer does not have to earn much on the product during the promotion, as long as many customers purchase all their products at his store and not only the promotional item. Also special assortments that can only be purchased at this store, such as organic or gluten-free food, can be traffic builders.

Impulse

These are categories that are designed to increase the shopping cart or basket. Often impulse products that are not on the shopping list, but to which you are tempted in the shop. Impulses should be found in a conspicuous place in the store, or near a complementary planned purchase. Impulse categories form an important group with products that sometimes are temporary or seasonal available, like vegetables, fruit or decoration products. The shopper thinks these items fit the format and he is willing to buy something extra. The margins on Impulses are higher than average. Price is not a decisive purchase argument. The reduction in price during promotions can therefore be lower. Getting attention is often enough to make a purchase. About 40% of all purchases are impulse products, so without this category the shopping cart would be much emptier. In online purchases, smart software brings impulse categories to the shopper's attention.

Convenience

These products are perceived as 'useful' by the shopper if they are part of the total assortment, but they are not essential to be a good store. Non-food kitchen items are for example convenience goods in a supermarket. By achieving consumer value, they strengthen the retailer's full-service position as a preferred store. This is often the peripheral assortment like bird feed, Valentine presents, christmas decoration and so on. In DIY stores, bottled drinks or chocolate at the checkout are convenience goods.

Different views on the category roles

To choose from the various options seems simple enough. The best choice, however, can only be made after all the roles have been properly considered and seen within their position in the market and strategy. After that, to determine which role is the best help for achieving the established goals, the financial ratios will be dominant. With proper coordination retailers can use dozens of categories to increase the attractiveness of their stores. Determining a relevant category role has two main advantages:

1. This creates greater consumer value as we manage categories according to the value consumers attach to it;
2. This creates maximum benefit from investments by retailers and suppliers because of the efficient, targeted allocation and use of shelf space, marketing time and money.

As described previously in this section, there are several marketing tools that can be used to determine a category role. Below we will explain them briefly.

- **Shopping basket analysis:** what do consumers purchase during a visit to the store? How do you ensure increasing shopping cart conversion through stronger links between different categories?
- **Consumer information:** which preferences do the most active consumers have? Which categories are most important to them?
- **Consumer panel data:** what percentage of consumers who buy a particular product, do you attract? What percentage of consumers also purchases from another retailer and how much time & money do they spend there? How can you attract more consumers and ensure that their transactions grow in a particular category?
- **Point-of-sale data** (including the size and growth of the category): how do the nationwide sales relate to the local sales? Does the category grow or shrink? Are price increases driving the growth of categories or do consumers actually buy more or fewer products in a particular category?
- **Occasional or impulse purchases:** this you need to know to determine the contribution of a category during holidays and other events. Are your consumers actual 'do-it-yourself bakers' who purchase flour and yeast, or are they hasty mothers who buy simple cake mix and decorative products; or are they both?
- **'Fair share' - demand gap:** the difference between what a retailer should sell based on its market share (fair share) and the quantity that he could sell (above fair share). For example, how many core consumers who like strawberry ice are in a particular area; how much do they consume and how much could you sell? Or how many activities do 'soccer moms' organize in a particular area and what percentage of them could you attract?
- **Financial analysis:** for example numbers sold products, sales, difference between cost and selling price and activity based costing. This analysis is intended to allow a retailer to reflect on the investments made in a particular category role. It is important that this analysis, if possible, is done bottom up, to achieve realistic figures.

These instruments show that the determination of a category role is developing into a consumer oriented, analytical process. In order to properly determine this role, it is important to have an in-depth knowledge of the retailer's strategy. We must also have knowledge of the consumers and their behaviour in certain categories. To bring the retail strategies to life, retailers determine the category roles that support the retail strategy and goals.

6.4 The category's objectives

The goals are determined by the category roles. The goal may be focused on sales, volume and margin, but also on customer interest, thus filling the basket or making customers loyal. In case the category is a traffic builder, it is important to know how many customers it draws to the store, but also how many additional sales it attracts. Did a promotion lead to higher sales in the category or to more additional sales? How high is the receipt amount of customers who bought the promotion?

Goals are both qualitative and quantitative, and vary according to the category role. Quantitative targets are always expressed in numbers and a combination of sales, volume and margin. For a routine category units sold and margin are important, for an impulse category margin while for a traffic builder units and sales are more important than margin. Qualitative objectives have to do with the desired effect on the consumer. This often is in particular true for destination categories. Quantitative targets can be expressed with the following KPIs:

- Market share / fair share
- Increasing the number of customers
- Increasing the customer spending, basket value
- Increasing the frequency of shop visits
- Increasing loyalty

An objective for a category is never stagnant

Determining the category's objective is never a matter of a simple snapshot. You should at least put the most important factors in one model:

1. The question whether an item is financially attractive to a retailer (the vertical axis 1 in figure 6.7).
2. In addition, the question whether the category (or the product) is appealing to the shopper (the horizontal axis 2 in the diagram).
3. And third, the question what the category (or product) does with the retail brand's positioning (the rearward-going axis 3). If this is correctly filled by category (or product) you can visualize the contribution of a particular category or product.

Gamma makes a destination category of paint

GAMMA

Background

In the recent years, do-it-yourself stores developed from product and supplier-oriented stores to much more customer-oriented stores with a clear format signature.
Paint and paint accessories are important categories for all DIY stores. Yet in the most stores these departments looked a lot alike. Each DIY format had the same brands (including Flexa, Histor and private label). And ready mix range was presented in brand blocks so the consumer could purchase the same color in different places in the store.
GAMMA's goal was not only to be the biggest paint specialist in the Netherlands, but also the best. It therefore decided to make a real destination category of paint, a category for which the customer would especially go to GAMMA.

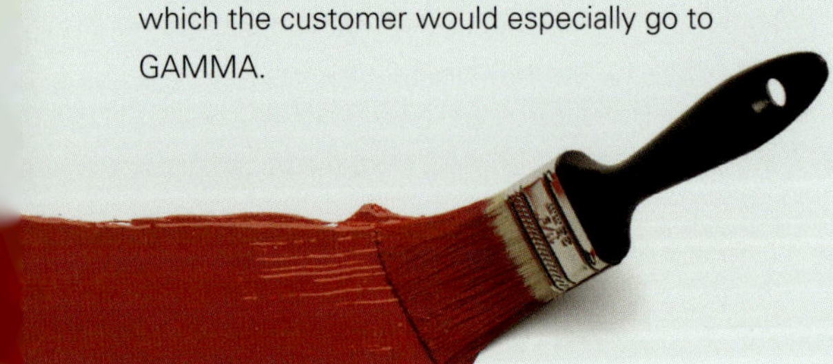

Analysis

In 2011, GAMMA conducted a consumer and shopper research together with its suppliers. The research revealed the following: in painting the consumer selects by color and he likes to be inspired. Moreover, the consumer has less knowledge about chores and painting and therefore needs advice. Often the consumer chooses for a specialist store because it sells professional brands, which also are used by the professional painter. Research also showed that the average paint job requires approximately five additional products in painting supplies next to the paint itself. Precisely these products make the transaction profitable for the retailer but GAMMA was unsuccessful in filling the shoppers basket with the paint accessories.

Core problem

- Little inspiration
- Presentation based on brand blocks instead of needs and shopper decision tree
- Not enough advice
- Little differantiation from other stores

CASE

Approach

GAMMA put down an innovative concept based on three pillars: extensive assortment, expert advice and inspiration.

- **The color selector wall and advice desk** The shopper decision tree showed that color is the first and foremost selection criterion, followed by where it is used (inside, outside) and finally the application eg. on wood or wall. GAMMA therefore abandoned its brand blocks and created a large color selector wall. Here the consumer can choose from 1.500 colors, presented on extra-large color samples designed to fully support the consumer's purchase process. Shoppers encounter this wall immediately after entering the store and it gives an instant WOW effect. You have the impression that 'if I can not succeed here, I will not succeed anywhere.' All colors have clear samples available, with information on the backside about which brands provide that color and for what spaces and materials that paint can be used. There are a number of displays with particular styles or special paint brands such as paint of the Dutch designer Jan de Bouvrie, Loving, but also professional paints. Inspiration is not only offered by the color wall and displays but also by the videoclips playing on the huge LED screen above the atmospheric advice desk.
- **Expert advice** To be able to give the consumers the right advice, GAMMA developed a special training course for its staff in collaboration with training for professional painters. During this training, all painting techniques and paint types are explained professionally. GAMMA also created an advice desk that invites customers to ask for advice. And in cooperation with suppliers they organized special 'Color advisory days' on which customers can get advice of an interior specialist in the GAMMA store.
- **A comprehensive range** The assortment has been expanded with exclusive brands at the top. The private label range is renewed. The selection process in the entire range has been made easier because the presentation is based on the shopper decision tree. It is divided into 'Inside' and 'Outside', then by application and then by brand. Additionally, duplications in the product range were cleaned up and the overall range has become more clear.
- **Shop Presentation** Concerning the in-store presentation, the right painting supplies were presented next to the appropriate paint. Anyone who buys paint, also needs some painting supplies, such as brushes, turpentine or tarpaulins. By presenting them together, you help the handyman. You make sure he purchases all and the right products and thus increase the shopping basket and the receipt amount.

Result

Customers were very enthusiastic. And although GAMMA cut in its absolute number of SKUs, the customer feels that there is much more choice than before. Customers are attracted by the 'Interior advisory days' and see GAMMA as the paint specialist. The market share of GAMMA has risen accordingly.

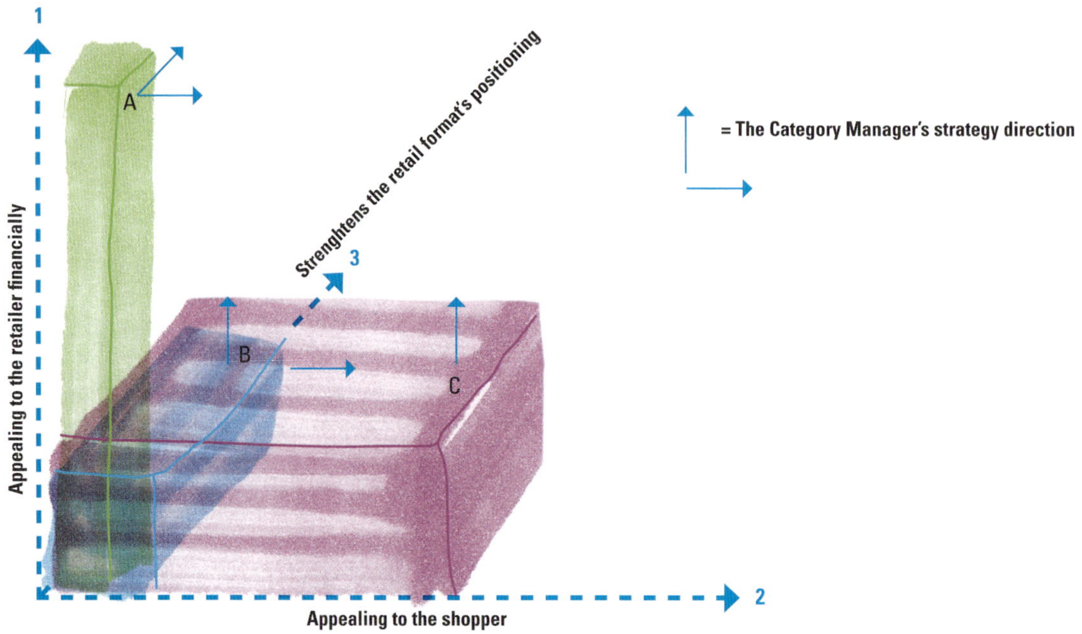

Figure 6.7
N.B. This is a 3-dimensional graph. Financially attractive for the retailer: vertical (1). Appealing to the shopper: horizontal (2). And attractive for the retail brand's positioning: the line backwards (3)
We have drawn 3 categories in this model: A, B and C
Category A is financially attractive to the retailer, but it does not interest the shopper and the retail format does not improve.
Category B is not profitable for the retailer and does not appeal to the shopper, but it gives the format its own identity.
Category C is slightly more profitable than B for the retailer, is very interesting for the shopper and the format's profile is strengthened.
It is clear which development directions a Category Manager can chose. If choices are to be made, then Category A and Category B will lose against Category C.

Consistency between categories
When we are focused on dealing with the objectives of a category, we can forget that the relationship between categories is sometimes more important than measures within one category. To associate ice cream and dessert toppings with each other can be more profitable than to optimize dessert toppings.

Evaluating: to measure is to know

Establishing the category's objectives also means that you should be able to measure them. Virtually all processes, activities and interventions at a retailer can indeed be expressed in targets and often in concrete numbers. To measure also means that all available sources of information should be able to be combined with each other. This also applies to the Category Management process and cooperation between trade and industry. The exchange of data is of great importance in this cooperation.

How to measure SMART?

Category Management is about achieving goals. The way Category Management projects are executed in the Netherlands, generally achieve positive results. Nearly all of these projects involved the tuning of assortments and shelves. Promotions, introductions and logistics optimization are addressed in some of the projects and so, there is still a potential for growth.

Performance measurement is necessary, but complex

Measuring performance improvement has been proved to be difficult in a number of projects and it took more time than expected. This can happen for a number of reasons, like:

- External factors like the weather strongly influence the revenue of certain categories. Therefore it is not always possible to precisely determine a project's impact
- A large product introduction within the category during the Category Management project has a strong influence on the performance;
- A change in the setup of the format and commercial actions such as the number and length of shelves available makes measurement based on comparison with the original setup difficult. For example, a retail organization may have grown during the project. For this, the turnover data must be readjusted, but this can never be 100% correct.

It is obvious that it is necessary to take the targets to be measured into account and to define when the test is successful. Before starting the test the starting points must be defined, in order to measure the results afterwards. This may sounds logical, but it is often forgotten. Without a clear objective and starting point, results cannot be measured.

SMART measuring means that the recorded objectives must be:

a. **S**pecific (clear);
b. **M**easurable (expressed in numbers);
c. **A**cceptable (it should be feasible);
d. **R**ealistic (both in real time and in terms of objectives);
e. **T**ime-bound (over a defined period).

What can be measured in Category Management?

In the summary on this page, you can find all the important elements that need to be made measurable in the Category Management process. They are divided into four columns. This includes effects: on the shopper, on the market (competitors and suppliers), on its own productivity and of course on profitability. The horizontal bars named 'category performance' focus on the four major ECR measurement techniques: the effect of changes in assortments and shelves; the effect of pricing; the impact on product launches and the impact on replenishment. With this method it shows, for each quadrant, a number of measurable factors.

Table 6.3 **Necessary indicators and financial parameters for Category Management**

		Shopper	Market	Productivity	Financial
	Results company as a whole	• Household penetration • Average basket • Loyalty shoppers in%	• Market share	• Operational costs in % of revenue • Revenue on stocks and cash • Revenue per m² • Turnover	• Turnover • Gross margin • Net margin • Operating cash flow
Category performance	Efficient assortment & shelf optimization	• Assortment reduction costs • Average purchase amount in category • Loyalty (share total needs) • Out-of-stock	• Category share	• Revenue per m² • Turnover rate • Costs staff • Return on investments	• Revenue category • Profit contribution category • Cash contribution category
Category performance	Efficient price & shelf optimization	• Category value rating (rank in category value list)	• Price differences competition • Category share	• % Accurate forecasts • Costs of markdowns, price changes and promotions	• Promotion volume as % of turnover • Incremental volume of promotions • True profit contribution by category
Category performance	Efficient product introduction	• Category revenue share in total store	• Market share of new products • Share in the category	• Success score of new items • Cost introductions and fase out old items • Time needed to achieve distribution goal	• Turnover share of new products • Sales growth category • Profit contribution category from innovations
Category performance	Efficient replenishment	• % Out-of-stocks • Reliability deliveries of DC to store • Waste	• ECR scorecard	• Operating expenses in % of revenue • Time to sell store supply • % full trucks • Billing accuracy	• Category sales growth • Profit contribution

Matrix functions with the company's objective

Establish SMART goals

Follow with Category Management Scorecard

The enumeration in the light green areas is the result of several ECR tests.

6.5 Determining a category vision & strategy

To reach a category target you must essentially have a clear vision on how this can be done. The analysis of shopper trends and category development has shown that ideas evolve around chances and solutions. Revenue and profits are the results of a good response to the shopper's preferences and converting them into good (format- and) category policy.

Determining a category vision is probably the most important and influential decision a Category Manager may take. It determines the category's direction and growth for next few years. This chapter highlights key aspects of the visioning of categories.

Figure 6.8 **Determining a category vision**

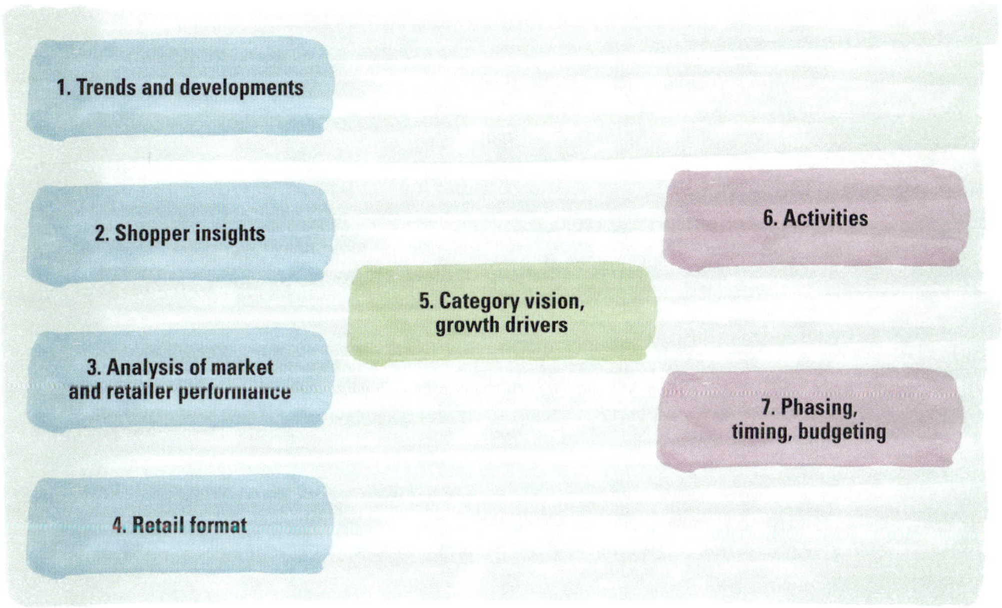

In this figure, on the left, you can find the various components of the analysis. For each component you should determine what influence it has on your category and how you can make the most out of it. From the analysis we derive 4-6 growth drivers, platforms for growth. For each growth driver a number of activities is developed each year. The activities are appropriate for the position and problems of the retail format. At the end, phasing, timing and budgeting are set. (Category & Trade Company)

The cooperation between retailers and suppliers is often on short-term basis and limited to introductions and promotions. There is not enough attention for the long term - where more profitable growth can be gained. This requires time, preparation and a different focus from both parties. As for the short-term, in which last year results count, we need to have a shopper and retail brand vision. To do that, we start examining the long term trends, shopper insights and long term developments in society and market and link these to the brand values and objectives of the retail format. Thus, we can discover the growth drivers based on trends and the shopper's needs, which fit the retail brand.

Drivers are growth platforms that can help to enlarge the category for the following years. This may consider more solutions for consumption on the go, or anticipation on trends such as obesity and dieting. By annually initiating a number of activities that give meaning to the growth drivers, you will achieve both short term and long term goals. The category will not only contribute to the short-term objectives, which are of course important, but will also contribute to the format by realizing what is expected from it in terms of products and brands. This is why customers do not only visit a retail store for promotions but also because a format suits them.

In the future, brands and products will be less important and the focus will be on providing solutions for the customers. No massive range, but 'customization'. Not product but 'solution centered'. In the United States, you can see these trends translated into format concepts. There are intermediate forms of catering and retail in a supermarket. For example, you can get hot or cold soup. You can take it with you, eat on the spot or even have it delivered to your office. 'Blurring' and online shopping will gain importance.

The difficulty in having a vision is based on the fact that Category Management is not a rational science and a vision cannot be determined with a 100% rate of certainty. However, by studying the analysis thoroughly and using the knowledge of specialists and partners, you can develop a strong vision. Pilot tests, tracking of results and finding out which adjustments are necessary, are essential to implement a good policy. And failure in responding to the shopper's ever changing needs, means you are too slow in adjusting to new developments and competition. The category will loose its attraction on shopper and retailer and eventually price erosion occurs. Another mistake is to appoint growth drivers that resemble the 4 P's. However, the 4 P's are no growth drivers, they are the implementation of activities of a growth driver. A strong vision can be recognized by a number of pillars, Over the years, these pillars can be supported by several activities and lead to a healthy growth of the category.

Determining a category strategy

A clear strategy is needed to achieve the desired category objectives and targets. In retail, seven marketing strategies are widely used. They have partly a direct relation with the category's functions we have described above. But there are some more functions:

1. **Increasing traffic:** getting shoppers to the store, aisles and category.
2. **Basket value optimization:** increasing the size of the average receipt.
3. **Optimize profits:** increasing margin and volume to get higher profits.
4. **Generate cash:** create immediate cash with high turnover rate.
5. **Create excitement and incentives:** grow interest and enthusiasm among shoppers.
6. **Strengthen image:** reinforce the consumer's impression of the retailer.
7. **Prevent consumers switching to other retailers:** making the category stronger than competitors. Mainly for routine categories – Compact product range, covering bottom range by budget label and discount packages

Below you will find the seven strategies and the impact they have on the shopper's behaviour within the category:

Table 6.4 **Category strategy and the impact on shopper behaviour**

Category strategy	Features of the category as effect of shopper behaviour
Traffic building (attracting customers)	Effective for items that are planned purchased by many customers, generating high sales.
Check out deposit optimization	Large packaging or high priced items provide a higher check out deposite. Offers for impulse purchase. When selling, cross-selling activities.
Profit optimization	Items with higher profit margins and higher conversion.
Generate cash	Effective on products with a high rotations, purchase amount and purchase frequency.
Create excitement and incentives	Suitable for impulse purchases. Lifestyle-oriented. Seasonal assortments.
Strengthen image	Bought frequently. Strongly promoted. Impulse buying. Unique products. Seasonal products and so on.
Prevent switching	Ensures that retailers are able to maintain a traditional primary base of customers.

This model sums up the seven different strategies with corresponding category features.
(The Partnering Group, Inc)

These strategic choices can also be elaborated in a solid measures, and those measures can be used as a scorecard.
We can also relate these category strategies with the five marketing P's. See chapter 6.8.

Coca-Cola Enterprises and the shopper decision tree

Coca-Cola Enterprises

Background

The layout of a shelf has often grown historically and is not always in line with the shopper's changing needs. A major change in the deposit system for soft drink bottles in the Netherlands in 2006 (large soft drink bottles went from refillable deposit bottles in crates to single use bottles without returnable crates) triggered Coca-Cola to a major shopper research.

The soft drinks shelf was traditionally designed with the large packaging soft drinks placed elsewhere in the store then small packaging (cans and small bottles). This was based on retail operation (bulk presentation of bulk crate packaging) and in the assumption that large bottles were bought for indoor use and small packaging for consumption outdoors.

Analysis

Coca-Cola collaborated with various retailers for shopper research with focus groups and instore shopper interviews. This study showed that the shopper decision tree had changed over time: the majority of shoppers first chooses for a particular segment in soft drinks (water, lemonade, cola, ice tea, etc.), then for brand, package size (large or small) and, finally for regular or light. Thus the choice in packaging sizes is determined later on in the selection process. According to the shopper, it would be logical that large and small packaging are placed together on the shelf.

The shelf was designed like this:
package size → segment → brand

The shopper selects like this:
segment → brand → package size

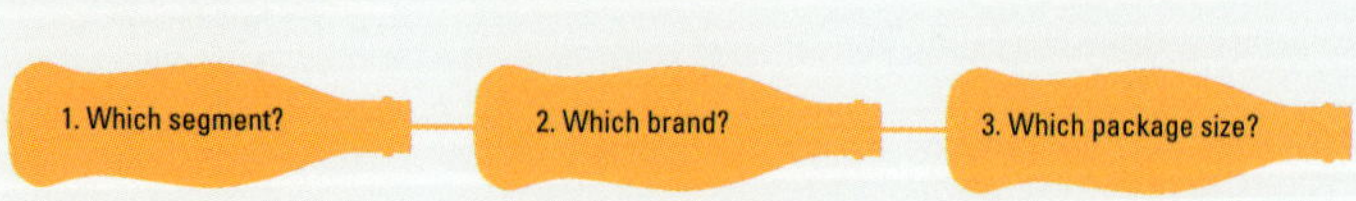

CASE

The average consumer only spends 9 seconds at the soft drink shelf to make a purchase decision, so a clearly arranged and easy to navigate shelf layout is very important. In addition, the category small packaging still had a lot of potential; penetration and market share of small packages soft drinks were relatively low in the Netherlands compared to other countries. The share of small packaging was only 23% of the total, while the average market share in Europe is 32% and in Belgium it is even 42%. Also, consumers could not find the small packages in the store. Finally, the assumption that small packs were only used on the road, was wrong. Research showed that more than 50% of the shoppers purchased small sizes for home consumption, for example for their convenience.

Core problem

- Presentation not in line with shopper decision tree
- Difficult to find small packaging soft drinks in the store
- Suboptimal margin mix

Approach

These shopper insights led to the idea of a rigorous change of the shelf layout; an 'integrated shelf' in which large and small soft drink bottles and cans would be presented together. This presentation is divided into distinct segments (water, lemonade, cola, ice tea), and then in brand blocks in order to give an optimal assortment choice. The small sizes are placed at eye level considering their revenue and margin potential.
The direction was clear. But in order to be sure that this concept shelf vision would actually provide success on the shop floor, Coca-Cola initiated a store test in cooperation with five national retailers. The goal was not only to see if the theory would really work in practice, but also to gain valuable feedback from shoppers and store operation at this stage. The test included a quantitative analysis, as well as video observations and interviews with shoppers and store employees.

Results

Shoppers appeared to be very satisfied with the new shelf! The new shopfloor presentation made products easier to find. And the shopper's choice perception increased because all sizes of a brand are presented together. The sales of the small sizes increased. Retailers were also excited about this sustainable growth impulse in sales en profitability for the category and the increased shopper satisfaction. On top of that, the store test had added value for the suppliers and retailers involved, because it allowed them to further sharpen the shelf vision and explore operational challenges before the full rollout. Since the conversion had a major operational impact, the rollout of this shelf vision has eventually taken a few years, before all retailers had changed to the new planogram.

New shelves at Albert Heijn.

6.6 Category management in fresh produce

Some years ago, Category management was still reserved for branded products and non-perishable packaged goods. Now we see that Category Management's importance is growing also for Fresh Produce. Fresh produce companies are not used to work with Category Management. However it is an opportunity for these companies to respond to and work with this.

EFMI Business School commissioned by LTO Netherlands and Albert Heijn conducted a study with a number of interesting conclusions. The study was conducted for four reasons: the damaged consumer's confidence in food, demands for transparency, predicted scarcity and the fact that supermarkets look for differentiation. One of the conclusions is that there will be different ways of cooperation in the future between the chains. This will be more demanding for the fresh produce companies. Every collaboration has its own characteristics and rules and has thus its own demands for skills for collaboration.

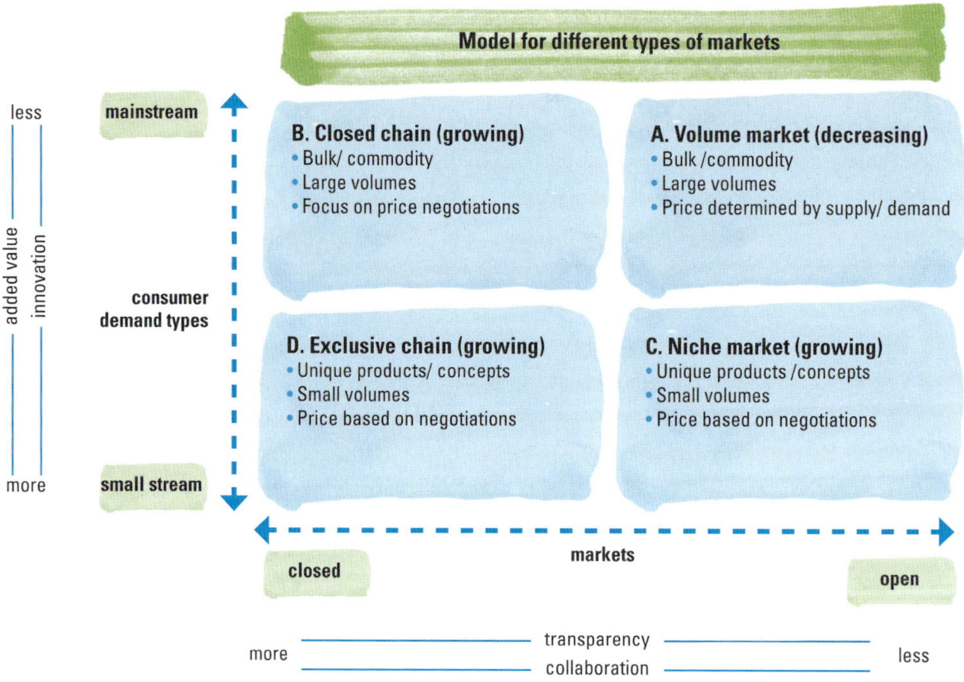

Figure 6.9

Mainstream versus small stream and open markets versus closed chains based up on a Delphi survey (June 2013, n = 64) (EFMI Business School)

The four different types of market described using two main questions

a. Does it focus on mainstream products (mass) or more special products (niche). That is the vertical axis.

b. Is it operating on an open market (everyone can buy this product) or does the supplier work for a limited number of customers? That is the horizontal axis.

We identify four types of markets: the volume market, the closed circuit, the niche market and the exclusive chain.

The volume market is the traditional way of doing business: supply and demand determine the price. This type of market will decline because more closed systems and small stream systems will arize and there will be more cooperation. In the volume market cost leadership is a prerequisite for success, because the price is largely determined by supply and demand. Because this market declines, the price pressure will increase if the quantity offered on the market is not reduced.
The closed circuit will become the largest quadrant. Supermarket chains are securing the supply of fresh products with purchasing in the closed circuit. This gives the chain more transparency and clear quality standards can be arranged so the quality is also better.

Retailers have four reasons to cooperate in the more exclusive chain:

1. Certainty in the supply: sufficient products.
2. Opportunity to get speciality products.
3. To protect the image of the company by monitoring the working methods of the suppliers.
4. Remove unnecessary costs from the chain.

The niche market is not estimated to be big but it gives good growth perspectives for added value concepts. Here innovation takes place, added value is created and sustainability is developed. As soon as the products are successful in the niche market, in general, they will move through to the volume market.

The exclusive chain grows fast and is as big as the niche market. Because supermarkets are looking for differentiations, it is expected that the exclusive chain will keep on growing rapidly. Here, the partnership is long and intense. Chain partners invest in each other's organizations, and good evaluation is possible and it creates distinctive abilities with innovative concepts.
To fit in the closed market, niche market and exclusive market as a supplier, it is necessary that you have good knowledge and application of marketing and Category Management. The consumer is mostly searching for solutions and many suppliers (and Category Managers) are still product minded. Retailers expect their suppliers to engage in finding solutions for the shopper, in the differentiation and competitive advantage for formats. This is an expertise that will be strongly developed in the next 10 years and with a large growth potential.

Table 6.5 **Impact on collaboration, valorization and sustainability**

	Collaboration in the chain	Valorization	Sustainability chain
Market type A **Volume market** 2013 50% → -34% → 2023 33%	• Limited or no collaboration	demand > supply • Relatively high prices, high valorization opportunities supply > demand • Relatively low prices, low valorization opportunities • Cost leadership is crucial	• Only if the whole chain raises the standard • Complying to laws • Social pressure from society
Market type B **Closed chain** 2013 33% → +24% → 2023 41%	• Intensive collaboration (made possible by an integrated chain)	• High valorization opportunities by cooperation • Product remains mainstream • Cost leadership remains advantageous	• Sustainability as competitive advantage • Other parties follow, under pressure from external parties or from a competition perspective
Market type C **Niche market** 2013 8% → +38% → 2023 11%	• Intensive collaboration is possible, not conditional	• Good opportunities for valorization by added value concepts	• Sustainability as added value encourages a sustainable supply chain • If a small stream product becomes mainstream, sustainability can be rolled out in other chains
Market type D **Exclusive chain** 2013 9% → +67% → 2023 15%	• Intensive collaboration (made possible by integration within the chain)	• Good opportunities for valorization by existing customer • Limited national growth opportunities • Possible dilemma with other purchasers	• Driven by sustainability as added value • Sustainability can be rolled out at exclusive chain partner

This table shows the prediction on the growth of each segment and the main characteristics for each segment. (EFMI Business School)

6.7 Category management in online stores

As already explained in Chapter 5, the shopper and the products in clicks and bricks are the same. However, the Category Management rules change significantly. Just the fact that the online shelf is indeed elastic and that there are no fixed planograms, already show the need for a different approach. It may even be that the category's role differs online and offline. We will work from the assumption that the category role remains the same. The effect of a category role continues to work in the online channel. Because through online you know more specifically who your audience is, you can be much more specific in showing products.
On the other hand, the space used to show products, for example, in a banner or email, is often more limited than in a promotion flyer so there should be a sharper selection of the products displayed. The direct link between media and shopping trip makes this choice extra important. For example, an email which contains only routine or convenience products does not lead to the highest conversion. You attract the consumer to your store with traffic builders and destination categories. If the consumer is in the store and puts a product in his basket, you can proceed to fill the basket, for example, with routine products or impulses.

Figure 6.10 **E-commerce fundamentals**

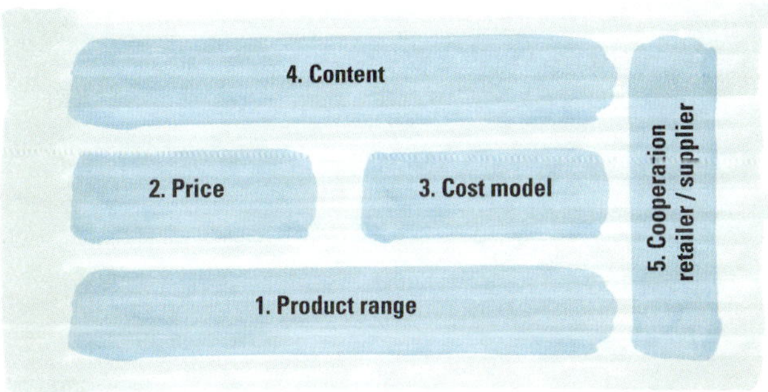

To conduct category management in an online environment, five elements must be completed and optimized continuously. We will refer to these five elements as the 'e-commerce fundamentals'

1. Product range
If you choose a product range, you should first take the format positioning in mind. Do you want to be a DIY store that attracts the die-hard handyman? Then, make sure you have those products in your product range. Are you a service supermarket? Then, make sure your product range is wide enough to cater the consumer's needs. Start with a complete product range and learn how to optimize it according to the online variables. In an online operation it is common to work with an activity based costing model that affects every transaction in the operational chain. If for example the cheap products are not profitable, the model should be optimized. You could increase the minimum order quantity of a product bundle products or sell from the cartons.
Use the loss by (operational) unprofitable products as a profit. Force yourself and your organization to sell those product ranges that actually belong to your retail brand. Sometimes, consumer unfriendly choices are made in the range, for example cutting it to a minimum margin or minimum selling price.

From the perspective of the retailer this may be obvious, but in practice it means mostly that the fast moving products are not available. The consumer will settle this with the retailer by spending less or even not proceeding with the purchase at all. Another challenge is to entice the shopper to fill his basket, because of the absence of a natural routing through the store. Especially considering that the cost model of a mix margin plays a key role in the range. If a consumer is tempted inside by a traffic builder, which often does not have the top margin, how do you make sure that the customer still will be profitable before leaving? By making the right choices in the selection you make sure the consumer is able to create a profitable basket. To actively control this and make this possible a Category Manager can optimize baskets by assembling them from categories which are often purchased together. This optimizes your margin for example by adding a profitable fabric softener with a detergent with a low margin, or for example to add drill bits with drills. The online channel offers great opportunities for increasing the basket by (virtual) bundling products or making clever cross-sell combinations.

For the consumer there is no difference between the virtual product bundle and a 'normal' product. With one click, the bundle goes in the basket. This makes it possible to test different combinations of products before bringing them physically together. It is also possible to create volume promotions from the standard product.

Figure 6.11 **Example of a virtual product bundle**

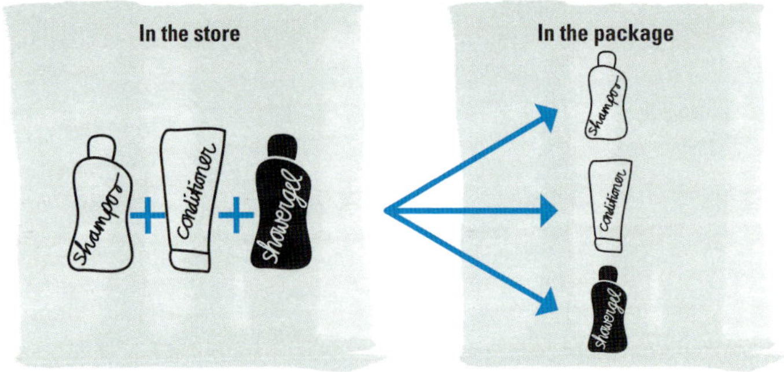

Figure 6.12 **Example of a promotional bundle**

The products are presented and supplied separately to the consumer. In order to entice the consumer to fill his basket, bundle discounts are offered.

2. Price

Transparency in the online channel creates a compulsory review of the pricing strategy. It becomes indeed easier for consumers to compare prices with other players in the market, even with those who were not previously included in the competition. For the local supermarket which is used to work with a mark-up for small-scale shop management, the discounter becomes suddenly a direct comparison. Consumers initially will not look beyond the price of the product. In some cases it is not possible to see more than the prices, if the products are viewed in a price comparison. Many retailers that make the transition from bricks and mortar to online overestimate the strength of their retail brand as influence on the consumer's buying intention.

Thanks to the increased transparency the online consumer shows a strong focus on price and value perception. The choice concerning pricing has a major impact on the overall management of the store, both online and offline. But the cost model (see point 3) plays an important role in the pricing.

As mentioned it is the starting point to assemble an attractive assortment for the consumer. Consequently some products cannot be sold profitably due to the high shipping or handling charges. Perhaps it is necessary to differentiate between the product's shipping costs because some are too large for ordinary postage like selling garden fences which can be delivered only on a pallet.

Or products that only can be sold in certain quantities to get them effectively to consumers. For example; screws can only be sold efficiently in a large box, not per single item.

When it is necessary to use such pricing mechanisms, it might also be necessary to give a small price incentive to the consumer in order to get them to purchase the larger box.

Picnic, the online supermarket 2.0

Online shopping is one of the fastest growing elements in retail. Customers have more options than ever to shop when and where they want and that is exactly what they do. One of the sectors that is lagging behind where online shopping is concerned, is groceries.

Buying groceries in a supermarket is different from most other purchases: customers buy an average of twenty to thirty products instead of just one or two. And there are several barriers for consumers to buy their groceries online. The main barriers for consumers to buy their groceries online:

1. Delivery cost
2. High prices
3. Staying at home for several hours to wait for delivery

Picnic is an online supermarket scale-up, that wasn't founded by a traditional supermarket organization but a new pure player that has built its entire business model and tech platform 'from scratch'.

Dismantling barriers

How did Picnic dismantle the above barriers and how did they design their business model? Consumers find that doing groceries at a supermarket is a hassle, however most of the consumers have to visit a supermarket two or three times a week. Altogether this easily costs two hours. Moreover, after shopping, customers must carry their heavy bags back home. Picnic makes these household tasks easier and faster because it deliveries groceries right at your doorstep. Three years before launching, Picnic started preparations, and developed a platform that made quick and easy online grocery shopping possible. Picnic's brand positioning is: Guaranteed lowest price & Free delivery. Picnic takes away the following thresholds:

1. No delivery costs
2. Lowest price guarantee
3. Using the Picnic app, the delivery vehicle can be followed minute by minute, so people don't have to wait for hours

CASE

Waiting list

The start was promising: Picnic started in one neighborhood in the Dutch town of Amersfoort. As soon as it was announced that people all over Amersfoort could become customers, there was a waiting list to be admitted to the Picnic app. In its first market in Amersfoort Picnic learned what customers want and developed the platform, app and assortment together with their launching customers. After that, the scale-up began. Faster than expected, the company became quickly known through word-of-mouth and many consumers across Amersfoort wanted to shop at Picnic. Currently, Picnic operates in six Dutch cities and is expanding rapidly.

Customer determines the assortment

Picnic's assortment is defined together with its customers. A typical Dutch supermarket sells about 15.000 items. Picnic customers ask for approx. 5.000 items, especially because they want to shop quickly and don't want to be bothered with just another sea salt brand. Initially Picnic started with a standard assortment of about 4.000 items, sourced via an existing supermarket's supply chain. From that starting point Picnic carried out changes to the assortment based on their customers demands and anticipated on specific wishes customers expressed via the app. In particular, customers requested to add organic products,

CASE

which were added rapidly and increased turnover accordingly. A disadvantage of offering a supply-driven broad assortment is that it causes choice anxiety. Picnic has, therefore, opted to maintain a focused, relevant assortment, based on the customer's demand. As soon as several customers request a specific product, Picnic adds it to their assortment. And if a product does not generate sufficient sales, they phase it out and inform customers accordingly. In addition, if a product is not available, Picnic offers an alternative. The assortment is adjusted continuously, based on consumers shopping behavior.

Limiting the range

Why is the amount of items Picnic carries lower than a traditional supermarket while it offers everything their customers ask for? A traditional supermarket has many categories with an extensive assortment, but not all of these products matter to the consumer. The Pareto curve is very steep. Approx. 10% of products account for 90% of sales. No customer wants to choose from twenty types of sea salt. Picnic customers are offered only two kinds of sea salt: a salt grinder and a 200 grams packaging. It appears that customers find this sufficient. What additional value does a third variant or brand have? Apparently none to their customers. Also, Picnic has opted not to carry certain bulky products such as beer crates. Although traffic drivers for offline supermarkets, these products suffer from very significant promotional pressure and are often sold at a loss.

Fresh sales

Picnic shows a high share in sales of fresh goods. Consumers must have confidence in an online-only supermarket to buy fresh food as they prefer to inspect the fresh groceries before purchasing. Picnic provides several guarantees to ensure their customers that their fresh goods are really fresh. For example, they give clear indications about the product's shelf life after delivery. And Picnic only sources what has been ordered: every evening at 10 pm they order only those fresh goods they need to deliver to customers the following day. This guarantees the highest possible quality of fresh goods and the lowest possible waste in the supply chain. Because products are often a couple of days fresher than via the traditional supermarket supply chain, customers also throw less products away at home.

A narrow assortment: win-win-win

According to Picnic, there are several advantages of defining the assortment together with their customers and thus creating a demand driven assortment instead of a supply driven one. First, it reduces choice anxiety for customers so they can shop quickly and easily. It enables them to order during the commercial break on TV. Moreover, it enables Picnic to become a truly personalized grocery store, as their app adapts to the customer's habits, allowing them to order more effortlessly. Also for the logistics a narrow assortment has many advantages: less choice means less space for pallets in the distribution center, less inventory and less operational management.

Delivery at set times

Most online supermarkets work with many different delivery times per day. Picnic offers their customers every day one specific delivery slot. This allows their electric delivery vehicles to drive efficient routes. And Picnic indicates in advance when the delivery van will be at the door. Delivery time windows of 20 minutes are communicated early in the morning and the customer can follow the delivery vehicle via the 'grocery radar', a feature in the app allowing customers to track the delivery vehicle in real-time on the map. Payments are made at time of ordering, so no time is wasted at the door on payment during delivery. This results in shorter delivery times so Picnic can deliver approx. six orders per hour instead of the two to three some supermarkets manage to achieve. Picnic uses small electric delivery vehicles instead of diesel trucks. Next to reducing pollution their vehicles are significantly smaller than regular trucks, allowing traffic to pass in the street instead of causing congestion.

Picnic reinvented online shopping. It is not a copy of the traditional supermarket but a clear choice, based on consumer and shopper insights and smart costs.

No traditional marketing

Picnic does not use traditional media for marketing. They mainly use social media, newsletters and word of mouth. Also, the electric Picnic vehicles stand out as they drive down the street. And at Christmas time the Picnic cars are for example decorated with Christmas lights. If these cars drive down your street, you get curious or neighbors tell you about Picnic, which incites you to give it a try.

Results

Picnic has many fans. Consumers embraced the concept and Picnic is growing rapidly and expanding to other cities. This translates into a local higher proportion of online shopping where Picnic is present. In Amersfoort, Picnic's first market, they have a ~5% market share of the supermarkets' total sales. The share of total Dutch online supermarket shopping is 1-2%. In Amersfoort, Picnic has a dominant market share in online grocery shopping.

Picnic operates like a software company as they develop all mission critical platforms, systems and algorithms internally. For the time being growth in the number of customers and expanding is the target. Picnic seems to the be on the right path to revolutionize the grocery retail landscape.

3. The cost model

Insight about the costs concerning the sales of the range is crucial in an e-commerce operation. The storage and handling of the product and shipment of orders play a major role in the success of an online proposition. Promotions on the wrong products (big and/or heavy products or products with a low gross margin) or a range that is not optimized for online shopping (products with high operational costs as a percentage of the sales price), are reasons why online shops fail. The challenge lies in the operation of a bricks & mortar retail chain in which the category manager seldom has to deal with operational and logistical costs. In the online business these costs make the difference between profit and loss. The famous last mile, the transport of the product to the consumer is the most important and forcing factor.

To begin with, size and weight have impact on the choice of the range. They determine which shipping method is chosen. The composition of any order also depends on the size and the weight. For example, is it wise to do a promotion on a parasol and a concrete parasol base? It goes almost without saying that this is very challenging because you have a very big product and a very heavy one. These two cannot possibly get combined in one parcel and you do not want to worry yourself and your consumers with unnecessarily high shipping costs. Right choices and combinations of products and delivery methods are decisive in this.
Because in the physical channel these two elements do not often occur, only a few retailers have this information available. Even suppliers are not always able to provide this information. Exemplary is a major A-brand manufacturer who filled in 1.55 mm for the size of his 'soup in a bag'. That was the size of empty bags in the manufacturer's system. It is understandable what is going wrong but it has a major impact on the entire chain.
Stock is a challenge for every retailer, even today and in the online model it plays an important role in the realization of the cost model. The unpredictability of the online sales in a geographical area is that it is constantly balancing between out-of-stock and high storage costs. This makes forecasting more important because, certainly in the case of central fulfillment, it has a major impact on the operation. Operational pressure is no longer only distributed to all the stores, but concentrates in one location for the incoming stocks, as well as the outgoing flow of goods to the consumer.
Therefore reducing operational costs should be one of the Category Manager's focus points. Supported by a business analyst, the category manager must constantly keep an eye on the operating stock. It is a whole new way of working that requires a major adjustment in the Category Manager's way of thinking.

4. Content plan

The importance of product information has greatly increased compared to the bricks & mortar stores. Since you cannot touch the physical product and read the label, the information has to be given online. To give a proper information, it is important to make choices. We defined five levels of product data (figure 6.13). How far to go with enrichment of product information and for which ranges? Here, the category roles again is a key factor. Is it necessary to include all the information for the entire range, or is there a distinction between (sub)categories? In the content plan it is all about making choices. It is good to first write down the principles for the content plan. In the content plan the category roles are used and product information for each role is defined. Different roles may request other information.

In practice most attention is given to the destination categories, in which the retailer wants to stand out. But at least the 'consumer-friendly' level must be filled for all category roles. Either way, for every product at least the information must be given to make a product sale-able. In addition, assortments keep changing and it is necessary to deal systematically with the data. The Category Manager plays a role in gathering and determining the product information needed by category (based on the category roles). This information can be supplied by the manufacturer (see 5), or by capturing the knowledge of different products and categories yourself.
This makes you wonder who is responsible for creating and optimizing content. Traditionally in the 'old world' Information Management ended up in noncommercial departments such as IT or data management. This is because it is close to the Data Management activities and is often process oriented and mechanical. With the increased commercial interest for (product)information, there is a switch going on and that is often accompanied by a struggle and uncertainties. A successful content strategy starts with defining the roles and responsibilities. It sounds obvious, but who is responsible for product information in your organization? The final responsibility of the entire product content should belong at a commercial department. So Category Management, the department for e-commerce, a commercially oriented data management department or a combination of these.

5. Cooperation with suppliers

A number of trends ensure that the cooperation with the supplier has been reinterpreted. The foregoing fundamental, product information, is one of those trends. Product information plays a very important role in optimizing the online environment. To optimize would be to make sure that a large part of this information is supplied by the manufacturer. This rule of thumb can be applied that all non-price related product information should come preferably from the manufacturer. It is for the retailer, however, important to observe that there will be no distinction between retailers when the only information used is supplied by the manufacturer for both the consumers and search engines. The content plan needs to take into account the differentiation in this area.

Images are a great challenge for an online retailer. Especially if different suppliers are active in a category, it is difficult to use images that are delivered by the manufacturers. Photos that are taken from different angles and with different colours give a cluttered impression and do not contribute to a rapid selection of the desired product by the consumer. Especially in the supermarket where the consumer is very much accustomed to make his choice based on product shape and colour, uniform photography can be of major importance. In many cases therefore to take product photos yourself as retailer still is the best way to make product photos.

Ranges can be optimized in conjunction with the manufacturer. Perhaps it is possible for the manufacturer to offer a virtual bundle also physically which can lead to cost savings throughout the supply chain.

As explained before, traffic to and ability to find the online store and its products are great challenges. Often the manufacturer has its own platform and its own campaigns to market the product. By making each orientation moment into a possible start of the buying process, the consumer can be better served. There are already good examples in which the consumer on a supplier's platform is assisted in the purchasing process.

The importance of data

In the offline world the importance of product data was limited to logistic information. A product had to efficiently distributed to the store and had to be identified by the retailer so that it could be planned and followed throughout the chain.

The online channel has created three developments which increase the need for information drastically. The consumer needs more information because he cannot hold, feel and touch the product. The retailer wants to offer more information that helps the conversion and the sale and the supplier wants to offer information that strengthens the brand and differentiates the product from the competition. Finally the entire effort surrounding the product information should lead to higher conversion and thus, sales. Hereby the saying 'Features tell and benefits sell' is important to remember when making choices in the product comparison. In practice, relatively a lot of attention is given to the description of the product's features even though this does not have the most impact on the conversion. Here too it is important to give both equal attention.

Figure 6.13 **Five levels of product data**

1. Logistic Data
   All information necessary to adapt a product into the assortment
2. Consumer-friendly information
   Clear item description, descriptive product attributes (such as colour, material, packaging), but also a good consistent product image
3. Descriptive information
   Additional information in order to increase the conversion as commercial enrichment (features and benefits), usage attributes and technical characteristics
4. Cross & up sell information
   Any information that contributes to increase the basket value like alternative products, adjacent products, bundles, accessories etc.
5. Rich and social media
   Rich additional information such as videos, configurators, and reviews in the online shop or on Youtube, Facebook, Vimeo, Vine, and so on.

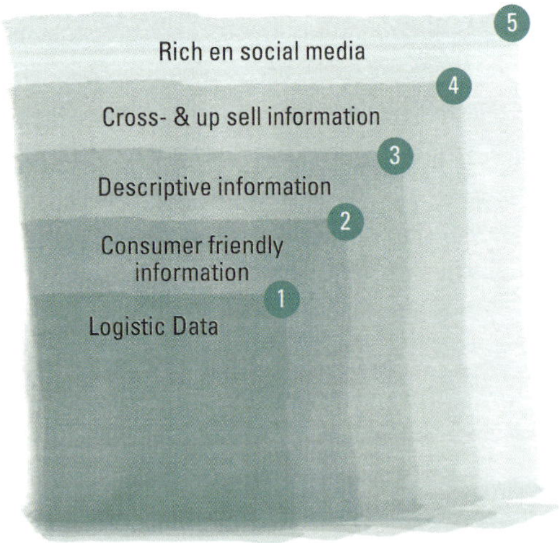

Online optimizing

Because there is only a temporary reality in the online world due to continuously changing circumstances, it is a complex matter to optimize an online store. It is possible to change all elements of an online store within a relatively short time frame. In a bricks & mortar store you need months of preparation to convert a shelf while in an online store, in theory, this can be realized within minutes. All the changes should have as goal to improve the results. But the question is what really needs to be adjusted first and has the greatest impact. A simple rule is that optimization should always lead to a higher turnover or lower costs. This seems obvious, but in practice it often happens that it is optimized on subjective goals. Just like a physical store, an online store's primary target is to sell products. The possibilities the online channel offers such as inspiring consumers often confuse this objective.
The e-commerce fundamentals in the game of increasing sales and lowering the cost are of great importance. For that reason, the Category Manager often plays a key role in optimizing the online store. Too often, this is still mainly the domain of a e-commerce manager, online marketer, content manager or someone in a similar position. For Category Managers it is necessary to know the basics of e-commerce to contribute in this debate.
But where do we start in optimizing an online store and e-commerce fundamentals? To answer this question, we first introduce the concept of the funnel model. The funnel model is a linear simplification of the path the consumer follow into a website. It is not just about the model as we introduce it here, but also about learning the mindset of going through this path in the search for the greatest optimization opportunity.

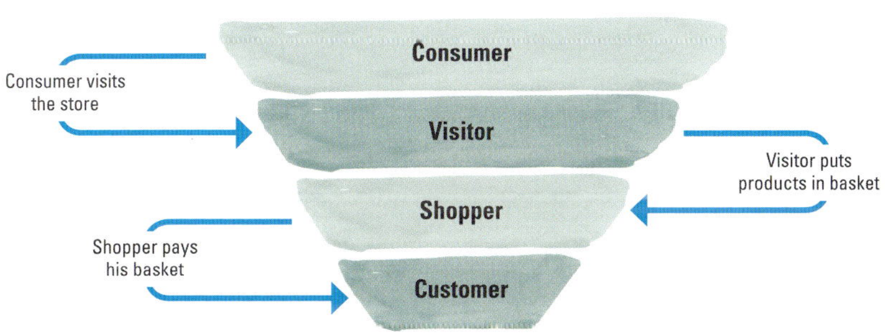

Figure 6.14

The most basic funnel model consists of the path from visitor to customer (figure 6.14). The first step is creating traffic for the online store. The realization that not every visitor to the store will buy something is extremely important. In a supermarket, an average of 95% of the visitors is here to purchase. Online, this percentage is between 2% and 3% for a well optimized e-commerce environment. Focus on increasing the number of visitors is therefore of little relevance as the 'shop' is not well and can, by definition, never be a standing objective in itself. Conversion improvements will rather be in tenths of a percent and depends on the interplay of many factors such as the previously mentioned e-commerce fundamentals which plays an important role. Adding relevant product information can lead to very significant improvements in conversion.

Figure 6.15
Including the right product information can have great impact on the conversion. Adding the right features and benefits can add up to 1,5% conversion on product level. That means doubling a normal conversion of 1,5%. (Truus.nl)

So it starts with bringing in the right visitors. The visitor's needs should connect to the assortment and the chosen prices. When these three are not aligned, then this will lead to low conversion rates. After one has been able to get the right consumer in the online store, and has therefore a visitor, it is important to get him to put something in his basket. It is the Category Manager's task to increase the store's conversion. Does he make the right choices for the price and range? Does he align this with the online marketeer for the right target audience? And does this together with the right product information, lead to conversion?

An important measuring unit in optimization the online store is the 'gross margin after delivery and fulfillment' or the GMDF. Simply said, it means that the margin is made once the order is on the consumer's kitchen table. Till then the Category Manager has a clear impact on the margin. Both the cost of collecting and of compiling the order as costs for sending it to the consumer. Considering the great influence that the Category Manager's choices have on this, is it important to be at least aware of the related methods of calculation of costs of e-commerce.
If we follow the simplified income statement of an e-commerce operation (figure 6.16), we see that the turnover is made up of 'visitors x conversion x basket size. The Category Manager has a direct impact on the revenues of the online store. Conversion rates and basket size are significantly influenced by the his choices.

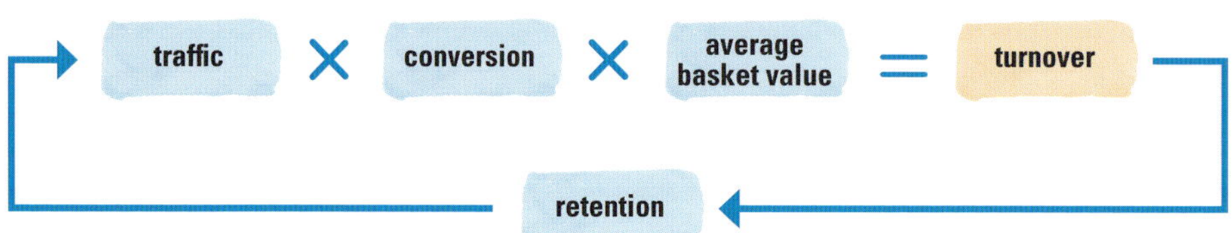

Figure 6.16

In the cost of sold goods, a number of factors are specific for online sales. For example, products with low sales price are, because of the cost model, rarely profitable online. For these products, it is necessary to see how they can be sold efficiently. One option is to consider selling products per carton. Even when a small price incentive is given to the consumer – to get them to buy more units or a larger case– the product may be more profitable. Therefore, it is important to see the online sales of a product through the profit & loss account of online sales and not just on the level of gross margin. In the variable operating costs there are also important differences between clicks and bricks. Other proceedings are required to get a one product to the consumer and they have their own price. If a category manager understands this cost model, he shall be able to make better choices in selection and promotion. Think of bulky products, different dimensions or heavy products with low margins. As with home delivery the impact of assortment and promotional choices is very large. It is only possible to set up a successful e-commerce operation and to maintain it if all departments involved throughout the profit & loss account work together on optimizing the operation and the profitability.

Figure 6.17 **Anatomics of an e-commerce P&L**

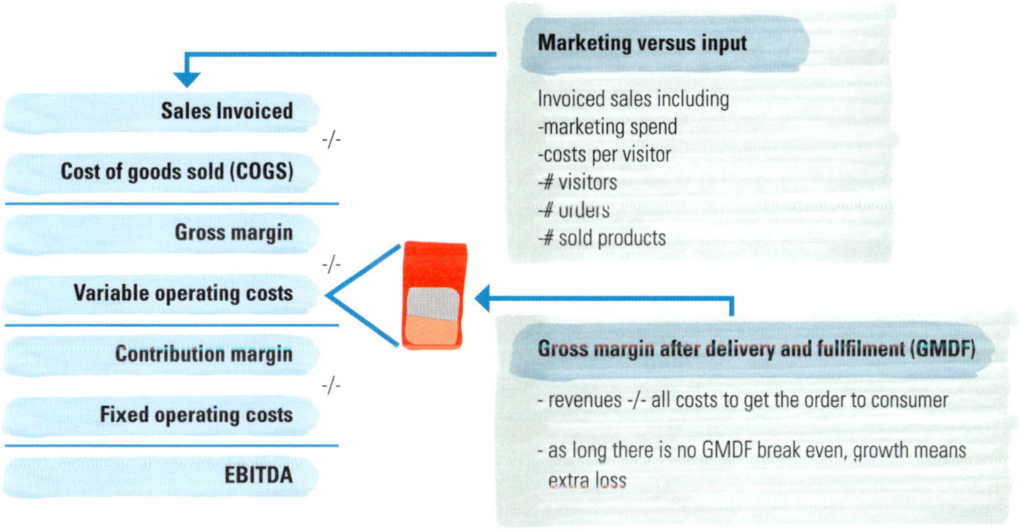

6.8 Tactics and measures

Many retailers are inclined to quickly take action. However, success needs not only a good vision and strategy, but is also dependent on a good execution of the plan. This is covered in this chapter with tactics, the business case and continued monitoring and evaluation.

Category tactics

The category tactics is about completing the P's of product range, instore presentation, promotions, price and personnel. The policy of a category differs greatly depending on the category role.

Regarding the assortment, with a destination category, the retailer wants to distinguish himself through it, because he wants customers to visit his store especially for those ranges. He wants to be famous for that. In this range you look for special products, or extremely tasty and good products. That means you are willing to invest in the costs to make this happen in your destination group.

For example, if bread is your destination category, you can offer more luxurious breads. However, it may also be that you have items in terms of availability that you make promises to your customers. Making sure that fresh bread is available until closing time, for example. That does indeed cost money but it also ensures that regular customers who know the bread is available until closing, will come shopping and will probably buy the rest of their groceries also at your store.

A destination group is displayed in a prominent place in the store, so people can see it well. Often that is at the entrance. It defines the image of the store. A destination group also gets a lot of attention in the communication process, where you should preferably not only communicate on price but rather on the unique characteristics or the unique product range. Here you can stimulate all the senses (when it comes to food) to let them taste. For DIY categories, you want to show, try, touch and organize workshops for shoppers. The price must be in line with the retail format policy. The P 'personnel' must be considered as well in a destination group. Product knowledge and sales expertise are prerequisites.

A large part of the store's assortment, about 50% of the range, is covered by the routine categories. These are important categories such as soft drinks, margarine or drywall. They are big and bought a lot, but it is difficult for a retail brand to distinguish itself with these products. The items are on the shopping list so often planned purchases. In these categories the large volume of sales gives the larger part of the margin. Category Management is about a compact, good assortment and a good shelf presentation that allows people to easily and quickly select the product of their choice. The pricing is competitive because you want to avoid costumers switching to other retailers. Volume promotions also fit into this category. Promotions are aimed at the purchasing frequency and to fill the customer's basket. Staff should ensure that items are in stock and that shelfs are refilled in time.

Traffic builders are categories that attract customers to the store. These are categories in which the purchase price is relatively high because otherwise the effort of the store switch is not worth it and for categories which are purchased by many people or which can create large flows of customers. Good examples are meat, beer, laundry detergent and in DIY paint. A strong traffic builder is a category or product that attracts many people, but also one that causes people to buy more than just the traffic builder itself. The promotions on a traffic builder should be sharp, presented in a conspicuous place in the flyer and there will be only a small margin on it. That is not a problem if customers buy the rest of their groceries at your store. The presentation should therefore not be in the front of the store, but in the middle or at the back. You want people to also pass other product categories and purchase them. For the staff, it is important to keep the stock on level and to prevent out of stocks. Customers who come for the traffic builder, should be able to purchase it. One important aspect in the choice between traffic builders is the shopping basket the clients leave the store with. If they only purchase the traffic builder, the promotion did not succeed. But if they leave with a full basket then the traffic builder's promotion was successful.

Impulse products mostly are not included on the shopping list; shoppers buy them because they were tempted in the store. Impulses are the brushes and turpentine with the paint, the cushions with the chairs or the cakes at the bakery. The range is appealing; it is presented in a good place in the store, in a high traffic location, or near planned purchases where this is additional. The products are visible and creatively presented. The extra sales make the basket value suddenly more interesting, as does the margin. Impulse categories should yield a higher than average margin. Price is often less important as you think it is a good addition to your other purchases.

Finally, convenience categories. The convenience products are products that you do not necessarily expect at the retailer but if they are present, they are convenient. Think about seasonal products such as suntan cream. Convenience categories are presented in a prominent place and generate a lot of margin. No promotion is done on these items.

Table 6.6 **Categorie tactics**

	Assortment	Presentation	Price	Promotion	People/ staff
Traffic builder	High rotating articles, bought by many people	In the middle or the back of the store	Sharply	Promotional high share, deep discounts	Prevent out-of-stocks and often replenished
Impulse	Seductive Impulse Conspicuous, surprising Matching	Presentation at high traffic location, in sight. Near a matching planned purchase.	Creates margins	Promotional low share, demonstra-tions, tastings	Able to present creatively
Routine	Compact assortment with runners, bottom or benefit packages to avoid customers switching to other retailers.	Throughout the store in alleys	Competitive	Average	Prevent out-of-stocks
Convenience	Additional supplement to 'normal' range associated with store type	Should stand out and seduce	Creates margins	Non	Non
Destination	Unmatched in quality or choice	Prominent in store, location in sight	According to the retail format's strategy	High with limited discount	Advice, tastings, demonstration. Training important

In the vertical column you will find the category roles that can be translated horizontally into the 5 P's of marketing. That way you will see the tactics that are important for success in execution.

The translation of category objectives into marketing techniques

In chapter 6.5, we discussed the different strategies for Category Management. Those seven strategies can be translated into tactics, the 5 p's. This means you have to consider which activities will bring the realization of each category objective. Those activities are divided into the five Ps of marketing.

Table 6.7 **Category strategies and the marketing P's**

Category strategies	Price	Product	Promotion	Place	Personnel
Traffic building (attract customers)					
Optimize check-out transactions	25% price reduction on the purchase of tri-pack suntan lotion	The three most common protective factors in one foil package	Through displays, window posters, advertisements and leaflets for mothers	On display at the checkout and in the non-food section	Instruction how the display can be easily maintained
Optimize profits					
Generate cash					
Create excitement and incentives					
Enhance image					
Avoid customers switching to other channels/stores					

Example of the category strategy's translation into the marketing P's in practice.

This is a tool to translate the various category objectives into marketing activities. We have completed for one objective (Basket value optimization) the practical options for each marketing P.

6.8.1 Assortment composition and pricing

Stretching the price variation

The composition of a category has one basic rule. Consumers usually choose in the middle of a range. So if more higher priced items are added to the assortment, the average selling price will go up. No because a lot of people buy the most expensive product, but because the perceived price range has gone up. Most people do not want to buy the cheapest product, nor the most expensive one. They buy from the middle segment. That's why good, better, best is the assortment strategy for many ranges. However if you can add some exclusive or organic items to the top of the range, your average price will rise further.

Particularly in supermarkets, we see that within the range of categories, the number of price value variation increases a lot. The diagram below is an example of the composition of a peanut butter range at Albert Heijn. There are five different price classes for peanut butter. At the top, there is a premium product and a budget brand is at the bottom (AH basic). In between we find three other players: the AH private label, the market leader brand and a special label like organic. The premium product is, per 100 grams, almost four times more expensive than the budget brand. Whereas often good-better-best is used in ranges, especially service supermarkets add more levels to their ranges. This because it underpins their overall image as an assortment choice champion. For supermarkets the build-up in two or three layers is standard. Tesco and Sainsbury have strategic ranges from seven to nine layers (health, vegetarian or organic ranges, regional products, child-friendly product variations; allergen products etc…).

Figure 6.18 **Category Management and value creation**

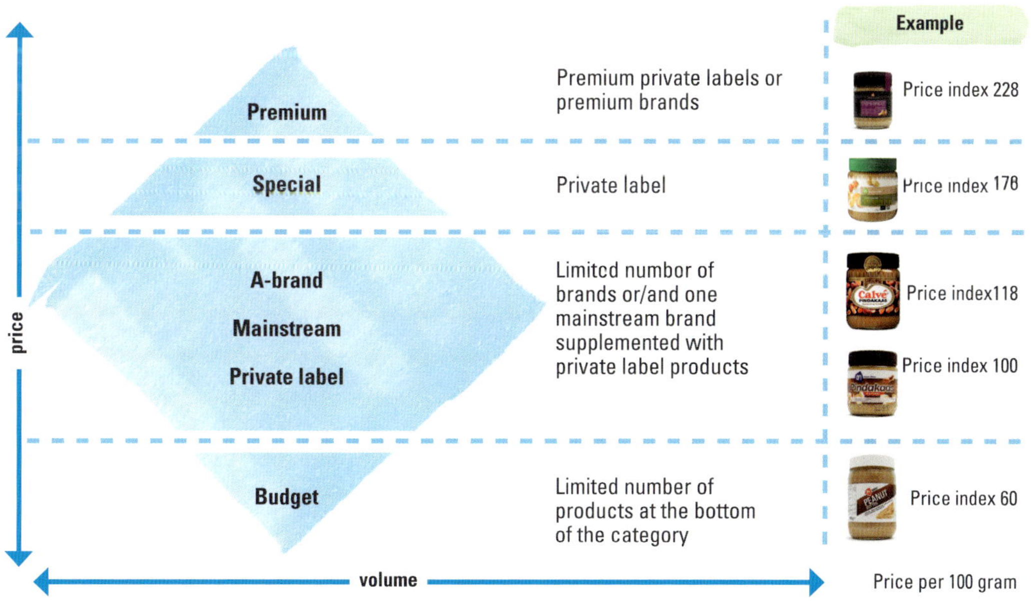

(EFMI Business School)

The composition of an assortment category in full service supermarkets contains more often five layers in which the most expensive (premium) products costs up to 500% more than the cheapest. This tactic has been widely accepted as successful in the UK and France. In this example, you see the structure of the sub category peanut butter at the Dutch supermarket Albert Heijn.

Does this also apply for fresh produce? This is the price composition for potatoes at Albert Heijn.

	Content (grams)	Consumenter price	Price per kg	Index
500 g petite potatoes	500	€ 1,29	€ 2,58	338%
1 kg biological potatoes	1000	€ 1,79	€ 1,79	234%
1 kg Pommes Primeur AH Excellent	1500	€ 2,49	€ 1,66	217%
1 kg firm cooking potatoes	1000	€ 1,59	€ 1,59	208%
3 kg firm cooking potatoes	3000	€ 2,29	€ 0,76	100%
5 kg firm cooking potatoes bulk packs	5000	€ 3,39	€ 0,68	89%

Table 6.8

For a small household, a 1 kg pack of potatoes is much more convenient than a bag of 3 kilo. And a pound oven baked petite potatoes with rosemary and garlic is totally different from cooked potatoes and has more added value for consumers.

Price elasticity is of great importance to retail

When do consumers find a product expensive and when not? To answer that question, you cannot only proceed with pure logic. Pricing is primarily a psychological process. Raising a product's price is attractive if the competition allows it. But the question is what happens if you raise the price out of the blue? Or conversely, if you let the price drop, will that automatically lead to increased sales?

Many scientific studies on price elasticity have been published. The EFMI Business School has studied the price elasticity. In that context, hundreds of studies on price elasticity have been taken into account and added to their own experiments. We will briefly give some practical conclusions that EFMI supports with their studies.

The main conclusion from the studies is that the price perception of shoppers can be managed without having to change prices. A central role is played by the (internal) price reference: a kind of internal standard when shoppers use their 'normal' price to evaluate the price level of goods in stores that they visit. As the price reference is higher, the shoppers will perceive a product or store as being more advantageous. As illustrated by one of the EFMI experiments, retailers and manufacturers can influence the price perception of shoppers with the assortment: a 'premium' range allows for an increase in the (internal) reference, causing consumer to consider prices less rapidly as being uneconomical. However, the addition of discount brands in a range just seems to have the opposite effect. The diagram shows how all these factors affect the consumer's final price perception. Price perception is not established only inside the supermarket. The emergence of other providers, for example discounter like Lidl, plays a role. Discounters put products sometimes on a completely new low price level with a quality that exceeds expectations, making the pricing of 'normal' supermarkets suddenly seem high and switching the purchases in this category to discounters.

Figure 6.19 **How price perception is established**

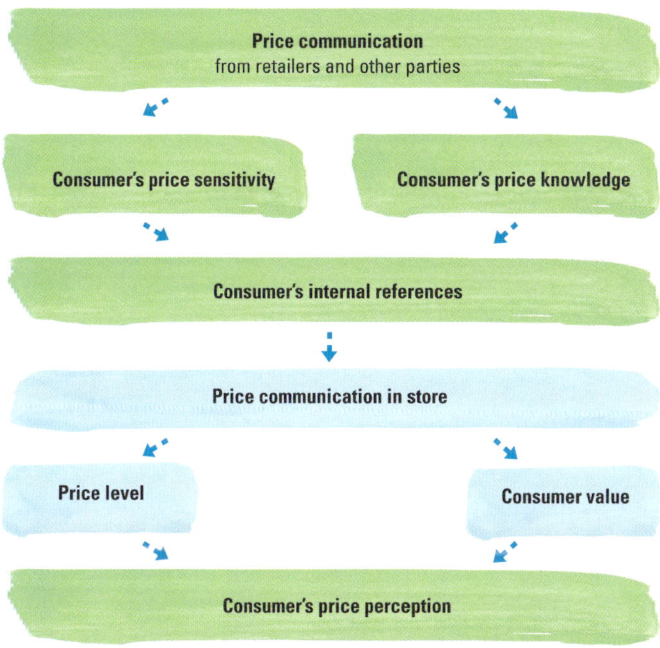

Consumers are constantly exposed to price communication, especially in supermarkets. What effect this has, has to do with two main factors: the consumer's price sensitivity (and, depending on the economical or personal situation, these can be very unstable); and on the other hand, the consumer's price knowledge which is also variable. One consumer may know all about coffee prices and nothing about the price of desserts or meat. And for another consumer it is the other way round. But both factors mean that consumers will build their own internal references. In the shop they are brought in contact with products and prices. And their personal reference becomes a way of weighing the price of an item and the importance (value) that they attach to it. This results in a price perception. (EFMI Business School)

How price perception is established

Less price sensitive consumers have a higher (internal) price reference than those who are price sensitive. They will not often perceive a price as 'unprofitable'. Consumers tend to be less price sensitive when products or stores are considered to be 'unique' or when they associate it with quality and exclusivity. Innovation and strong, distinctive (quality) brands or retail formats can provide that lower price sensitivity.

Manufacturers and retailers can influence the price perception with the assortment structure: a premium range causes an increasing (internal) price reference, so retail prices are less likely to be perceived as 'unprofitable'. The opposite is true for a discount range.

Psychological pricing affects the price perception. Consumers consider € 2.99 to be a much lower price than € 3.01. Communicating a relative price change (in %) has, especially at relatively low priced products (like many supermarket products) a greater effect on the consumer's price perception than absolute price change.

Consumers who are confronted with relatively few price communication, have a low price knowledge. Consumers with low price knowledge usually estimate the selling price higher than it actually is (they overestimate). In other words, they evaluate prices based on a higher reference price, which makes their price perception more favorable.

Manufacturers and retailers can influence the price perception with their assortment's price level. Driving up the assortment's price level causes an increasing price reference. Consumers assess future prices on a higher reference price, so the price perception has become more advantageous. The opposite is true for lowering the assortment's price level.

As consumers experience more 'value', their (internal) price reference rise and prices will less likely be perceived as disadvantageous. Building strong brands or retail formats and developing innovative, distinctive products or stores optimize the consumer's perceived value.

(EFMI Business School)

The extensibility of pricing

We have already indicated that extensibility of the pricing is determined by many factors. The following figure describes the significant upside and downside potential for price fixing. It is also important to realize that the creation of a dominant product with a (high) price reference, can increase the overall price -value perception. For a A-brand can green beans, € 1.19 seems less expensive if there are also very luxurious green beans for € 3.39 on the shelf. If that is missing, and only mass brands or 'budget' brands for € 0.69 and € 0.89 are presented, that same A-brand can suddenly seems expensive.

Figure 6.20 **The playing field of pricing**

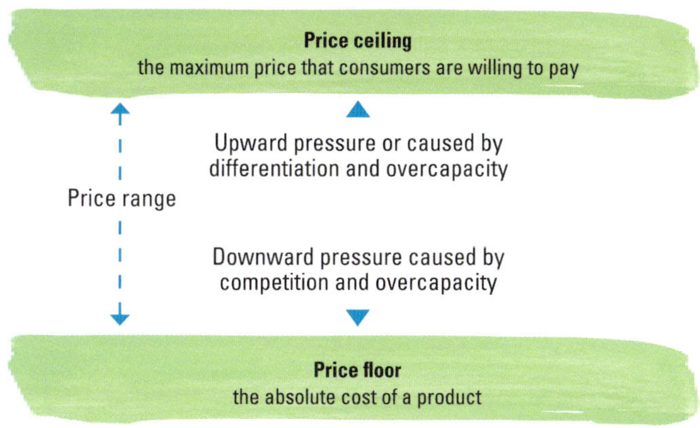

Pricing is determined by many factors in both upward and downward direction.
(EFMI Business School)

Price sensitivity varies widely

Based on the above we can see that the degree to which consumers are price sensitive may vary by period, consumer group, product category or even by brand. In general we can say that consumers are less price sensitive when one or more of the following situations occur (James, 2003):

- Consumers perceive the product as 'unique'. *The price is less important with products that have unique, distinctive properties;*
- Consumers associate the product with quality, prestige and exclusivity. *The price is less important when buying a Bentley than when buying a Daihatsu;*
- Consumers are not (well) aware of substitutes. *The price is less important if consumers feel that there is no other choice;*
- The determination of the product quality is difficult for consumers. *If it is difficult to determine the quality, the price may give an indication for product quality;*
- Purchase price is (relatively) low. *The price is less important as it is a smaller part of the available budget;*
- Purchase price is low compared to the total cost. *The price of matching socks is less important when purchasing an expensive tailored suit;*
- The product is used along with a previously purchased durable product. *Because the price of the durable product is higher than the price of the complementary one, the latter is less important (for example, printer and cartridges);*
- The product cannot be kept in stock. *As it is difficult to keep a product in stock, the price is less important.*

Product introductions

In the food sector, about 80% of all invented product introductions fail. It is therefore clear that any method that manages retrieval from 10% of the failure rate will save a lot of costs.
Increasingly, product introductions are part of the consultation between Category Managers and Format Managers, because all retailers are eager for distinctiveness. If product launches are properly dealt with, they can be very beneficial to a format.

Check list for new products

A check list for Category Managers in the various ECR cases is designed to help to objectively assess whether a product is really new. With this check list, a Category Manager can add a measure (what to do) that suits his organization. Moreover, this check list is an excellent way to get into a conversation with a supplier and come to a mutual position.

Figure 6.21 **Judging new product's innovation value**

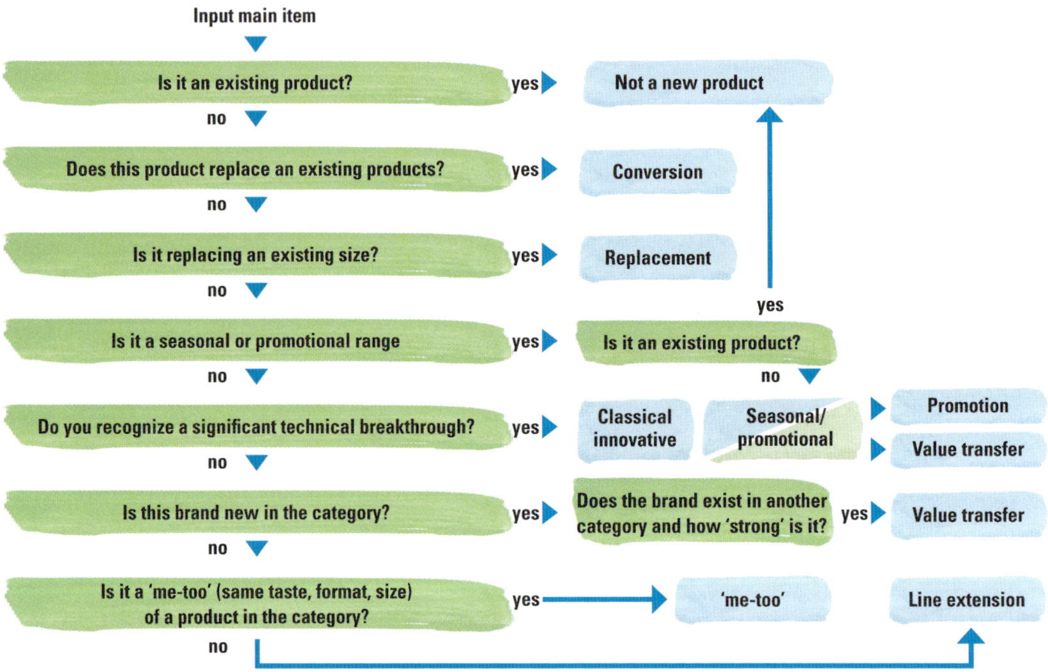

The chart above looks like a selection box system that determines whether an item is new or not really new. In order to agree on a new product's potential value, filling in this figure may be a good exercise for both supplier and Category Manager. A correct assessment of a new product is of great importance in the Category Management process.

The conclusion that an item is not new, does not mean that the item is not interesting for a retail brand. An important question is: what is the advantage of the introduction for this category? Is it the introduction of a strong brand? Is it supported by mass media and will a customer ask for it? Will this grow the category, or does the yield go up? Can it prevent relapse of the category? Or can a retailer distinguish himself with it because he introduced it before other retailers did?

Rationalize the assortment

Rationalizing ranges is essential to ensure the store's transparency and efficiency. A regular clean up of the range is therefore good. Note that it is necessary to reorganize an assortment on the following principles:

- 'Need' versus 'Want' products: if there is a high brand loyalty or product loyalty, people will have more difficulty to buy alternative products. For commodities like sugar, brand is usually irrelevant but for soft drinks it is a key factor. If you want to reorganize an assortment, you should know whether alternative products are available. Many novice Category Managers make the mistake of cleaning up an unique product that is not a big seller but fills a specific need or does not have a substitute. Based on customer inquiries, usually it is quickly back on the shelf.
- Reorganizing the range in small steps, like regularly replacing a small segment, is not a problem. But if a large part of the assortment disappears at once, and the consumer misses a number of products during his shopping trip, it can cause dissatisfaction about the whole store. In addition, at first someone may purchase a product at another store, but over time they usually find an alternative in their primary supermarket.

Considerations for assortment and pricing

Category Managers who deal with selection process in their assortment and wonder what price tag they should use, should consider the following tactical questions:

- Was the assortment balanced across the different value segments?
- Do the growth segments have enough SKU's?
- Does it make sense to add larger sizes of fast moving products?
- Do we reorganize overlapping brands or products?
- Is there enough, too much or too little choice?
- Can I add premium or special products?
- Does the low price segment prevent customers to switch stores?

6.8.2 Planogram power

The only place shoppers and product meet is on the shop floor.

A large number of purchase decisions in the store are taken in front of the shelf. And simply said, if the product is not found, it cannot be bought. The layout of the store and the shelf is therefore of great importance. The professional areas concerned with this are the Floor Planning and Space Management. Space management directly impacts purchase decisions and shoppingexperience of every shopper.

The shopper buys on average 150 different items in a supermarket per year. He has to select them out of 20,000 other items that are often offered. This is a big task. The better the shop - and shelf layout, the more satisfied the shopper will be. We have to ensure the shopper that the shelf is accessible, the products are easy to find, the articles are in stock and that they can complete their shopping list in your store. Aside from the items on the shopping list, it is important to seduce them to impulse purchases. Beside the impact on the shopper, logistical and financial aspects play a large role: how easily can I refill the shelves? What is the correct size and place of every department in a store? It is obvious that the retailer's department of Space Management has been rapidly professionalizing in the recent years. Space Management changed from a part of the activities of Category Management to a knowledge and expert centre in the field of Planogram Management and store layout. Space Management develops planograms, among other things, and has the following objectives:

- Optimal availability of articles
- Optimization of the supply chain
- Minimizing stock and thus reducing capital costs
- Increasing customer satisfaction
- Increasing conversion
- Larger baskets
- Prevent out of stock
- Stimulate up selling and cross selling

Shelf layout and pleasant shopping

Shoppers are in a hurry: they spend on average 21 minutes to shop at a time and 90 seconds in a convenience store. One of the major preconditions of a shelf is therefore a good and logical layout, allowing the customer to shop quickly and comfortably. Items must be found quickly and the shelf should also be right, financially and logistically as well as in the presentation.

Floor Planning

The layout of the store is often designed by the retail format department together with the store. There often is a clear division into categories, but the cohesion is not always optimal. How easy is it to find your entire meal consisting of vegetables, meat & sauces? Are the products placed near each other or are they far apart? Does the shop layout only work for large shopping trips in which you go around every aisle in the store? Or does it also facilitate the small shopping trip and is it optimal designed for that too? For DIY stores, it applies even more strongly. Shops are often classified by category, but not necessarily on the job. So to buy everything for your new door you have to be at 4 or 5 different places in the store. The doors are a separate category, but the hinges are part of the hardware category that is somewhere else. The convenience for the shopper can be increased significantly and therefore also the size of his basket.

The following model visually indicates which influences there are on the shelf and with which stakeholder Space Management has to deal with:

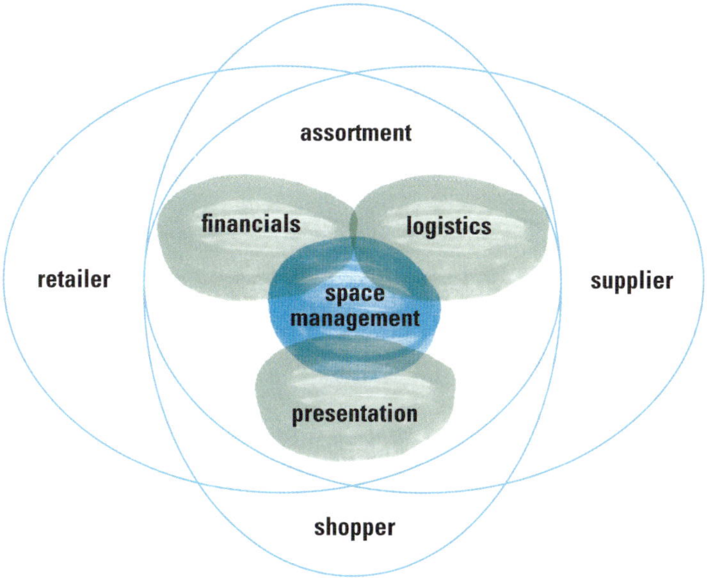

Figure 6.22
Retailer, supplier and shopper affect the assortment. Space Management is developing planograms, while looking at financial, logistical and presentation factors. (Category & Trade Company)

A shelf can be well presented and logical, but it is also important that it is financially and logistically correct. The Space Manager should determine, as an independent party in the Category Management process, the right balance between these forces and stakeholders.

To introduce consistency in the shelves' structure and appearance, a retailer should develop guidelines in presentation througout the store. For example, to standardise the positioning of private label or the cheapest products. In addition, you can determine a maximum height limit for the top shelf. Some shelves are 190 cm high and the products are therefore even higher. Many people cannot reach them or find them hard to reach. In addition, as soon as the first product of that top shelf is sold, the shopper cannot see the remaining products, we call this visual out of stock. For suppliers these format presentation guidelines are a fundament to develop thorough and well considered proposals. For the shopper a shelf must be accessible, interesting and attractive. By using the appropriate classification based on the shopper decision tree, strict segmentation in vertical blocks can be used to divide the shelf logically for the shopper. The shopper can find his products quickly and there will be a higher conversion.
In contrast, the wrong shelf layout prevents the shopper from finding his product and thus from buying it. Also a lack of important information can cause the consumer to leave the store prematurely without any purchase. The absence of price communication is an example. If people do not see or know the price, they will not buy the product. In a DIY store you need much more information about a product. Alas is this information often hard to find or not available. For example roller blinds: the customer cannot see the product's colour, its specific mechanism or how to assemble it, nor can he feel, touch or try it. A good shelf provides the following: it is easily accessible, it provides the right information in order to decide about the product, it is on stock and with that it increases the conversion.

Week-part meal solutions: Inspiring shopper choice in fresh poultry

SUPERVALU

Green Isle
2 Sisters Food Group

Background

Packaged fresh meat offerings remain relatively under-developed in most supermarket environments. Packaging is largely functional, merchandising and layouts basic, with the main focus being on product visibility in-pack and SKU availability. Packaged fresh meat in most supermarkets is often one of the most boring fixtures to shop, void of any inspiration. Alongside these issues, the bulk of fresh raw meat is sold as retailer own label, and thus unbranded. While some retailer own brand stories carry great quality messaging, in general branded offerings are not core to the category.

Manor Farm provide most of the raw poultry meat to the Supervalu business, and most of this hits the shelf unbranded. In advance of their 2014 re-development of their own Manor Farm branded offering, they decided to undertake a significant shopper project to optimize the impact in-store. Similarly Supervalu had invested significantly in their 'meat quality' story with shoppers, with the bulk of this focus and messaging on their fresh meat butcher counters in-store. To mirror this investment, they also wanted to optimize the on-shelf pre-packed offering. In 2014 both parties partnered together to optimize the packaged fresh poultry category, uncover quick wins and develop a best-in-class approach in a relatively under-developed area in-store.

Analysis

As raw meat suppliers tend to be more operations and production focused, investment in things like space-planning, shopper insight and shopper marketing tend not to be top-of-mind. Manor Farm have always challenged this norm and added value to their retailer relationships (in what is otherwise a commodity product) through an investment in shopper marketing.

In 2014 they commissioned Ireland's first significant multi-methodological shopper and consumer study on raw meat, capturing both the in-store behaviour (HOW shoppers buy) and connecting this with a national household usage diary study covering WHERE shoppers bought raw meat, HOW OFTEN, HOW they

CASE

used it in the home (meal solutions) and WHAT they thought of the category. This 360-degree approach ensured that any arising solution would focus not only on selling more (to shoppers) but also focus on getting shoppers to use more in home (consumers).

Key problem

The arising key findings of the study were as follows:

- 1 in every 3 shoppers in-store engaged with the category and then simply walked away without buying anything. While some of these lost sales were picked up by the butcher counter or other raw meat categories, many others were not. Poor merchandising, an absence of navigational signage and a lack of inspiration at the point-of-purchasing was resulting in fresh poultry sales being lost every minute of every day.
- Of those who were buying, the large majority were only buying one SKU. This made little sense when the in-home diaries showed that most households cook at least 6 meals using meat every week. Multi-SKU purchasing at the fixture was thus extremely low.
- On examining the diary information it was apparent that actually shoppers used a large number of stores and butcher shops to fulfill their fresh meat requirements for any given week. This meant that any fresh meat sale lost in-store today (through a lack of inspiration or visibility) was most likely to be lost to a competitor store due to this promiscuous meat shopper. Shoppers were buying SKUs one-by-one throughout the week and, as it was unlikely the shopper would be in the same store every day, meat sales were scattered across the competitive set.
- Considering fresh poultry was made up of many sub-categories, each meeting different meal solution needs (chicken breast, breaded chicken, chicken legs/wings, whole chickens and duck, turkey or quail), then the 'single SKU' shopping behaviour was even more worrying. Most shoppers were simply interacting with one product area and moving on, never considering other sectors or product types beyond what they 'routinely bought'.
- The time spent at the fixture was very low, functional and lacked the type of browsing behaviour that tends to drive incremental sales. Shoppers described it best as a 'sea of plastic'.
- Interestingly dual-site locations (aisle ends and floor-fridges earlier in store flow) accounted for nearly a third of all SKU sales. Due to the single SKU shopping behaviour, these shoppers were then de-listed traffic from the main fixture, but this finding also offered further opportunity to use the secondary sites more strategically, instead of just price promotion.
- Diary usage information showed that poultry was the second most used raw meat in meal solutions but there was significant growth potential across both traditional and modern recipes (as consumers were relatively limited and unimaginative in their use in home). For example, few households were cooking a traditional whole chicken for Sunday lunch, while most shoppers agreed that they would do this 'more' if they remembered to buy in-store.

The SEA OF PLASTIC

- Shoppers agreed that coming up with meal solutions everyday was challenging and that they rarely planned the weeks meals in advance – the majority only planning 2-3 days ahead at best.

With these challenges, it was clear that the arising action needed to be a TOTAL CATEGORY SOLUTION as opposed to just focusing on the sub-categories in which Green Isle had strong product portfolios.

Objective

The shopper marketing initiative needed to reduce lost sale walkaways, encourage category interaction and browsing, drive meal solution and ingredient experimentation, and put fresh poultry 'on the shopper map' for every shopper. Every additional sale would not only be a win for the supplier but also a sale stolen from a competitor store later in the week. To achieve this, shoppers needed to be jumped from their auto-routine product focus to a more engaged meal solution focus around fresh poultry. As the majority of meal planning is completed in the 'fresh' area of the store, additional meal 'wins' here would also have further sales impact in the rest of the store for the retailer.

Approach

The final project had two distinct executions. The first was the simple re-design of the main fixture, clearly segmenting the category and navigating the shopper through the various category sub-sectors. Using brand colours, meal occasion imagery and a segmentation designed around cooking time, the products became easy cook meal solutions. Segmenting by cooking time had been a decision arising from the shopper insight – shoppers were planning meals standing at the shelf, and 'cooking time' was a key factor. Were they looking for a quick healthy meal convenient to prepare or a more indulgent family meal? The arising segmentation, navigation and colour coding made the category more engaging and easier to navigate.

The secondary sites were also converted into Meal Solution Stations (instead of fridges full of price promoted product as before). Each fridge showed a meal solution idea, housing all chilled and ambient product required to make it. Alongside the image-laden header board, recipe leaflets were housed on the fixture making it easy for shoppers to buy in-store and follow at home.

The unique approach taken to the frequency of the meal solution changes in-store is what makes this case more unique. Shopper missions and needs change through an average week, and looking at the home diaries it was evident that a single meal solution was not going to satisfy shoppers across a 7-day period. For example from Monday to Wednesday, shoppers were more likely to want easy, quick and healthy meals allowing them to live their busy varied lives (maybe a Chicken Caesar

CASE

Salad), while on Thursday and Friday they were more likely to be motivated by more indulgent foods (Chicken Fajitas). Lastly on Saturday and Sundays, shoppers were more likely to be seeking meal solutions involving friends and family, recipes requiring more involvement (and thus Whole Roast Chicken).
The meal solution approach was thus designed along a week-part agenda. The meal solution proposed to shoppers changed 3 times a week in-store. Quick, healthy and convenient meals showcased on MON-WED, indulgent meals THU & FRI and family/friends and togetherness meals on SAT & SUN. This meant that all POS (header boards, recipe leaflets) as well as all adjacent products needed to be re-merchandised 3-times a week. Week-Part Meal Solutions meant that shoppers were always inspired by a meal solution that met their shopper mission on that particular day. In a retail environment that usually works on 2-3 week long promotion cycles, this was a unique proposition!

Results & learnings

There was an immediate effect on multi-SKU sales once the main fixture received its re-fresh. While pre-test those shoppers buying more than one SKU at a time was only at 8%, this jumped to 25% post-implementation. Being able to see all the products available, the colour coded shelves and sectors and presenting the products by cooking time allowed shoppers to 'think ahead' and build meal solutions for later in the week (which of course resulted in bigger overall baskets for the retailer also). It should be said that doing the basics right (category signage, segmentation and navigation) still return impressive results. Sales of packaged fresh poultry increased by between 30-50% post-implementation. Changing the focus to meal solutions (both on main fixture and secondary sites) had reengaged shoppers and thus stolen share from competitor retailers. The meal solution focus also fitted perfectly with Supervalu's own 2014/5 'Good Food Karma' overall marketing campaign (focusing on family and food).

Rotating the meal solution fridges 3 times a week proved too much of a logistical challenge (with all the associated ingredients for the recipe, POS changes etc). In the end, two rotations were achieved a week, although the original three rotations remain planned. Also getting the store to buy-in and own the project was key. Ultimately the store had to keep these secondary meal solution stations stocked, not only of poultry products but also of ambient and other fresh product. Early project on-boarding proved to be of major benefit in making this happen.

Manor Farm ended up growing retailer sales, getting more of their own new branded offering listed and increasing poultry use as an ingredient in meal planning for consumers. Supervalu, by encouraging more meal planning in-store, benefited not only from the higher poultry sales and share, but also from the bigger 'meal' baskets arising. And the shopper went home inspired with different recipes to cook. The win-win-win we so often preach about in Shopper Marketing but rarely see!

Shelf analysis

In addition, during the maintenance time, the Space Manager analyses the shelf and identifies opportunities and threats. Opportunities like increasing the number of products with a high rotation but a low distribution so the revenue can be optimized. You can achieve that by giving products with low shelf stock and high rotation more shelf space to reduce the out of stock. And by cutting down the space for products with a high shelf stock, so the losses because of waste or redundant, outdated products are reduced A Space Manager should ensure that the fast rotating products are on eye level. Finally, Space Management can recommend which products can be reduced in the tail of the assortment (because of a low rotation).

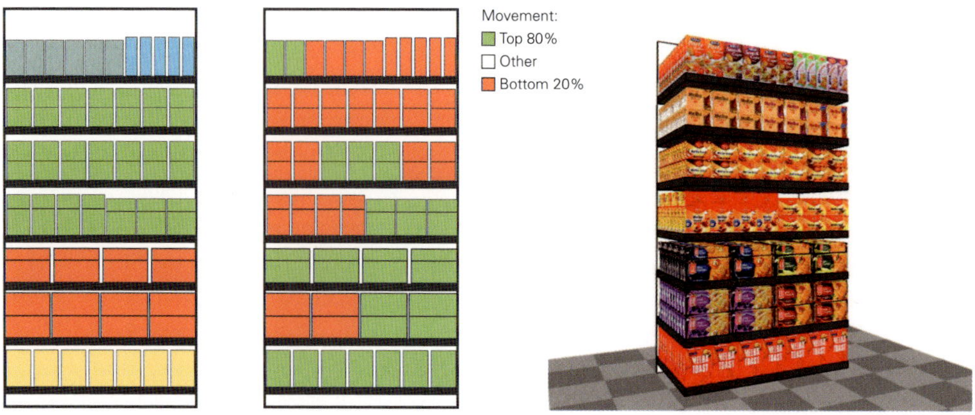

Figure 6.23
With help of spaceplanning software analyses can be made of a shelf. The first illustration analyses the category on segment level, to determine whether the segments are clearly positioned on the shelf. The second analysis is a top bottom analysis on circulation speed. This shows where the fast runners are situated. The thirth analysis is a 3D-represenation of the shelf. (Symphony EYC)

Developments in Space Management

Because no single shopper or target area is the same, the layout of planograms should not be equal either. Currently retailers develop often generic planograms to be implemented everywhere, but a shopper in a big city is not same as one in the countryside. Even within cities large differences in income, ethnicity and buying behaviour appear.

The current trend therefore shows that supply and demand in planograms can be more specifically matched. This may be a better response to the differences between the shoppers and using those opportunities within the planogram will increase the retailer's turnover. With new smart software solutions, a generic planogram can easily be adapted to a local store. We see a tendency to cluster stores with an similar customer behaviour and make cluster planograms. On one hand, these cluster planograms respect the category goals, but they also respond to the local situations and sales opportunities.

Furthermore, promotions is an important part of the total sales. Most stores determine themselves where to put the various promotions, how wide, and which combinations. Some stores are very good at it while other stores aim for margin and let the consumer search for the flyer items. Yet another uses good place to clear old stocks. Planograms for promotions create more satisfied customers and leads to increased sales.
Besides the planograms for the regular assortment more and more retailers also offer planograms for end of the aisle promotions and combinations in promotions.

Checking planograms:
When delegating a planogram the Category Manager has to check the final plan on the following points:

- Is the segmentation logical and based on the shopper decision tree?
- What is the balance in Share of sales / Share of shelf?
- Can the out-of-stock be reduced?
- Can the loss by exceeded shelflife be reduced?
- Can the stock be reduced?
- Which barriers are there to buy the product?
- Is the case size optimal in relation to the turnover rate?

Digitization
Thanks to digitization and the emergence of smartphones the selection process will be supported with smart applications in store. We can find more and more product information online, like product specifications on allergies or competitive price information, but we can also arrange our shopping list in the order of the store layout.

6.8.3 Optimizing promotions

A lot of time, money and energy is spent on promotions. To spend that money effectively, it is important to consider your desired achievements carefully and measure the effect of the promotions. The retailers and suppliers goals can vary in this case.

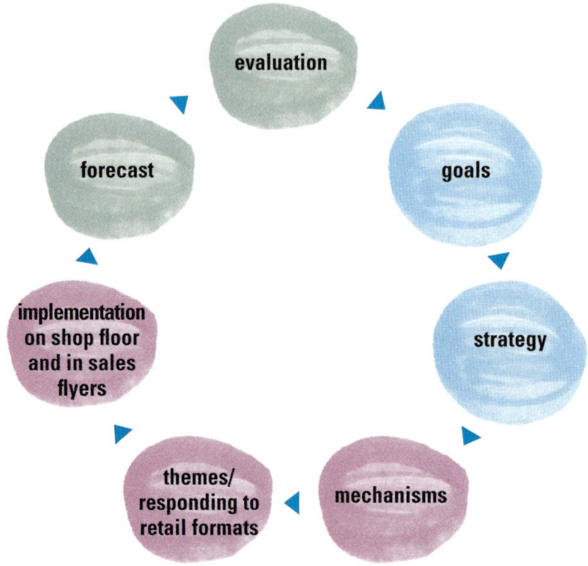

Figure 6.24
This model includes the steps to make promotions increasingly effective, by evaluating the effects of establishing a clear objective and effective implement that in your policy.
(Category & Trade Company)

Often, too little time is taken to analyse the shopper's behaviour and evaluate promotions. Because of this you do not know what the effect is or how high the costs are.
Creating a good promotion strategy starts with defining the objective. This depends on the category role. A traffic builder promotion will have to draw customers to the store. The number of visitors or purchasing visitors is the standard, as is the basket size of these customers. Do they buy the promoted item in your store along with other groceries or do they buy only the promoted item? If a traffic builder gets a lot of customers who buy a lot more products, you do not need to earn a large margin on the traffic builder itself. In case of an impulse category it is different, because this is a product that one decides to buy in the store. For this, it must be presented in a location with a lot of traffic. Being printed in the flyer is less important. The margin should be good. For routine items, the objective is usually to keep up the level of sales and market share.
For suppliers, the motivators to cooperate in a promotion are sales, volume and market share. In addition, penetration, purchase frequency and quantity per purchase play a role.

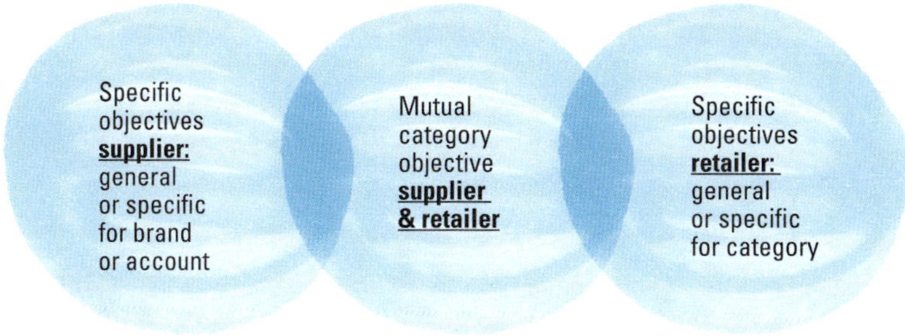

Figure 6.25
As well retailers as suppliers have objectives for an action. The best way is to formulate joint objectives if possible. (Category & Trade Company)

For both the manufacturer and retailer, there are three basic objectives: sales, volume and margin. In addition to that, retailers and suppliers have different objectives. The most usual ones are:

- Supplier; for A brand increasing the:
  - Penetration (acquisition)
  - Loyalty (binding)
  - Frequency/volume (filling)
  - Market share

- Retailer
  - Increasing number of customers
  - Increasing basket size
  - Making fans (loyalty)
  - Market share

If the goal is determined, the next step is to determine best fit in policy.To do so, an evaluation of the promotions is necessary. The assessment of any type of promotion's impact is mainly based on this evaluation. Use external data from IRI or Nielsen for the evaluation, but also use of internal and store data.

For manufacturers and retailers the evaluation will answer the following questions:

- What promotions are successful in relation to the relevant KPIs? To what extent is the forecast or objective realized?
- What did the promotion do for the entire category?
- Did it lead to extra sales instead of regular sales?
- Which promotion technique works best?
- To what extent was there forward buying?
- To what extent was there brand switching?
- To what extent do we subsidise customers who would have bought the product anyway?
- On which brand or retailer should we use the remaining promotion budget?
- Did it take place in all the stores or just in some of them?
- What can we improve in the execution on the shop floor or the communication in the flyer?

Based on the evaluation, you can optimize the current promotional approach by concluding:

- What to stop?
- What to improve?
- What to continue?
- What to learn from competitors and other categories?

What to stop? - Examples:

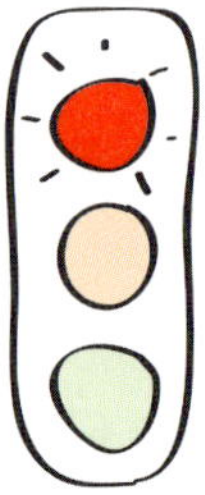

- TV advertising investments in relation to a brand A or mechanism 'X' for retailer 1. The additional investment does not provide a lifting effect.
- Promoting a segment of the assortment because of the high costs for flyers and poor profitability for suppliers, only if it is necessary for example, to obtain distribution.
- After using the same theme continuously, it might wear out. Initiate brainstorming sessions with colleagues and retailers, in order to find new or better themes.

What to improve? - Examples:

- Spreading the promotion throughout the year and anticipate on the right moments
- Reconciliation of suppliers' promotion proposals and planning of retailers' themes. Deployment of the promotion in a theme week, because generally it has more impact than in an ordinary week
- Increase effectiveness of the promotion by adding other assortments of brand A or private label.
- Improve the design and attractiveness of the display in the store.

What to continue? - Examples:

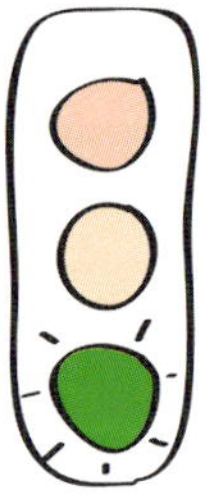

- Price theme 25% off, an elastic theme with reduced markdown. Deeper prices-offs usually do not give better results.
- Combining the promotion of brand A in category X with brand B in category Y.

In addition, also promotions can wear out. After a few years, they are perceived as normal and contribute less and less. Creativity and innovation can increase the promotion's effect; new promotions stand out more and generate more impact. The counterpart is of course that new promotions require more work than repeating old ones.

Considerations for promotion:

- How often and how long we should promote a category?
- What times are most suitable for promotion?
- Are we going to promote the entire category, or just one or a few items?
- Is an introduction suitable as attention grabber for the entire store?
- What kind of promotion is best for the category or the product?
- Do we focus on introductory discounts (a low try out price) for a new product or do we stimulate multi-buy (3=2)?
- Which medium is best suited to communicate the promotion?
- Is the promotion supported by a flyer, leaflet, website, TV-commercial, Facebook, Twitter?

- And in the shop, is the promotion supported by displays or tastings?
- Should we consider cross promotion (with a totally different product)?
- What is the timing in relation to the TV campaign and competition?
- Is the promotion designed for all retailers or can we differentiate?

Price promotions are often major disruptions in the regular processes for both retailer and supplier. Therefore, organizations with Every Day Low Pricing (EDLP) create a lot of cost advantages. They promote less or not and optimize well-defined and standardized processes. Various tests proof that all costs in logistics and stock replenishment in the store, can be 10 to 15% cheaper with EDLP. The question is how to keep attracting customers and increasing the conversion. Other types of communication and promotions should be devised for this.
Some cost advantage can be achieved with a perfect promotion plan between retailers and suppliers. The following model shows all activities related to promotions at both retailer and supplier. The model also indicates the areas in which precise interaction (exchange) should take place in order to achieve optimization.

Because retailers are very eager on differentiation, and thus on speciality products or promotions (what can suppliers do to strengthen my format's image), this subject will gain in importance during the annual contract agreements.

Figure 6.26 **Promotion interaction areas between retailers and suppliers**

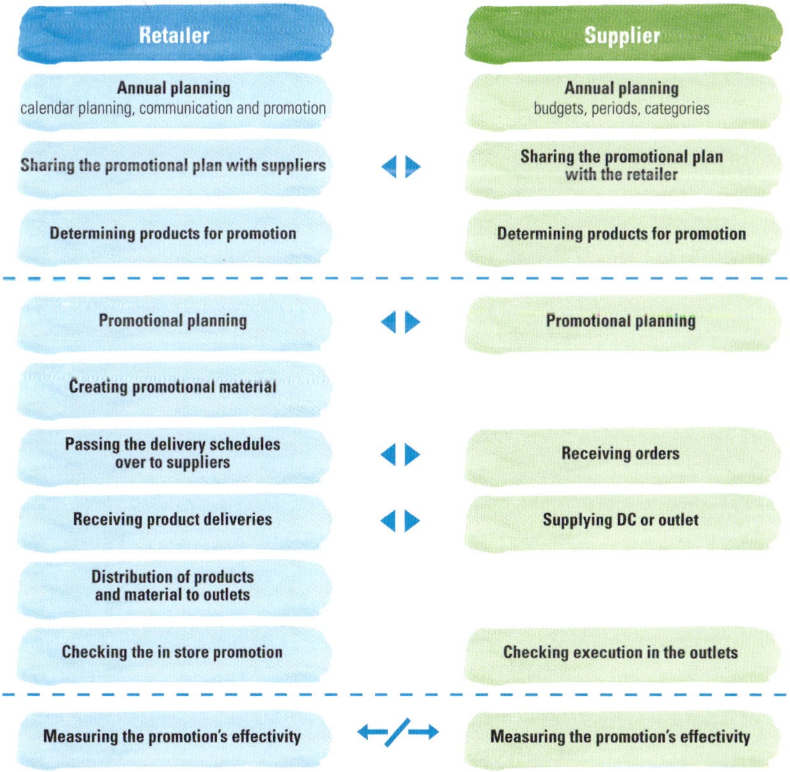

Retailers and suppliers have their own area of interests. Retailers have a lot to do with the execution of the promotion in leaflets, logistics and on the shop floor. Suppliers focus more on orders and delivery.

6.8.4 The Business Case

If the plan is created, it is important to get the management's approval before we can proceed to implementation. The business case is the estimate of the profitability of the measures and investments as well as the costs and effort needed for it.
The investment plan will be weighed against other plans. Its profits will be measured by their potential: where will these revenues come from? The result is a revenue and market share growth, and can be split between more customers or a higher spending (number of items, more expensive products, and more side sales). The revenue growth can also be specified per store.

The costs are the costs that have to be made for new store materials, communication in leaflets, on TV or social media, as well as training activities for staff, and also in cleaning up obsolete inventories and write off old materials. As the impact of a plan gets bigger, it is more important to have a good support for it in the business case.

6.9 Implementing the category plan

Every good plan is made up of 2 phases: it is conceived first and than it is implemented. We call it secure and deploy. This includes a lot of work and there is a lot that can go wrong. Suppliers often overlook the implications of a plan and what it means for the procedures at the stores. To execute the plan, it means that something will be changed in the store itself. The same applies to the composition of the assortment, the shelf, the way of ordering, the stock in store and inventory in the distribution center, and so much more.
It is very important for a retailer to make a kind of standard script for his own organization in which all the practical elements to be regulated are written. Those can be divided into several types:

- Anything to do with criteria for the retail brand and the building blocks for positioning;
- All types of information that can enhance the understanding of the quality of the analyses;
- All the elements that have to do with the physical store such as planograms, assortments composition, display locations and so on;
- Everything that has to do with data management: article code, shelf code, shelf cards, distribution and order code, administrative changes, payment policies and so on;
- Everything that has to do with financial controlling; impact on margin mix in the store, discount schemes, promotional fees, payment terms and so on;
- Everything that has to do with logistics; changes in ways and moments of ordering and delivery of goods;
- Modifications in assortment and promotion. The impact of assortment adjustments and promotion on the buying behaviour of customers and the handling in the store and at the checkout

The diagram on the following page provides a basic scheme that can be developed into an overall roadmap.

Figure 6.27 **Implementation of the category plan**

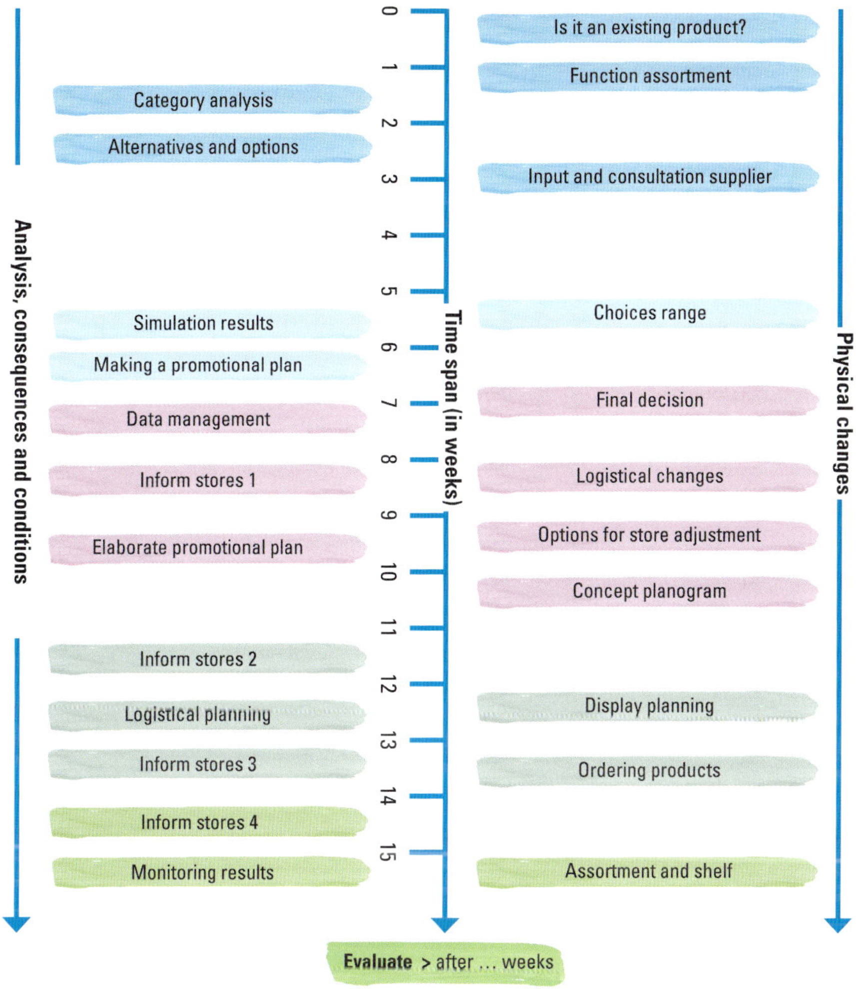

This is a schematic representation of the steps that should be completed for an implementation plan, divided in physical changes (left) and other measures.

Focus points for information:

- Who needs to be informed on shelf changes? Franchisers? Store managers? Department managers? Store employees? Format managers? Sales agents of suppliers?
- Is the product adapted in the database?
- Has the planogram been adjusted?
- How far in front should we provide information?
- How often should we inform everybody?
- Which media do we use for our message?
- Can sales agents play a role in the communication?
- How important is sufficient support on the shop floor for all these changes?
- Should I create support for innovations with sampling or employee premiums?
- When does this information has to be removed from the shelf?

6.10 The evaluation of the plan

Figure 6.28 **Everyday Category Management focusses on four aspects:**

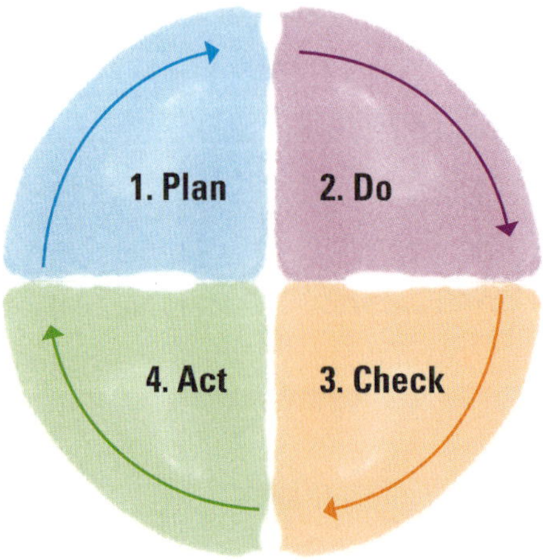

1. **Plan:** develop the category plan
2. **Do:** implement the category plan
3. **Check the results:** what is done well and what can or should be improved
4. **Act:** adjust the plan and activities in response to the results

In fact, an evaluation plan is no more than on a previously agreed time to double check all originally made plans with the original objectives. You must use the same forms, the same check lists, the same templates as those used at the beginning of the operation. But now (so to speak) with a red marker, in order to make it easier, you have to make a base matrix which can be used as a framework for an evaluation.

In advance a Category Manager, in consultation with Format Managers (and where possible, suppliers) defines the criteria which should be measured. Mostly, they are the following:

1. The qualitative targets which are difficult to measure with turnovers. That may be the format's image; the positioning of the retail brand relative to the competition; customers become ambassadors;
2. The objectives around shopper behaviour are: more customers, fuller shopping carts, loyal customers. The format's objectives. That has partly to do with the qualitative goals, though these targets are measurable. For example, price distance with respect to competition, number of primary customers and so on;
3. Market share and fair share, how are we doing in relation to the competition and to the retail format as a whole?
4. The turnover, volume and margin goals are obviously to be measured very well. Certain categories may deliberately score a low margin, to be able to score better on other ranges.
5. Results of promotions, introductions and new planograms.

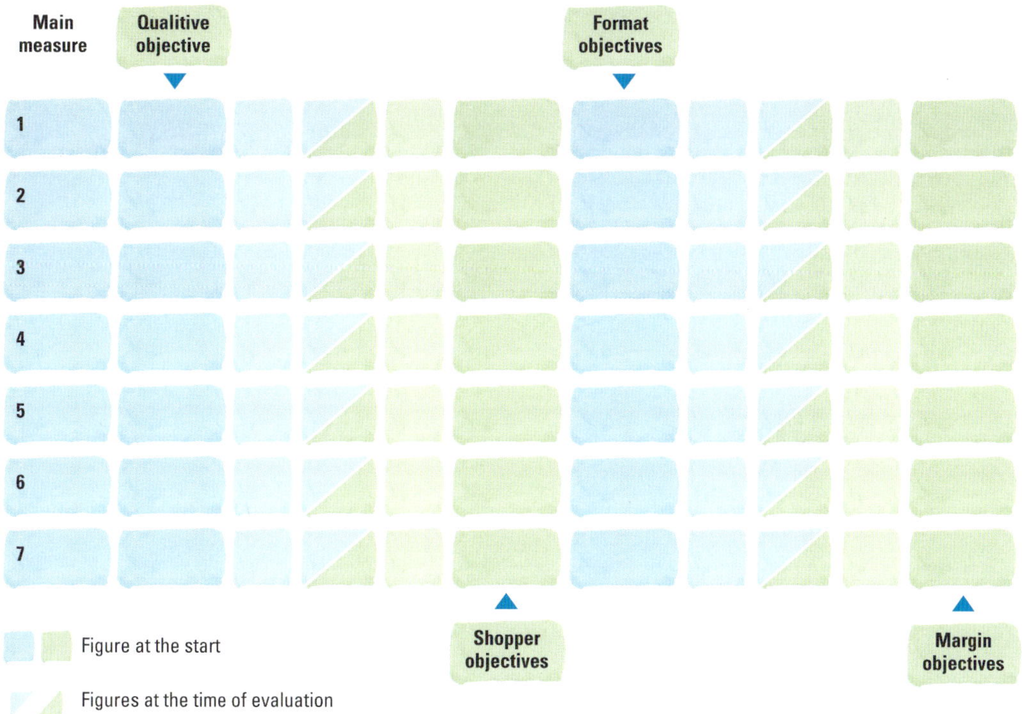

Table 6.9

Basic figure for evaluation divided by criteria that can be measured.

When to evaluate?

It is customary to let the frequency of evaluation depend on the function of the respective category. The more important an assortment group is, the more frequent we need to evaluate it. Rule of thumb is that very important categories are evaluated on a quarterly basis (or per promotion) and that stable categories in which not much has changed, are evaluated only once a year. An evaluation secures also the plan: in addition to the hectic pace of the day, we pay attention to the long term progress: are we on schedule with planned activities from the category plan? Are the activities undertaken effective or do we need to adjust the plan to realize our objectives? And so, we will perform a little better every day.

Chapter 7

Category Management and the organization of retailer & supplier

Not all retailers have a whole department for Category Management; this applies to retailers in food as well as non food. In fact, some retailers comply with a purchasing-only department while others deal on the detailed level with their supply chain and arrange supplier audits before delivery. These differences between retailers ask for manufacturers that are flexible enough to deal with each one efficiently.

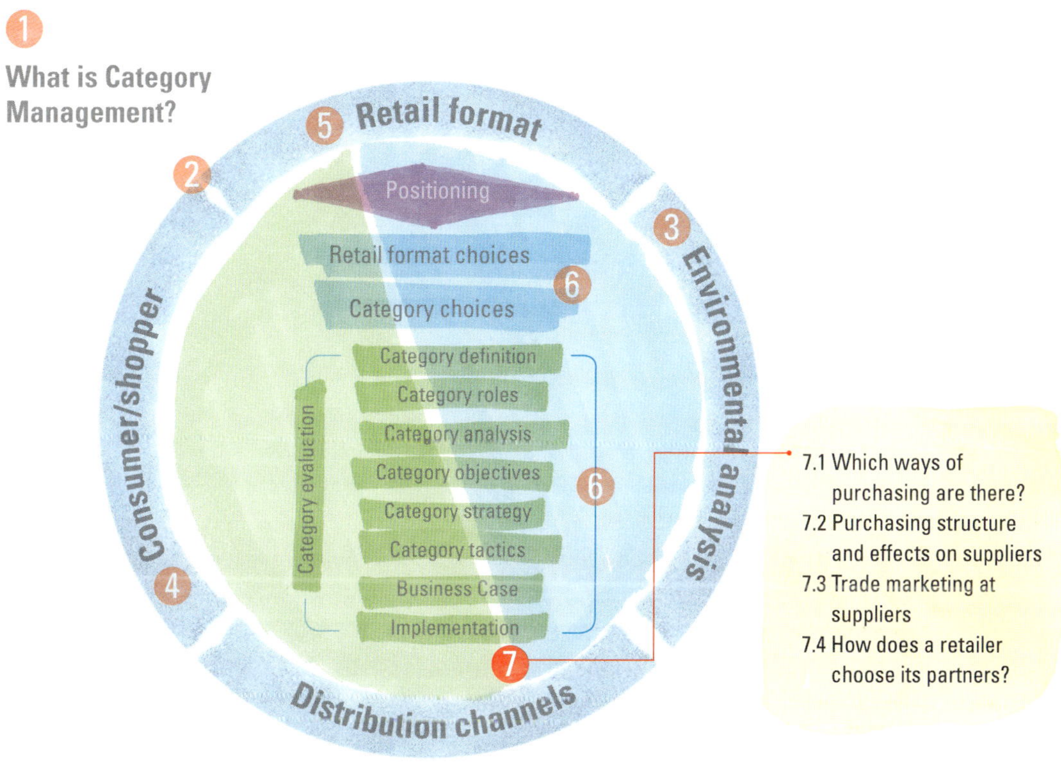

In this chapter we describe the various processes of procurement and their effects on retailers and suppliers.

7.1 Which processes of procurement are there?

The organization of the retailer determines the scope of the supplier.

The organization of the retailer determines the scope of the supplier.
Retailers with a strong price focus (hard discounters) concentrate primarily on the purchasing process. All other functions of the Category Management procurement process will be executed 'along the way'. Some organizations are so intertwined with their suppliers that there is hardly room for a free negation Examples of these organizations can be found in the car and airplane industry. In the food industry companies like McDonalds are vertically integrated and conduct business through an open book system with a lot of suppliers. This situation is totally different for hard discounters like Aldi, with simple criteria for annual agreements, an effective procurement system about the product quality, the purchase price and the volume of the purchases. Aldi adheres to the purchase amounts and expects its suppliers to fulfill the quality and price agreements. During the year, nothing needs to be changed and there is no need for additional agreements. Between these two extremes, many variables are possible.

The way a retailer is organized has its limitations for both retailer and manufacturer. We will discuss that in this chapter.

If not only the purchasing department decides
Many retailers are organized in a way that not only the purchasing department decides on agreements between retailer and manufacturer. Several other departments can be involved (from retail format to logistics). In that case, there is a Decision Making Unit (DMU) that affects the commercial process between retailers and suppliers. Suppliers often underestimate the complexity of this internal process. We summarize the different ways in which retailers are organized; these are four additions to the pure procurement process. Then there are five different areas of interest surrounding the selection of ranges, each with its own implications for suppliers:

1. The classic purchasing function focusses on selecting suppliers, assortments and purchasing prices. A low purchase price and related fees are central to the purchase process;
2. Broadening the focus from purchasing to merchandising and promotion. Agreements on flyers, displays and events are subjects added to the field. Sometimes this is done by separate staff members; sometimes it is part of the buyer's tasks;
3. Retail format management. This mainly concerns the determination of and/or filling in the formats selected building blocks. For this function in the purchasing process, somebody from retail format management is added periodically. For example during the annual targets, terms and conditions negotiations with priority or key suppliers;
4. Logistics and business control. Especially when large assortments and a constant high flow are important, reducing logistics costs and inventory formation and simplifying of processes are essential. In this situation, the purchasing team is therefore provided with extended expertise in logistics and control. Every little possibility to make the total distribution more efficient will be evaluated separate.

5. Quality control. These are experts with knowledge about the primary process in the chain. They do not negotiate purchase prices, but negotiate with knowledge about the way of producing, about raw materials. They know if a manufacturer is productive enough, whether there are enough quality safeguards in his process and so on. Some retailers have a number of specialists in company or they hire these experts. It is used in those ranges that are essential for the retailer's format, like fresh produce or private label, and when it involves unique assortments. A retailer usually has four goals with this additional staff position in the purchasing process:
    1. He wants safety and guarantees for those products that could harm the retail brand.
    2. He wants to be sure that he really gets the necessary volumes for the format, also in the longer term.
    3. He wants to eliminate unnecessary costs from the supply chain.
    4. He wants to create unique products (special recipes).

Table 7.1 **The various ways in which retailers purchase**

Involved in the purchasing	Consequences for Category Management	Consequences for suppliers
The purchasing department only	All the authorization to take decisions (depending on management). Also runs greater internal risks on loss of credibility.	Focus on negotiations and providing assistance to the Category Manager so he can take defensible decisions.
+ Merchandising and promotion	Extra emphasis on income for promotions and the attractiveness of the format's promotions on shopper behaviour.	Spreading the budgets well and focus on realization of agreements made on the shop floor.
+ Format Management	Extra emphasis on what influence assortment decisions have on the power of the retail format. Asks for unique promotions and assortments.	Supplier will have to prove more that he knows the format's secrets and that he can provide tailor-made solutions that are beneficial to the format.
+ Logistics and control	Extra emphasis on reducing complexity and costs and increasing service levels.	Own logistics (or production) specialists necessary to be able to also realize the complex arrangements.
+ Chain control specialists	Pre-selection and monitoring of suppliers' possibilities are made and criteria are provided by specialists.	Transparency of internal processes and production methods is necessary.

The five ways in which retailers organize their purchases are in the model mentioned above in the blue segments. The most simple method is the pure purchasing department. In fact we can describe the other four methods of purchasing as an extra dimension on the pure purchasing. Mostly, the responsibility of the purchasing department grows as the responsibility for merchandising and promotion is added to their department. In the next step, the purchasing department works more intensively with the retail format and will be co-responsible for the administration of typical retail building blocks. And again the next step after that will be when the purchasing department is involved with the logistics and finance departments. On the last step the chain, quality control specialists are active to supply the buyers of information about the suppliers themselves. This list is of course only a summary of a complex practice. Each retailer can be different from this setup and in practice; these steps will be combined in different possibilities.

International purchasing makes the process more complex

These five factors play similar roles at large retailers and also outside of the food sector. When we put those five variables in a scheme with, on the vertical axis, the different possibilities of purchasing (from local purchases to international buying desks), a list of the most common ways how retailers are organized, is created. Aldi and Tesco are good examples.

Table 7.2 **How does Aldi purchase?**

	Purchasing	Merchandising and promotions	Format Management	DMU with logistics and control	Chain control on core assortment
Local purchasing	A 3%				
National purchasing	A 84%				
International purchasing	A 8%				
Buying desks	A 5%				

Here we filled in Aldi as example. A = Aldi.
In the left triangle you see the percentage of the total purchase volume in value.

Example Aldi

Aldi has a very simple method of purchasing. They purchase internationally but on the basis that other independent distribution centres of Aldi can join in. The quality control is done under the supervision of the purchaser. This applies also to other criteria. Furthermore, local purchasing activities (of one distribution centre) can be rolled out to other distribution centres.

Table 7.3 **How does Tesco purchase?**

	Sheer purchasing	Merchandising and promotions	Format Management	DMU with logistics and control	Chain control on core assortment
Local purchasing	4% T	3% T	3% T		2% T
National purchasing	66% T	40% T	30% T	50% T	20% T
International purchasing	25% T	20% T	5% T	20% T	10% T
Buying desks	5% T			3% T	

The left triangle shows the percentage of the total purchasing volume in value (estimation). The numbers in the 2nd to the 5th column are a part of the total percentage for the purchasing column. Different ways of purchasing can occur at the same time, which is why on the horizontal beam the total percentage can be bigger than 100%.

Example: Tesco

Tesco is a worldwide retail organization that has the most advanced commercial department's setup. They have the possibility to purchase locally and Tesco stimulates this (mostly on the advice of the Format Manager). Tesco purchases internationally too, sometimes through a buying desk. Merchandising and promotion are important decision making criteria for promotions with suppliers. Simultaneously there are agreements with specialists about the chain control and logistics.

7.2 What are the effects on the purchasing structure of the retailer?

Based on the five most important fields of interest that surround the organization of purchase, it is important to compare the direct consequences of each model which each other. This is important for the retailer, but also for the supplier who wants to do business with the relevant retailer.

We mapped the important differences in the model below here. It will be clear that a retailer can use different models for different product ranges. A retailer's use of chain control on the range will be limited. Usually he does that only for the ranges that are really strategic for the retail brand.

Table 7.4 **Method of organizing**

Way of organizing	Necessary quality of people	Desired output	Effect on the cost structure	Dominant business processes	Features of the commercial structure
1. Pure purchase	Orientated on negotiation. Deal making. Strong rational and commercial skills.	Low purchase price. Perfect value for money.	Low purchasing costs. Which does not always mean that the total chain cost are also low.	Measuring is knowing. Price measurements are significant for benchmarks and price guarantees.	Purchasing department dominates the business organization. Other departments are supportive.
With the addition of					
2. Merchandising and promotion	Commercial resourcefulness. Being able to switch fast. Creative.	Surprising and attracting customers with changing promotions. The retail format remains attractive.	Risks for peak costs and investments that are not easily translated into immediate profits.	Lots of room for deals, logistical peaks (loading supplies) and overstock handling.	Flyers and promotions are important, therefore sales promotions are leading in purchasing processes.
3. Format management	Strategical power. Being able to switch fast. Being able to see cohesion.	The retail format turns into a brand and is backed by solid and unique characteristics.	Value creation is an important goal so also less direct-profitable decisions can be made.	Long term focus is important and many small details in the operation will be raized to benchmark (to support brand building).	Format management is leading the organization (anchored at management level) and everything else is secondary.
4. DMU with logistic control	Financial and logistic expertise. Willing to bring quality in the mix.	Efficiency in all processes, low capital requirements, high inventory turns.	Will affect costs and cash flow.	Efficiency in logistics and all information processes is dominant. Prevention of peaks and process disruption.	Logistics and control are as important staff members involved in the decision-making on assortment adjustments.
5. Chain monitoring on (core) range	Food technology. Interested in manufacturer processes, recipes and raw materials.	Safety. Unnecessary costs are removed from the chain. Can select unique products.	A kind of open book system is being created. Users get substantive arguments if unnecessary costs are taken out of the supply chain.	The supply chain's transparency and testing out the candidate supplier's innovations are important.	Control specialists have a strong voice in selecting (potential) suppliers and are focussed on a long term relationship and transparency.

In this model, the descriptions of the staff member's core competencies are only briefly noted. We could devote a separate chapter to this subject only. Further training and assessment of actual or lack of competencies in the team, are essential on each of the five 'purchasing levels'.

Purchasing methodology has often five stages

In any way that a retailer organizes its purchasing department, at any given moment, differences of opinion will arize between supplier and retailer. It is a part of the 'negotiation game'. The purchaser who gets what he wants from a supplier within a minute, will wonder in the weeks after if he really made the best deal.

Tactics are also used in the 'game'. One of those tactics is punishing the supplier. In the diagram below, we show the corresponding tactic stages.

Table 7.5 **The five stages of Purchasing Methodology**

1	Negotiations
2	Threats
3	Completion of threat
4	Inventory of mutual 'damage'
5	Negotiations

If no agreement is reached in the negotiation (stage 1), then comes the next stage, the threat. That is the communication of the consequences when one of the two negotiating parties did not get what he wanted. When the threat does not lead to a result, then it must be put into action. That is the third stage which does not occur often. Sometimes the effects of carrying out those threats make it big into the news. But however long the effect of a threat lasts (example, a boycott), in the end the parties should sit together around the table again. This is when stage four occurs; determining the damage caused to both parties and when that has happened, the negotiations can start again (stage 5).

The effect on the supplier

A retailer sits in the 'driver's seat' in many situations. Essentially it means that the criteria and characteristics of the retailer are leading for the entire supply chain and especially for the supplier. This is not only about the demands that come by during the purchasing process. It also applies to the characteristics which the retailers is not totally aware of.

If a retailer thinks he has the knowledge about meat production and tries to act as a specialist during the negotiations and it appears quickly that he is not, it can then give way to complications in the purchasing negotiations. As a supplier would you tell him that he is wrong? Or would you try to benefit from the retailers' poor knowledge? Do you help him building up knowledge to fill the gaps or do you let him believe that he is an expert? All options for a supplier have their own advantages and disadvantages.

The stakes are high

One of the most important consequences of concentrating on purchasing in a chain is that for suppliers, there is a lot at stake. The number of suppliers is relatively big and the number of purchasers is limited. Furthermore a retailer has limited deciding moments - the suppliers know this and for them it is essential to make a deal. Retailers know that there is a lot at stake for the suppliers but underestimate the importance of those interests or are not able to see it as a whole. But they also know that the importance and the interest often are at the expense of objectivity. But the 'power' of the retailer decreases when one of the following developments occur:

- There is only power when there is overcapacity. If a retailer can choose the products because there are too many suppliers or because the volume of this product is too big on the market, the retailer will have the power. The other way around is true too; if there is less choice of suppliers or the supply volume is lower than the demand, the balance of power shifts to the supplier.
- If a retailer finds it necessary to have a certain quality, variety or supplier properties for his retail format, then the purchasing power is lower than in the previous case.
- If a supplier finds the quality and transparency of the production process very important for his own reputation, then the influence of the supplier is bigger.
- If a supplier possesses certain knowledge (about the market, about the origin or any other form of knowledge as well), that retailers do not have (but find very important), then the balance of power shifts to the supplier.

What does the choice of the purchasing model from the retailer in practice mean for the supplier? On the diagram on the next page (the same format as in the previous section) are the possibilities which are available to the supplier.

Retail organization	Necessary quality of account management	Desired output	Effect on the cost structure	Way of working within commerce of department	Support in the supplier's structure
1. Pure purchase	Orientated on negotiation. Strong commercial and psychological skills. Understanding what the bottom line is.	Sufficient profits and sales volume and good argumentation to defend a deal with other customers and internally.	Should not have a negative effect on your own fixed and variable costs that are not anticipated.	The negotiation process is a game that should also internally be played psychological well. Closing a deal within five minutes always raises questions afterwards.	The production specialists should provide input on the absolute basic prices. And for the psychological game a managing director may play his own role.
With the addition of					
2. Merchandising and promotion	Contributing to creative processes. Knowledge at hand from other countries. Knowing how large the playing field is.	Focused on sales incentives and repeat purchases of their own product or brand. Brand recognition needs to be stronger.	Must come from the budgets that are determined in advance and these costs are therefore previously weighed against the returns.	Determine which creative ideas whether or not add unnecessary cost and complexity.	A below the line advertising agency (or promotion department) can provide ideas. A database with ideas from other countries is a perfect backup.
3. Format management	Understanding retail strategy. Knowledge of the retail format's features and building blocks. Knowledge of all strengths and weaknesses and of what opportunities a supplier has to contribute to the format's growth.	Strengthening the retailer's format, also independent from the supplier's services and products.	If the result is that the retailer depends on the supplier, one should determine what that the value is for the supplier.	Continuous analysis of the retailer is very important and trade marketing is an important pillar to strengthen the supplier's position.	Trade marketing is the key to this layer. Knowledge of general retail developments and the retailer's SWOT-analysis should be up-to-date.
4. DMU with logistic control	Being able to deal with the decision-making process with several people and having the basic knowledge to assess logistical and financial impact of the proposals.	Making predictable and planable revenues and stable profits.	Will enhance the predictability of production and revenues and reduce excess inventory.	Account Management and Trade Marketing should take care of their own specialists in logistics and finance to be able to resist the supplier's thumb screws with rational arguments.	Production and logistics service providers can give input on annual agreements. Optio-nal cooperation with other suppliers with whom co-logistics can be realized.
5. Chain monitoring on (core) range	Having sufficient knowledge to as-sess the possibility of transparency and knowing whoro to pick up missing knowledge. Building a confidential relationship with the retailer.	Retailer's insights of the quality of the supplier's producing possibilities. Even-tually, one should have the idea that the retailer can't grow without this supplier.	Even with complete transparency, the supplier will have to make it clear why certain price adjustments are necessary	The retailer could be provided with new and good ideas and concrete plans should be tested under the supplier's direction.	Production specialists and R&D-departments should continuously be present in this process.

Table 7.6

Based on the five basic ways a retailer purchases, we can put five departments or functions at a supplier, opposite to them. In the diagram we have tried to summarize it. With the horizontal lines we display the official counter partners with the focus on the contact (main subject of the converzation). It does not mean that the involved staff members really meet periodically. But the experience of these members will be included in the contact between retailers and suppliers. Often the Category Manager (or purchaser) together with the Account Manager will coordinate the entire process.

Figure 7.1 **The Decision Making Units (DMU's) from retailer and supplier**

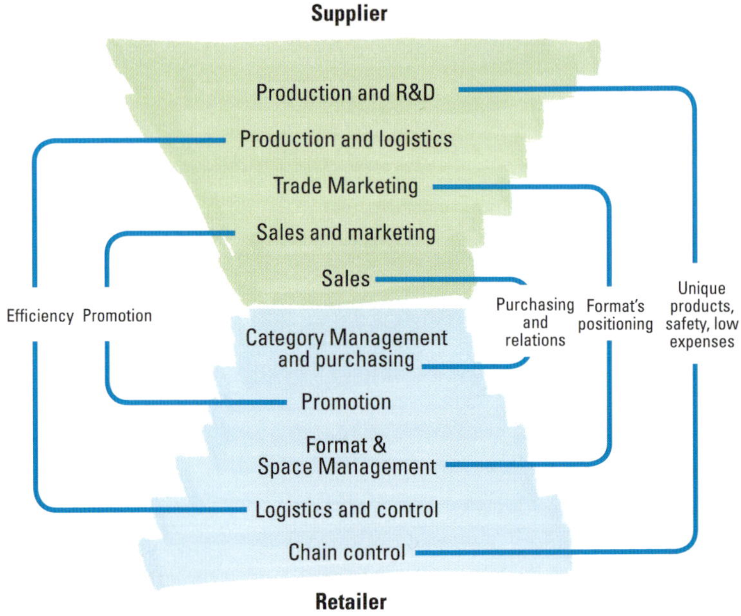

Tthe above model brings all departments (from both retailers and suppliers) involved around assortments into the decision. The lines indicate which departments of the supplier (top model) liaise with departments of the retailer (bottom of the model). However, the director of these interactions will often be the Category Manager.

Retailers and manufacturers look different at assortments

That a retailers view on an assortment differs from a suppliers view is obvious. For a retailer, the assortment is a way to make his store look different from the competitors. For a manufacturer, a range is efficient if he can sell one product to as many as possible different stores.

Figure 7.2 **Focus of retailers and manufacturers**

We summarize the differences between a retailer and a supplier as such: a retailer looks at the format and its customers. And a supplier looks at the consumer (the user) and at the various channels through which to reach the consumer and he wants to emphasize the identity of his own product (brand) as much as possible.

Potential conflicts often are unnecessary conflicts

Retailers and manufacturers who do not understand each other easily get into conflicts that would have been avoided if they knew and respected each other's role and position better. In figure 7. 2, we present the main sources of conflicts (and misunderstandings) in one overview.

Figure 7.3 **Specific considerations and sources of conflicts**

Retailer tactics and considerations	**Supplier** tactics and considerations
Minimize national brands and products	As far as possible all retailers get the same product
As much as possible unique products (including private label)	Minimizing separate and specific things for one retailer
More choices for shoppers	Fewer product variants per plant
Less disruption of the shopping process	Many promotions on the shop floor
Fast delivery and supplements directly from factory	Minimize production sites
No excess stock in the supply chain	Countries should only regulate local distribution

In an exaggerated way, we put the focus differences between a retailer and a supplier beside each other. Being honest and clear about it, will make the Category Manager's and Account Manager's work easier.

The key of many conflicts between retailers and suppliers is that differentiation is increasingly important for retailers. The retailer wants something that the other has not. But for the supplier standardization (offering all the same) is of major importance in order to keep costs under control.

In the future, we will see that vendors (including brands) will be able to resolve this paradox:

- Suppliers choose a retailer who brings in an innovation and the retailer uses this innovation exclusivity to differentiate the retail brand better;
- The scale needed for the supplier will be achieved internationally. What he does is exactly the same in the other countries;
- Gradually the supplier will even develop special products for a certain type of customer. Maybe even separate brands.

7.3 Trade marketing at suppliers

Virtually no manufacturer has its commercial departments set up the same way. And that means the work and the responsibilities of the commercial departments (account management, marketing management and trade marketing) can be quite different.

To summarize, we show how the supplier's staff member could have contact with the retailer's staff member.

Figure 7.4 **Splitting tasks**

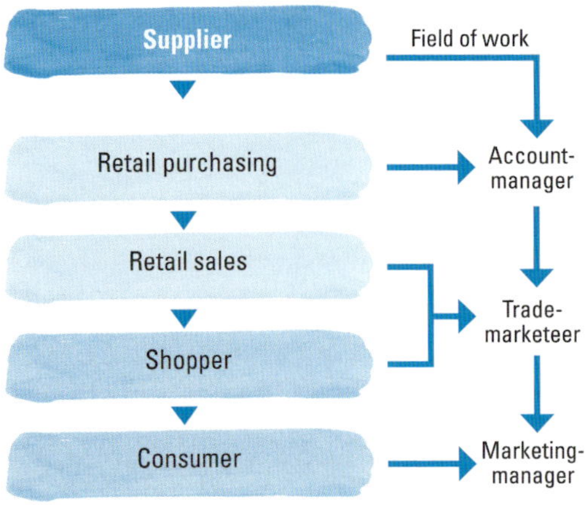

When we visualize the functional commercial chain of a supplier, he has to deal with four links after him: the retailer's purchase department, the retailer's sales department, the shopper (the purchasing customer) and the consumer. These four links all have different interests and a different way of looking at a supplier and vice versa. From these differences, we have put the work areas within from a suppliers' commercial department in the diagram above. The Account Manager interferes primarily with retailer. The Trade Marketer concentrates on the retail format's process and the way the shopper behaves. And the supplier's Marketing Manager looks primarily at consumers.

A supplier focuses of course on the field of the retailer, but also on the shopper's and consumer's behaviour. Those are four different components in the chain. The retailer's purchase department is in the field of the account manager. The way the items are sold from the supplier is in the field of the Trade Marketer and that goes also for the shopper behaviour. Sometimes the function of Trade Marketer is divided in other departments like Shopper Marketing and Category Management. And there are consumer behaviour and trends among consumers that concern the marketing department.

Trade marketing with suppliers varies greatly

For a retailer it is sometimes difficult to determine the supplier's commercial functions. He has to adjust his frame of reference of the supplier's staff member for each of the suppliers individually. Example: the freedom and professionalism of an Account Manager of manufacturer A with whom the Category Manager is in contact, can be totally different from the Account Manager of manufacturer B. The same applies to Trade Marketing, a phenomenon that appears at more and more suppliers. Roughly, there are four different ways to deal with trade marketing at manufacturers.

1. Trade marketing is besides Account Management and Marketing a fully independent department, responsible for the categories' growth in different channels and formats;
2. Trade marketing is part of the Marketing Department and it is mainly a analytic function that, especially with consumer marketing, analyses results of retail marketing and shopper behaviour;
3. Trade marketing is a part of Account Management and acts like a market analyst for the Account Manager's work and is responsible for formats;
4. There is no Trade Marketing and the work is done by Account Management.

In table 7.7, we disbribe the different models.

Table 7.7 **Trade Marketing can be done in different ways**

What does this mean for…	Trade marketing independently alongside Account Management and Marketing	Trade marketing as a part of Account Management
Qualities of Trade marketing	▶ Independent and proactive ▶ Own goals ▶ Understanding shoppers ▶ Understanding formats ▶ Long and short term strategy ▶ Decisive department manager	▶ Account oriented ▶ Derivative sales objectives ▶ Hardly insight into shoppers ▶ Understanding formats ▶ Short term strategy ▶ Analytical Sales Manager
Output (what to do)	▶ Channel Choices and Strategy ▶ Category Plans ▶ Category analysis within/of accounts ▶ Shopper research/insights/translation ▶ Retail Knowledge/insights ▶ Trade introductions	▶ (Contribution to) year/account plan ▶ Category analysis within accounts ▶ Retail knowledge/insights ▶ Presentations account (regular) ▶ Operational proposals on retail instruments
Internal collaboration	▶ Part of commercial MT ▶ Alignment marketing (consumer): introductions/ brand/product performance ▶ Shopper branding/communications ▶ Tuning Sales (retailer): assortment, promotions(pressure), pricing ▶ Presentation on the account level ▶ Tuning MT: Annual plan/strategy/budget	▶ Part of sales team ▶ Alignment marketing (consumer) ▶ Shopper branding/communications ▶ Tuning sales (retailer): ▶ Assortment, promotions(pressure), pricing presentation on account level, account presentations, annual performance appraisals ▶ Tuning sales team: support
Cooperation with retailers	▶ Provide analysis from shopper insights ▶ Provide analysis from retail tools ▶ Turn into concrete proposals on instruments ▶ Presenting introductions ▶ Strategic vision on retail instruments	▶ Provide analysis from retail tools ▶ Turning into concrete proposals on instruments ▶ Presenting introductions ▶ Contact often takes place via Account Manager (less direct contact)

What does this mean for…	Trade marketing as a part of Account Management and Marketing	Trade marketing, but the tasks are fulfilled by Account Management
Qualities of Trade marketing	▶ Product oriented ▶ Derivative marketing objectives ▶ View on (shopping) consumer ▶ Limited insight in formats ▶ Long term strategy ▶ Sales oriented marketer	▶ Pragmatic and reactive ▶ No Trade Marketing objectives ▶ Selective store data analysis ▶ View on sales operations at retail ▶ Short term strategy
Output (what to do)	▶ (Contribution to) marketing/strategic plan ▶ Category analysis per channel ▶ Consumers (poss. shopper) knowledge/insights ▶ Product/marketing presentations (regular) ▶ Operational proposals on marketing tools	▶ (Contribution to) year/account plan ▶ Category analysis within accounts ▶ Account presentations (regular) ▶ Operational proposals on assortment and promotions
Internal collaboration	▶ Part of the marketing team ▶ Reconciliation marketing (consumer) ▶ Product/brand presentation, shopper branding/ communication, interpretation brand in-store, consumer rights movements ▶ Tuning sales (retailer): (brand)introductions, consumer promotions ▶ Consumer pricing ▶ Tuning marketing team: support	▶ No regular consultations on trade marketing ▶ Ad hoc, reactive and short term agreements about: assortment, promotions(pressure), pricing ▶ Presentation at the account level, account presentations, annual performance appraisals
Cooperation with retailers	▶ Explaining introductions and promotions (minimal direct contact)	▶ Contact as an Account Manager with any additional information about assortment and promotions.

This table shows the four different ways in which a supplier organizes his Trade Marketing and the consequences this has for the tasks. Making this transparent helps a Category Manager to determine his own fields.

Figure 7.5 **Trade marketing at the manufacturer is being developed**

The value of Trade Marketing for a manufacturer appears to grow gradually. In the model on this page, we distinguish five different phases.

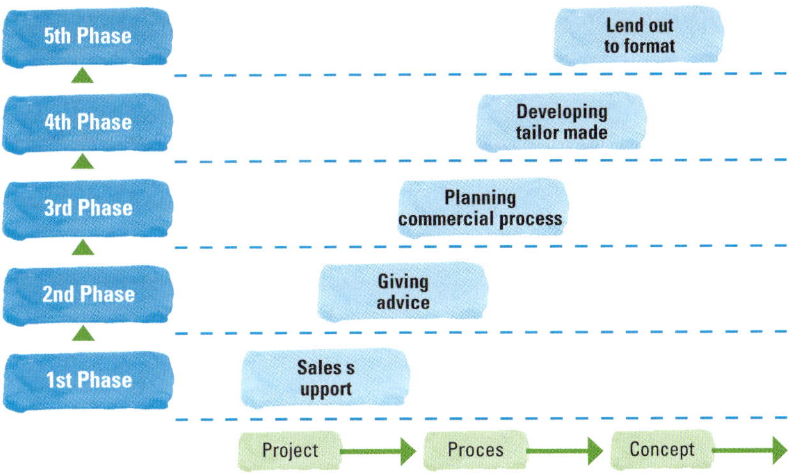

Trade marketing and its development process. It usually begins as a support function of the sales department. But in the end, it may become a function where a supplier is a specialist lent out to the retailer. Then this is no more a question of cooperation in the framework of a project. It is about a supplier as a co-builder of the concept (format) for the retailer.

In the first phase, Trade Marketing is no more than a way to support the sales department with analysis;

In the second phase, Trade Marketing is more mature and gives advice to the other different commercial disciplines;

In the third phase, Trade Marketing is responsible for the overall commercial process, but is still in a supporting role;

In the fourth phase, Trade Marketing is fully featured and presents tailor made ideas (nearly concepts) for a retail format or a channel;

In the final phase (it does not happen often but sometimes at major private label manufacturers) a Trade Marketeer is someone who is loaned to regular formats to help an important category of that format to be developed.

7.4 How does a retailer choose its partners?

A retailer's Category Manager always has too many focus areas, too little time for all those categories and little knowledge in each of these product groups. Then it is logical to think that he (if there are only three handicaps) can use the assistance of a supplier. However, there are some questions about that assistance.

First, there is the question of whether the supplier knows much more about a category. The second question is about the suspicion of alternative motives that a Category Manager is suspected to have of a supplier. Do I get, as a retailer, an objective advice from my supplier? On the other hand, a Category Manager has a lot to offer to a supplier, as he has knowledge about the shopper, the buying consumer. He is in possession of the sales data from the scanning data. He sometimes gets customer-card data from which an even better link can be made between the buying behaviour and the characteristics of a client.

That means that a trade agreement between a retailer and a supplier could be established easily, but a retailer is careful with that. A supplier will always delve into his clients. That should be the primary task of Trade Marketing or Account Manager or of both depending on how the supplier has organized his Trade Marketing (see 7.3).

Not always rational

A retailer does not always use completely logical or rational criteria when selecting his suppliers. Therefore it is not possible to give a good answer to the main question of this chapter. Sometimes the relationship between retailer and supplier is decided very high up in the organization. If a CEO or director/owner has certain arguments to give a supplier a preferred position then those are the circumstances a Category Manager has to live with.

It is clear retailers consider two things when they wonder if they should change their supplier. The first consideration is the question wether the operational consequences a change of supplier entails. What would it mean for the logistics? What would it mean for the frequency of delivery, for the automation or the processes in the shop? And so on. The second consideration is about all questions that cannot be expressed in terms of money such as the continuity of the supplier, the type of staff that the retailer has to deal with. Is the new supplier able to bring the retailer to a higher level in time? How dependant is the supplier of the retailer?

Discipline and invisible arguments

In addition to the considerations of an individual retailer sometimes the discipline appointments with its buying group play a major role. For the sake of the cooperation, decisions taken may not be the best solution for the individual retailer and he wholeheartedly acknowledges to the supplier that he actually would have been his first choice. In addition, historical ties often play an important role. A supplier may have helped the retailer to develop and that 'faith' from history is sometimes worth more than a few percent of benefits. And to make it even more complex, retailers can sometimes make irrational tactical considerations when choosing a supplier. The rational choice would make a manufacturer sometimes too powerful or the retailer can get too dependent on him. Furthermore, it can be a choice to have expected future development (a choice that can weaken the competition) or other logical considerations.

Regardless of these considerations there is still a kind of selection matrix to create. It is shown in tabel 7.6. On the horizontal axis are three key questions that apply to the retailer itself and which should be completed objectively, compared to competing retailers. On the vertical axis are five key questions which have an influence on the process of choosing a manufacturer in general.
In this way arize all sorts of combination questions that can facilitate a selection process. If the importance of the range for a retailer is very large and the craftsmanship of the retailer is low, then a retailer will want to choose a supplier who is very competent and committed to him. That is a kind of selection situation other than one at a low assortment interest and a skilled craftsmanship of the retailer. In the first case the dependency of the retailer grows and he would like to trust his supplier completely. In the second case he wants to exercize more power.

Figure 7.6 **Selection of the supplier by the retailer**

	Power of retail format: high or low?	Retailer's assortments importance: high or low?	Craftsmanship retailer: high or low?
Are there many suppliers in a category (international)?			
Is the supplier dominant through innovation and/or strong brands?			
Is the supplier a family business or a listed company?			
Has the supplier proven to be sustainable, successful and have sustainable relationships?			
Is the supplier skilled in sustainable development?			

The assessment of a base supplier is in relation to the characteristics of the retailer.

The retailer makes his choice not only by investigating whether a supplier is important in its sales and category, but also whether the supplier can help in distinguishing and strengthening the format.

Figure 7.7

If you are, as a supplier, indispensable because you make a major contribution to the revenue in the category, then you are a basic supplier. Retailers would prefer suppliers that are less important because they can be less dependent on this supplier. As a supplier, you can, however, also contribute to the growth of the category and format policy by sharing knowledge or contributing to strengthening the distinctiveness and the retail brand.

Interdependence

If a retail format is dominant and there are few suppliers, then the dependence of the basic supplier of that format is often very large and the willingness to invest in the retailer will be large. Conversely, the retail brand – as of the suppliers' craftsmanship is very large and has proven durable successes – cannot do without the supplier. This creates a strong mutual dependency.

How can Trade Marketing help the Category Manager?

A Trade Marketing Manager has a lot of knowledge of the category, the shopper and various sales channels and all the characteristics of those channels. He also has knowledge of the different formats in those channels. Often, that knowledge is more objective than the knowledge of the retailer in this area. But a Trade Marketing Manager will not always just make his knowledge available for any retailer. Here also applies a selection policy. A good Trade Marketing Manager will be selective in investing in a particular customer. Questions that a supplier will ask himself include:

- Is the format suitable for my range and for my brand?
- Does the format also have a long term chance of survival?
- Does the format grow faster than the market and also in the medium term?
- Does the format itself have much need for my brand and/or product range? Is there an open mind for my quality and strategic insight?
- How professional is the buyer?
- How professional is the Category Manager?

- How professional is retail management?
- How good are the franchisers and/or store managers?
- Is the information technology sufficiently adequate to provide better understanding and to promote interaction?

After all, the key quality of a trade marketing manager is that he is able to strengthen and improve the retail brand. Then you must, as Trade Marketing, also know to whom you will offer most of your knowledge.

Figure 7.8 **Selection of the format provided by Trade Marketing**

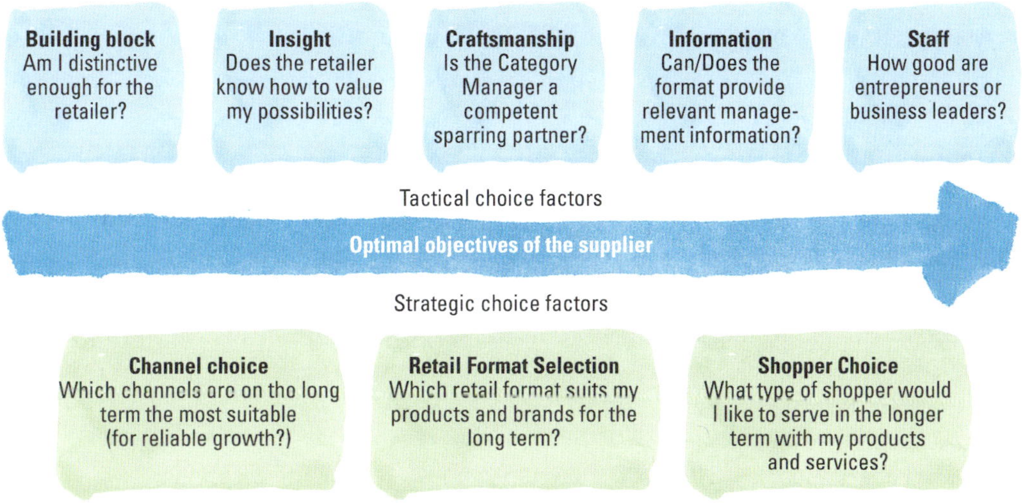

A supplier also has the 'power' to select a channel or format. Economies of scale can be achieved internationally with similar formats.

In the supplier's considerations, the consumer will always be at the centre. And the retailer is for the supplier only an intermediary. If the interests of a retailer and manufacturer are parallel then we can say that there is an optimal relationship. This is not always the case and there should be, besides strategic considerations, also tactical arguments (difficult to make a rational consideration) to consider a certain retailer as a primary relation.

The policy considerations

A good method for a supplier to anticipate to the Category Manager's way of thinking is table 7.8. It contains the retailer's different types of policy considerations (and consultation possibilities) on the vertical axis. On the horizontal axis are the expectations (and possibilities) for three types of suppliers. The absolute basic or priority suppliers are in the first column. These are the suppliers that enable the retailer to give an identity to his format. The other key suppliers are in the middle column and the regular suppliers in the last column.

Table 7.8 **What is expected of what sort of suppliers?**

Policy scenarios to manage suppliers	Priority supplier	Core supplier	Supplier
Management interference in the category policy	Each level	Selected levels	Partial allowed
Frequency of meetings	Monthly	Four times or twice a year	Twice a year
Making category plans with multiple suppliers	Yes	No, unless necessary	No
Uncovering the market strategy	Yes	Selective components	Only product supplier
Sharing necessary information	Scanning data overall category	On brand level	Limited
Annual KPI targets	Accomplished together	Negotiated and approved	Closing agreements
Promotion plans	First choice in options	Negotiation for free spaces	Negotiations

This table is a rule of thumb to put arrangements between suppliers and retailers in a real expectation pattern. A priority supplier may not only undertake much more in a relationship. He also has much more to prove. (This list of criteria is from the ECR experience of ten years collaborative projects between retailers and suppliers in different countries.)

Cooperation makes demands

Cooperation based on commercial agreements like the cooperation between any retailer and supplier cannot do without expectations and good arrangements. Good agreements in all measurable criteria are hardly a problem. Examples include agreements on terms, delivery, returns, promotional support.

But cooperation also gives expectations that are more difficult to express in solid numbers. Then we often talk about things as expectations about the quality of the staff at the suppliers. Are the Accounts Managers in a position to analyse a format; do they know what they are talking about when they come up with a value judgement on a competitive format? Does a Trade Marketing Manager have the ability to get things done in his own organization? All these questions can also be discussed and answered openly. But the same applies conversely. If a Category Manager agrees on something, is he able to realize that on the shop floor? Later, can he objectively evaluate or would he be under pressure from the franchisers or storemanagers.

A second expectation has to do with the extent to which a retailer and supplier are (or can be) straight to each other. Here too, there can be agreement on a number of neutral moments during the year on the mutual frankness. The hardest is to tell how much you trust each other.

And a third section with expectations concerns the way you work. What do they expect from each other? When does a retailer hear about plans for new items? When will a retailer analyse a range? When does a supplier hear that a competitor has made a quotation?

Chapter 8

Daily Category Management in 25 questions

Daily Category Management in 25 questions

This chapter is intended as a summary of the daily use of the insights into Category Management which are described in more detail elsewhere in this book.

Figure 8.1 **Category Management in conjunction**

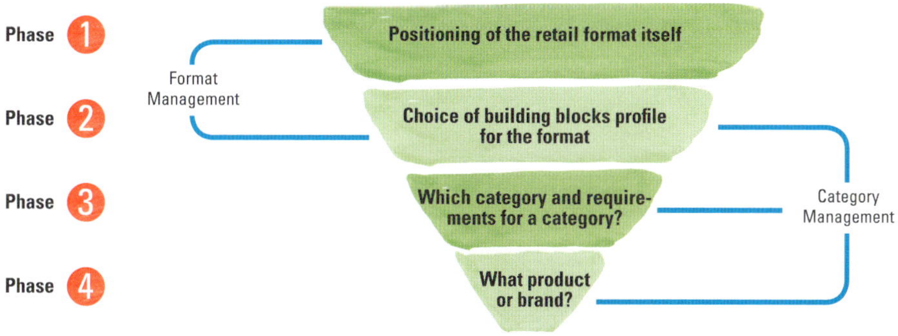

Category Management deals with assortment management and assortment selection. The overall policy consists of four phases as shown in the diagram. The first two phases are the work of the Format Manager, but provide an input for the work of the Category Manager. Phases three and four are the work of the Category Manager.

The phases in the above figure are worked out into a practical work plan for the Category Manager in figure 8.2. Phase two delivers the starting points of Category Management, but the Category Manager will be able to give his expertise (also from evaluations of previous experience) input to the decision-making phase 2.

Phase 1: Retailer Strategy

In this phase you set the component of the retailer's strategy that are important for establishing the category plan.

The key questions addressed in this phase:

1. What is the positioning of the format (the strong, distinguishing factors)? Is it still like a year ago?
2. In what areas did the competition make progress?
3. In what areas are threats for the next year?
4. What does that mean for the category concerned?
5. Has our target audience changed and do we still reach the same target audience?

Phase 2: Retail format building blocks

In this phase, you determine which categories are distinctive features of the format and which category components support the formats building blocks.

Key questions:

6. What are the strategic categories and category roles and what is the target audience of the format?
7. What categories/segments are important to the format and what role do they play?
8. Is there the need for new building blocks (if so, which ones) that give the format a better profile?
9. Are there enough suppliers to fill these new building blocks?
10. What are my requirements for those suppliers?

It is recommended to perform this analysis on an annual basis.

Figure 8.2 **Daily Category Management**

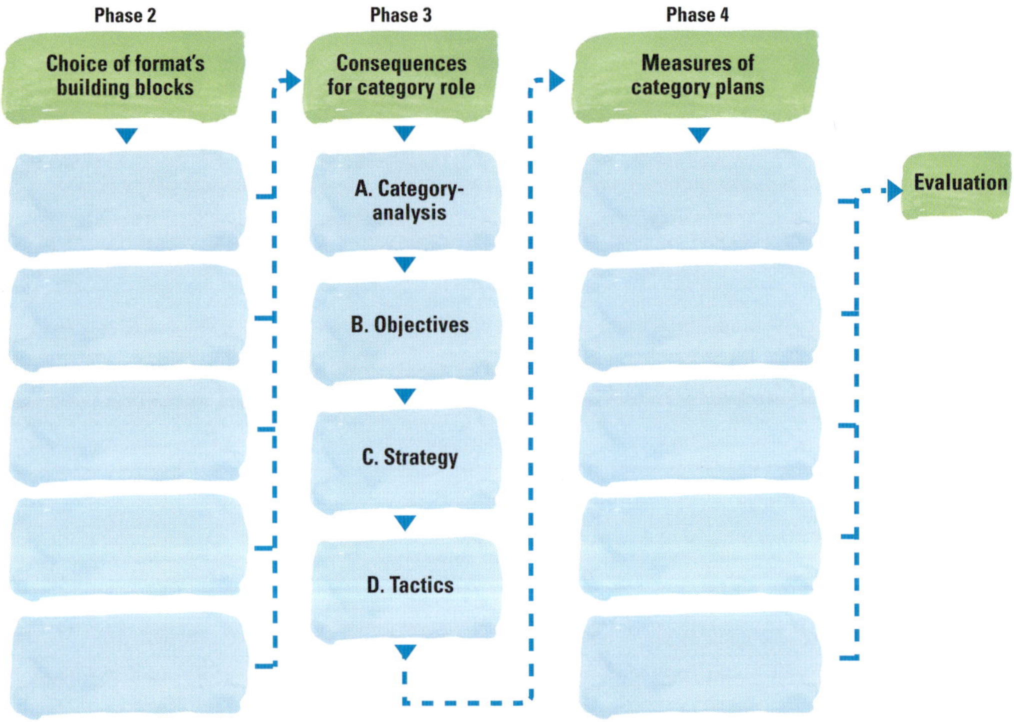

This is the basic diagram for daily Category Management as it functions for the Dutch retailers. The numbers above the scheme correspond to the numbers in the previous scheme. We have Phase 1 (positioning of the format) which is not more elaborate, because this is not an activity of category management. A format positioning is usually an element. The profile of a format requires building blocks. These building blocks are often products or categories. As a result, there are in fact already the first influential assumptions arising at this stage, with which the Category Manager has to deal. Then comes the choice for the role of the category (phase 3) and in the fourth phase the concrete measures. And finally, evaluation (see question 25).

Phase 3: Category plans

In this phase you go through four steps in which you (along with your main suppliers) jointly formulate the objectives and concrete action for the Category Management Plan and commit to them.

Step A: Category Definition and Analysis

Key questions:

11. What is the category definition according to of the shopper and which groups are included?
12. What are the trends and shopper insights that we know? What is the shopper journey and what is the shopper decision tree?
13. How should the SKU's be segmented within the category? Should this segmenting be different from what we always do? Based on consumer needs and decision trees.
14. What are the main competitors in this category?
15. How do the segments perform? Where are opportunities for growth?

It is very important to align this step with the needs of the shopper, buying behaviour, and the mutual influence of product attributes that affect purchase decisions.

Step B: Format positioning and category

The basic principles of phase 2 will be translated for strategic choices for the function that categories should (and could) have in the format. The category role must be implemented in the category strategy. That means determining whether a category (or subset) is a destination category (building block of the format), or from one of the other roles.

Key questions:

16. What is the format positioning and which strategic function does the category has for the format?
17. Which of the five roles (Destination, Routine, Convenience, Traffic builder and Impulse) fulfills the category (or sub category) now in the total assortment policy?

Step C: Category Objectives & Strategy

Here the choices made are translated into objectives. Objectives are set out in numbers to express quantity, but also qualitative goals of phase two.

Key questions:

18. What are the objectives to be achieved in terms of contribution to revenue and profit?
19. What are the objectives to be achieved in terms of shopper behaviour, shopper loyalty, format differentiation, brand loyalty and so on?
20. What are the main strategies to achieve the objectives?

Step D: Tactics category

You have defined a clear picture of your strengths and weaknesses, opportunities and threats; you have the strategy and also recorded which results to be achieved. In this step you formulate what specific activities and which marketing tools to take to accomplish your goals (eg. price reduction).

Key questions:

21. Product and price. Number of SKUs: what is the optimal product range for the format? What is the price positioning?
22. Promotion. What is the optimal promotion strategy for the category?
23. Location: presentation on the shop floor. How can the available retail space be used optimally? Can we improve the planograms? Is the information and inspiration correct and sufficient to optimize the conversion?
24. Personnel. What information or training or resources do we need to develop the staff on the shop floor or in the distribution?

Each question can add quite a few sub-questions which are described in more detail elsewhere in this book. You can by yourself, as needed, add them to this summary of 25 questions.

Phase 4: Implementation of category plans

The recommendations for the execution of the activities: after all, on the shop floor is where it happens.

The implementation is the most important phase, since here, the plans need to be realized. It is also the most difficult phase. A good plan is very important so as not to forget anything.

Figure 8.3 **Implementation plan of Category Plans**

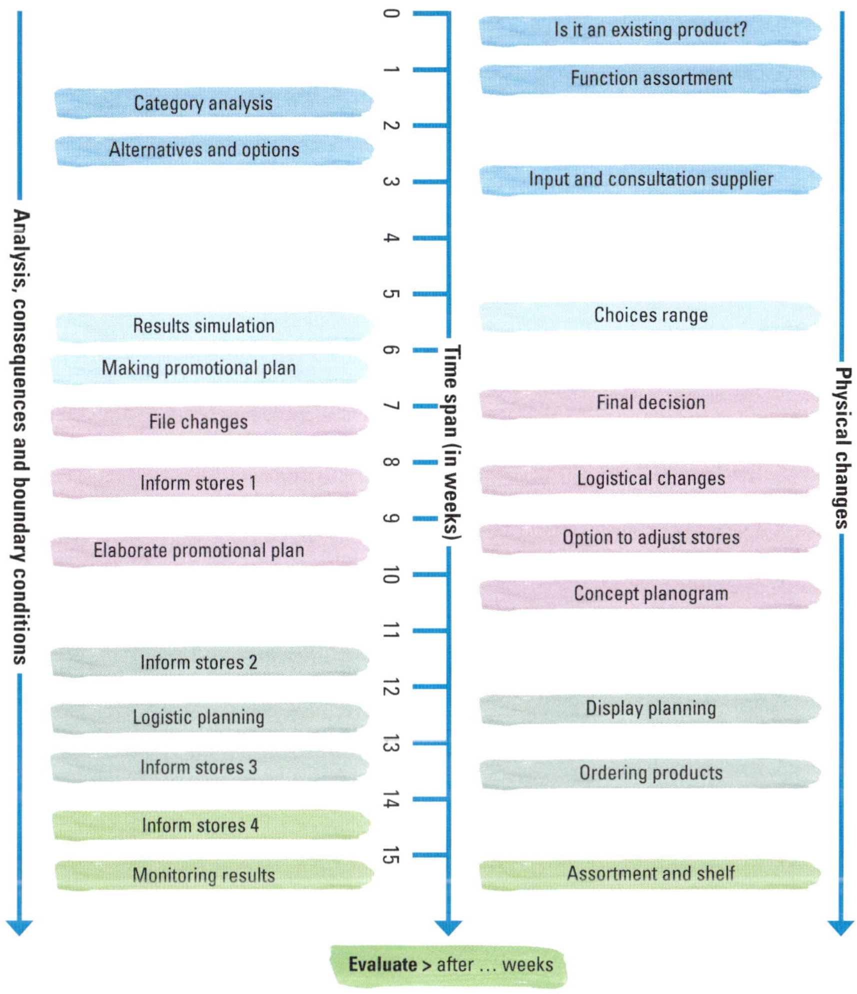

This is a schematic representation of the steps that must be completed in a Category Management implementation plan. The time-line shows in outline the necessary amount of preparation time that is needed. At the top of the scheme are the physical changes; on the bottom of the analysis you find the conclusions and the necessary preconditions.

Final Phase: Evaluation of the category performance

Periodically you have to measure whether the objectives of Phase 3 have been achieved and possibly adjust the plans. You have predetermined objectives. In this phase examination based on the score-cards are realized in the extent to which the targets are realized. For this purpose, a series of fill-in schedules are available. It is advisable to carry out this evaluation periodically.

Key question:

25. What lessons and which improvements can we pick of the recent practices and apply to the next period?

Score card Category Management

Evaluation is not just a matter of hindsight and taking a critical look at the results. Evaluation means that we are learning our lessons from it. And that should not be based solely on a sense of the retailer and on the final result. The supplier too has an opinion on the final result of the agreements made. A scorecard is a good instrument to express that opinion as objective as possible. Below you find a model that can be used and that both the Category Manager and supplier can complete.

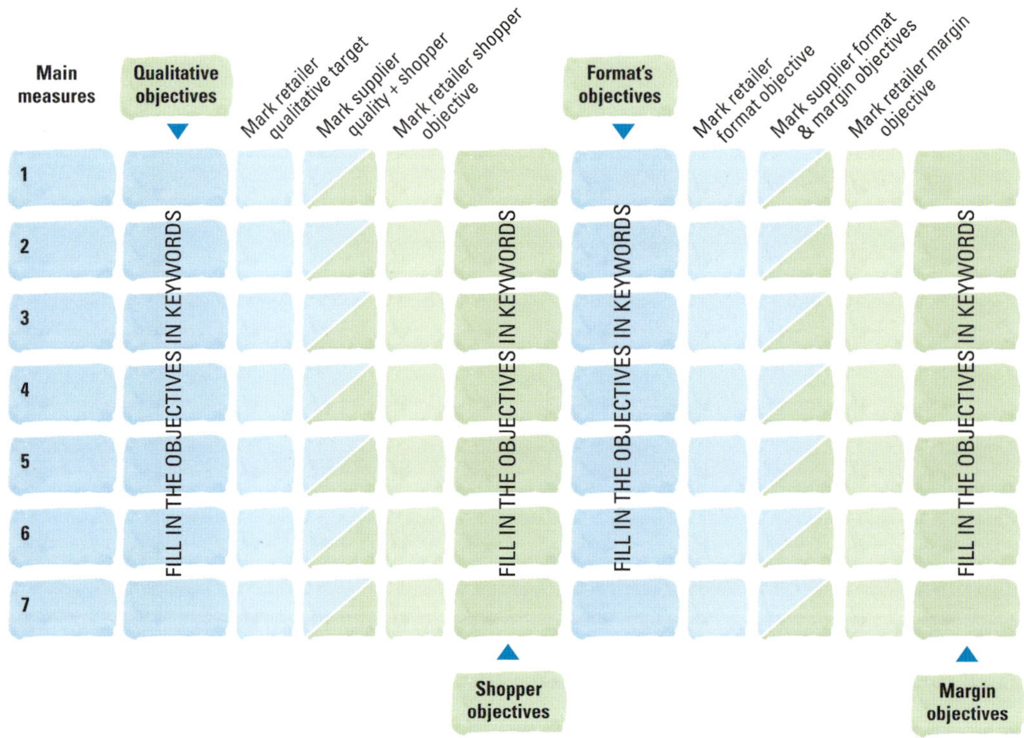

Table 8.1

In order to keep the outlines of the targets in mind while making choices regarding the assortments, it is good to review the main questions.

1. *What is the category doing in terms of sales and margins (right column on the scorecard)?*
2. *What does it do to the format?*
3. *What does it do to the shopper?*
4. *What are the overall qualitative objectives?*

By decree for each category this can be tracked in this scorecard. The four objectives should be written in keywords in advance. Thereafter, the retailer as well as the supplier gives a grade to the results. It is a good way to get the suppliers and retailers to discuss about the plans that have been made.

Bibliography

- ECR reports, all years, ECR Netherlands
- Report **'Demand Side Project Results'**, ECR Italy
- Report **'Efficient Assortment'** Best Practices Report, The Partnering Group and ECR Europe
- Report **'Efficient Product Introductions'**, The development of value-creating relationships, Ernst & Young, AC Nielsen and ECR Europe
- Report **'New Product Introduction'** Successful Innovation / Failure: A fragile boundary, Ernst & Young and AC Nielsen Bases
- Report **Optimal shelf availability**, Increasing shopper satisfaction at the moment of truth, Roland Berger Strategy Consultants and ECR Europe
- Report **'European Value Chain Analysis Study'**, Final Report, Coopers & Lybrand and ECR Europe
- Report **'Working together - a strategic imperative'**, Coopers & Lybrand and ECR Europe
- Report **'Assessing the impact profit or ECR'**, ATKearney, P.A.P. Consulting and ECR Europe
- Report **'Promotion Tactics: Adding focus, adding value'**, PricewaterhouseCoopers and ECR Europe
- Report **'Toolkit voor effectieve promotions'**, KPMG Netherlands and ECR
- Report **'Overview CEO effecient Consumer Response'**, Coopers & Lybrand and ECR Europe
- Report **'The praktijk van Category Management'**, KPMG Netherlands and ECR
- Book **'Consumer-Centric Category Management'**, How to increase profits by managing categories based on consumer needs, AC Nielsen with John Karolefski and Al Heller, 2006 Published by John Wiley & Sons, Inc., Hoboken, New Jersey, United States
- Report **'Category Management, van theorie naar praktijk'**, Chris de Groot and Pascal Hein, MFM - Thesis Series, EFMI
- Book **'The Trade Marketing Dimension'**, A Strategy Model for the Retailing Landscape, Ron Cijs, Regain van den Berg, with Peter Wolff, Sdu Publishers, The Hague, 2007
- Report **'State of the Art in Food'**, The Changing Face of the worldwide food industry, Jan-Willem Grievink, Lia Josten and Conny Falcon, Published by Capgemini and Elsevier, 2001
- Reports **'Quo Vadis'**, EFMI, FSIN and Rabobank, editions 2007, 2008 and 2009
- **Food Shopper Monitor**, FSIN 2013; FSIN Policy Monitor 2014
- **25 AH Franchisers, onderzoek naar meerwaarde profilering zelfstandigen**, 2008
- **Several publications and presentations on pricing and price elasticity**, dr. L. Sloot, EFMI Business School
- **Why we buy**, the science of shopping, Paco Underhill
- **What women want**, Paco Underhill
- **Selling with space management**, David C. King
- **Reorganize for Resilience**, Ranjay Gulati, Harvard Business Press, 2009
- **Shopper Marketing**, Markus Stahlberg and Ville Maila
- **Van alle markten thuis**, a study on cooperation and valorisation of the fresh chain, EFMI Business School April 2013
- **Popai Benelux**, model Shopper Journey
- **Marketing4Results**, model Shopper Journey
- **Thuiswinkel, CBS 2013** I Vergelijk.nl, kelkoo en beslist.nl
- **De koopknop**, Martin de Munnik, 2012